OPTICAL STORAGE FOR COMPUTERS
Technology and Applications

ELLIS HORWOOD BOOKS IN INFORMATION TECHNOLOGY

General Editor: Dr JOHN M. M. PINKERTON, Principal, J & H Pinkerton Associates, Surrey (Consultants in Information Technology), and formerly Manager of Strategic Requirements, ICL

M. Barrett & A. C. Beerel	EXPERT SYSTEMS IN BUSINESS: A Practical Approach
M. Becker, R. Haberfellner & G. Liebetrau	ELECTRONIC DATA PROCESSING IN PRACTICE: A Handbook for Users
A. C. Beerel	EXPERT SYSTEMS: Strategic Implications and Applications
K. Bennett	SOFTWARE ENGINEERING ENVIRONMENTS RESEARCH AND PRACTICE
A. C. Bradley	OPTICAL STORAGE FOR COMPUTERS: Technology and Applications
P. Brereton	SOFTWARE ENGINEERING ENVIRONMENTS
R. Bright	SMART CARDS: Principles, Practice and Applications
D. Clarke & U. Magnusson-Murray	PRACTICAL MACHINE TRANSLATION
V. Claus & A. Schwill	DICTIONARY OF INFORMATION TECHNOLOGY
D. Cleal & N. O. Heaton	KNOWLEDGE-BASED SYSTEMS: Implications for Human–Computer Interfaces
I. Craig	THE CASSANDRA ARCHITECTURE: Distributed Control in a Blackboard System
T. Daler, *et al.*	SECURITY OF INFORMATION AND DATA
D. Diaper	KNOWLEDGE ELICITATION: Principles, Techniques and Applications
G. I. Doukidis, F. Land & G. Miller	KNOWLEDGE-BASED MANAGEMENT SUPPORT SYSTEMS
P. Duffin	KNOWLEDGE-BASED SYSTEMS: Applications in Administrative Government
C. Ellis	EXPERT KNOWLEDGE AND EXPLANATION: The Knowledge–Language Interface
J. Einbu	A PROGRAM ARCHITECTURE FOR IMPROVED MAINTAINABILITY IN SOFTWARE ENGINEERING
A. Fourcin, G. Harland, L.W. Barry & V. Hazan	SPEECH INPUT AND OUTPUT ASSESSMENT: Multilingual Methods and Standards
M. Greenwell	KNOWLEDGE ENGINEERING FOR EXPERT SYSTEMS
F. R. Hickman	ANALYSIS FOR KNOWLEDGE-BASED SYSTEMS: A Practical Guide to the KADS Methodology
P. Hills & J. Beaumont	INFORMATION SYSTEMS: Management Implications for the Human–Computer Interface
E. Hollnagel	THE RELIABILITY OF EXPERT SYSTEMS
J. Kriz	KNOWLEDGE-BASED EXPERT SYSTEMS IN INDUSTRY
M. McTear & T. Anderson	UNDERSTANDING KNOWLEDGE ENGINEERING
W. Meyer & H. Walters	EXPERT SYSTEMS IN FACTORY MANAGEMENT: Knowledge-based CIM
U. Pankoke-Babatz	COMPUTER-BASED GROUP COMMUNICATION: The AMIGO Activity Model
J. M. M. Pinkerton	ADVANCED INFORMATION TECHNOLOGY
S. Pollitt	INFORMATION STORAGE AND RETRIEVAL SYSTEMS: Origin, Development and Applications
S. Ravden & G. Johnson	EVALUATING USABILITY OF HUMAN–COMPUTER INTERFACES: A Practical Method
P. E. Slatter	BUILDING EXPERT SYSTEMS: Cognitive Emulation
H. T. Smith, J. Onions & S. Benford	DISTRIBUTED GROUP COMMUNICATION: The AMIGO Information Model
H. M. Sneed	SOFTWARE ENGINEERING MANAGEMENT
M. Stein	BUILDING EXPERT SYSTEMS MODEMS FOR DATA TRANSMISSION
R. Stutely	ADVANCED DESKTOP PUBLISHING: A Practical Guide to Ventura Version 2 and the Professional Extension
J. A. Waterworth	MULTI-MEDIA INTERACTION WITH COMPUTERS
J. A. Waterworth & M. Talbot	SPEECH AND LANGUAGE-BASED COMMUNICATION WITH MACHINES: Towards the Conversational Computer
R. J. Whiddett	THE IMPLEMENTATION OF SMALL COMPUTER SYSTEMS

OPTICAL STORAGE FOR COMPUTERS
Technology and Applications

A. C. BRADLEY, M.A., M.I.E.E., M.B.C.S., C.Eng.
Technical Consultant
Congleton, Cheshire

ELLIS HORWOOD LIMITED
Publishers · Chichester

Halsted Press: a division of
JOHN WILEY & SONS
New York · Chichester · Brisbane · Toronto

First published in 1989 by
ELLIS HORWOOD LIMITED
Market Cross House, Cooper Street,
Chichester, West Sussex, PO19 1EB, England
The publisher's colophon is reproduced from James Gillison's drawing of the ancient Market Cross, Chichester.

Distributors:

Australia and New Zealand:
JACARANDA WILEY LIMITED
GPO Box 859, Brisbane, Queensland 4001, Australia

Canada:
JOHN WILEY & SONS CANADA LIMITED
22 Worcester Road, Rexdale, Ontario, Canada

Europe and Africa:
JOHN WILEY & SONS LIMITED
Baffins Lane, Chichester, West Sussex, England

North and South America and the rest of the world:
Halsted Press: a division of
JOHN WILEY & SONS
605 Third Avenue, New York, NY 10158, USA

South-East Asia
JOHN WILEY & SONS (SEA) PTE LIMITED
37 Jalan Pemimpin # 05–04
Block B, Union Industrial Building, Singapore 2057

Indian Subcontinent
WILEY EASTERN LIMITED
4835/24 Ansari Road
Daryaganj, New Delhi 110002, India

© 1989 A.C. Bradley/Ellis Horwood Limited

British Library Cataloguing in Publication Data
Bradley, A. C.
Optical storage for computers: technology and applications. —
(Ellis Horwood books in information technology).
1. Automated information retrieval systems
I. Title
001.5

Library of Congress data available

ISBN 0–7458–0557–4 (Ellis Horwood Limited)
ISBN 0–470–21488–0 (Halsted Press)

Typeset in Times by Ellis Horwood Limited
Printed in Great Britain by Unwin Bros., Woking

COPYRIGHT NOTICE
All Rights Reserved. No part of this publication may be reproduced, stored in a retrieval system, or transmitted, in any form or by any means, electronic, mechanical, photocopying, recording or otherwise, without the permission of Ellis Horwood Limited, Market Cross House, Cooper Street, Chichester, West Sussex, England.

Contents

Preface		7
1	Introduction	11
2	Write-once disks	22
3	Rewritable disks	55
4	Read-only disks	63
5	Automated disk libraries	87
6	Optical tape and card	98
7	Controllers, interfaces and standards	102
8	Packaged systems	113
9	Applications — data storage, back-up and archiving	120
10	Applications — data exchange, distribution and publishing	155
11	What next?	181
Appendix 1	Further reading	192
Appendix 2	Holography	196
Appendix 3	Sample data sheets	201
Index		214

Preface

This book is about optical storage for computers. It is mainly concerned with optical disk, including CD-ROM, but also covers optical tape and card. It does not cover microfilm or microfiche, and videodisk is only mentioned in passing.

My aim is to give system and application designers an understanding of the nature of optical storage, its strengths and weaknesses, and some of the ways in which it can be used in systems — from mainframes to PCs. The book will also interest students and users of information technology who wish to know more about modern computer systems. It is not written for the hardware engineer, and no engineering or mathematical knowledge is assumed; within this constraint a fairly full account of the workings of each device is included, partly for interest and partly to help explain its characteristics.

The emphasis of the book is on optical storage devices which are already in practical use, or close to it — particularly 'write once', 'read only', and 'rewritable' disk drives; but other devices which may be important in the future, together with a few which have fallen by the wayside, are also discussed.

The world of optical storage is one of diversity and of rapid development. No book can prescribe how particular devices should be integrated into systems; that information (in the absence of practical experience) must come from manufacturers, system houses and consultants, while more general current knowledge comes from technical conferences and journals. But in a more general way this book shows how the characteristics of optical devices make them more, or less, attractive for various applications, and suggests the most advantageous of these; points out how optical solutions compare with the alternatives; and illustrates this by describing some actual installations.

My qualifications for the task are a lifetime's involvement with computer hardware, and many contacts with the other branches of the computer industry. I have spent the last few years in following the development of optical storage and in interpreting it to system designers and software technologists, helping them to decide when and how to use this new technology to serve the user. This book is an extension of that activity.

The book is not based on specific technical papers or other publications, so there are no references in the text. A few books and journals of particular interest are described in Appendix 1, 'Further reading', and one of these includes a comprehensive bibliography.

The spelling of 'disk' is a matter of some controversy; the computer industry generally uses 'disk' while the entertainment industry prefers 'disc'. The *Oxford Dictionary of Computing* uses 'disk' and for consistency I have kept to that spelling throughout, except in direct quotations.

The dictionaries remind me that 'media' and 'data' are both plural, and I have followed this ruling in the case of 'media'. However, in a computing context the treatment of 'data' as always plural has come to look pedantic, particularly since 'datum' is used with a different meaning (i.e. 'reference point'). I have therefore treated 'data' as singular where this reads more naturally.

The usual problem of 'he' and 'she' arises. I have no prejudices in this respect, and am happy to recognize the part played by many ladies in the computer industry. Nevertheless I find the constant repetition of 'he and she' clumsy, and the available alternatives worse. I have therefore used male pronouns throughout, and ask the reader to expand each such pronoun to cover both sexes.

Likewise I have avoided the phrase 'at the time of writing'. 'Now', or the equivalent, implies early 1989.

Although I have not discussed particular commercial products in detail, I have used company and product names here and there without specific acknowledgement. I hereby acknowledge all trade names used within this book.

I owe thanks to many people for help with this work. In particular I would like to thank those who gave their time to showing and discussing the installations discussed in Chapters 9 and 10, including David Mawdsley and Jan Ellis of the Britannia Building Society; Nigel Hanwell of Barclaycard; Derek Mills of Bell and Howell; Mary Wilkinson and Paul Sturm of the Public Record Office; Richard Elsley of Bookland; and Steve Lee of Shareware Marketing.

For providing photographs and data sheets, and permission to use them (the copyright remains with the companies named), I would like to thank the following: Peter Allin of Maxtor Europe; Vic Drayton of Laser Magnetic Storage International; Alex Monro of Data General; George Dundon of Cipher Data Products: Phil Storey of Plasmon Data Systems: Mike Tate of Telephone Rentals; Nick Rogers of Hitachi; Derek Mills and Brian Hafferty of Bell and Howell; Creo Electronics Corporation; Tina Law of Vockrodt Projects; and Martin Bonner of British Olivetti.

I am grateful for information and help of various kinds to David Abbott of CACL; Sally Whitaker and Trevor Coe of J. Whitaker and Sons; Mr H. J. D. Magee of CCTA; Gary Grant of Lotus; John Hayley of ICL; and Mr H. Eastwood of the University of Leeds — and to others whom I may have forgotten to mention.

I have had unfailing help and courtesy from the staff of the publishers, Ellis Horwood Ltd, and particularly from the Series Editor John Pinkerton and from Sue Horwood and Jayne Willett.

And last but very far from least I must thank David Williams for helping in more ways than I have room to list. If it had not been for David I should certainly not have written this book.

All errors or other deficiencies are my own. A work of this kind is bound to be out of date even by the time it is published, and readers must bear with me in that respect. I should be very glad to be advised, via the publishers, of any other errors.

Congleton, February 1989 Alan Bradley

1

Introduction

For over thirty years, magnetic storage has been an essential part of the computer. Disk and tape have been unchallenged for on-line and shelf storage. Now optical technology offers an alternative, and the system designer has a new decision to make.

Optical storage also offers a new way to publish data; an alternative to on-line databases, micrographics, and even print. More decisions to be made!

Good decisions depend on sound information. This book aims to give to designers the understanding of optical storage, and of the opportunities it offers, that they need in making these decisions. It is also for those who may not have decisions to make, but would still like to know what it is all about.

This first chapter introduces the principles and the important features of optical storage, and shows how the many types of media and device can be divided into a few classes. The next five chapters look at each class in turn, describing the technology and the device characteristics that follow from it. Each of these chapters considers the strengths and weaknesses of the devices, and how they match up to the competition from other technologies; in the light of this, it suggests how optical devices can best be used.

Chapter 7 looks at controllers, interfaces, and standards, and Chapter 8 at packaged systems. After this, two chapters discuss applications in detail; these include accounts of some successful implementations of optical storage and publishing.

The final chapter takes a brief look at the history of optical storage, summarizes the present state of things, and makes some guesses about what the next few years may bring.

WHY OPTICAL STORAGE?

Computers need backing store. The working store of the computer is fast, with truly random access; but it is very expensive, and usually volatile. So two-level storage — fast working store linked with slower but cheaper backing store — was one of the first advances in computer architecture (Fig. 1.1). Two-level storage was accepted in the same spirit as the car gearbox, as an unfortunate necessity; systems to manage storage, like the automatic gearbox, were introduced to hide the details from the user.

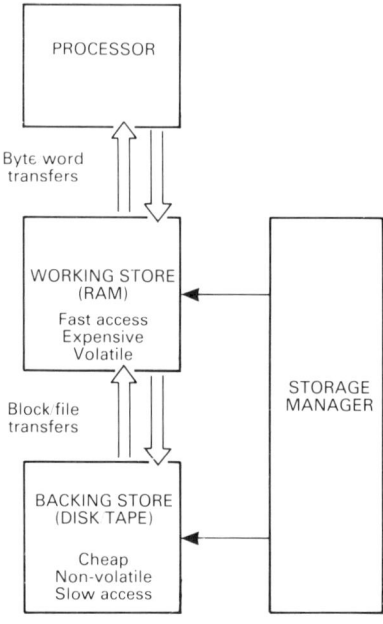

Fig. 1.1 — Two-level storage.

The vital properties of backing store are non-volatility, data integrity, and low cost. Also important are compactness, rapid transfer of data between backing store and working store, and reasonable access time (though it need not be as fast as the working store). Some applications also need the storage medium to be replaceable and cheap. Magnetic stores match these requirements well, although two forms — disk (or drum) and tape — are needed to cover the whole range. The development of computers has been closely linked to that of magnetic storage devices, and of the operating systems which support them.

However, as the power of computers increased, and with it their thirst for storage, it could be seen that magnetic storage had its limitations. Higher storage density became harder and harder to achieve; it involved such close head-to-media spacing that large drives could no longer use removable disks. As magnetic tape was used more for archival storage, its lack of long-term stability was found inconvenient and expensive. Engineers saw that optical technology had the potential to avoid some of these problems and offer denser storage than magnetic technology; so from the early 1970s much effort was put into optical storage research. Many problems had to be solved, in particular the development of media and of light sources. It was not until the mid-1980s, with a good deal of help from the entertainment industry, that optical storage became a practical proposition.

WHAT IS OPTICAL STORAGE?

Optical storage is like magnetic storage in many ways. It comes in disk, tape, and card forms; its performance is broadly similar to that of its magnetic equivalent; it serves many of the same purposes. The fundamental difference, the use of optical rather than magnetic technology, is at a level which does not really concern the end user. But the difference in technology does affect the characteristics of practical devices, and hence the support they need from the host system and the applications for which they are useful; and that is what this book is about.

Definitions, like statistics, can be used to prove almost anything; the definition of optical storage is more a matter of deciding where to draw a boundary than defining the technology itself. For the purpose of this book, then, *optical storage* is defined as *a technology in which stored data is read by optical means*. This is not precise; for example, if 'stored' were given its widest meaning the definition would cover bar-code scanners, which are well outside the scope of the book. But we have no need to be more rigorous.

Optical storage is often referred to as *laser storage*, and indeed the word laser is included in several product and company names. The laser has caught the popular imagination and the word helps to sell many things — some of which have no connection at all with optics. In fact optical storage and laser storage are not synonymous. The use of lasers is not fundamental to optical storage; other light sources have been used in the past, and may be again in the future. However, it is true that all those optical storage devices which are now on the market do use the laser. It has turned out to be a very convenient light source and, having adopted it, designers have used its properties in ways that would not have been possible with other light sources. The lasers used in optical storage are not, of course, the destructive devices of science fiction or 'Star Wars'; nor are they the high-powered gas lasers whose beams are used in outdoor displays. They are low-powered semiconductor lasers smaller than a pea, giving out light at the extreme red end of the spectrum. These lasers have been used widely in the entertainment industry, in videodisk and Compact Audio disk players. It is the low cost and long lifetime developed to suit that industry that has made them such useful components for optical storage.

PHYSICAL PRINCIPLES

At its most fundamental level, the requirement for data storage is that some property of a set of storage elements can be changed so that it represents the data to be stored; and that this property can be recognized at a later time, so that the original data can be reconstructed.

A number of different properties can be used in optical storage. By definition, the method of recognizing or reading the elements must be optical, at least in part; but our definition was carefully phrased so that the setting, or writing, of the elements need not be done optically. There were two reasons for this. Firstly, although nearly all optical storage devices do write with a light beam from a laser, the state of the storage element is changed by the *heating* effect of the beam rather than by a strictly optical effect. Secondly, the elements which are read may be copies made by mechanical means, albeit from masters which themselves were made (thermo-) optically.

Optical detection implies that some property of the light transmitted or reflected (or, in principle, emitted) by the storage elements is recognized; and also that it is translated into a form which the computer can understand, which in practice means into an electrical signal. The photoelectric detectors used in optical storage all respond to the intensity of the light that falls on them. However, data may be represented by some other property of light, such as its polarization; optical methods are then used to turn this into a change in the amount of light falling on the photodetector.

For practical reasons, nearly all optical stores detect light reflected from the signal elements rather than transmitted through them. The most common methods are those in which the *reflectivity* of the storage element depends on the signal (1 or 0) stored there; the reflectivity can be changed in several ways. Of the other techniques which have been explored, the only one widely used varies the *direction of polarization* of the reflected light according to the signal stored.

These writing and reading techniques will be discussed in more detail in later chapters, along with other aspects of the technology.

FUNDAMENTAL CHARACTERISTICS

In this section we shall look at some of the fundamental characteristics which are shared by all practical methods of optical storage.

The feature which led to most research into optical storage is the high data density that can be achieved; more precisely the high areal density, in the sense of the amount of data that can be stored on a given area of the surface of the recording medium. It is areal density that matters, because all optical storage media have a thin sensitive film carried on a thicker, inert, substrate — as do the competing magnetic storage media.

The storage density that can be achieved in *magnetic* disk and tape stores is limited by the technology; in particular, the manufacturing technology for media and recording heads, and the closeness of the spacing between head and media. Theoretically, much higher densities can be achieved; but every step becomes harder and more expensive. In *optical* storage, on the other hand, a physical limitation is imposed by the wavelength of light (at least while conventional optics are used); but it turns out that it is not technically too difficult to come quite close to that limit, and thus use much higher densities than are usual in magnetic recording. However, it follows that major increases in the density of optical storage will not be achieved simply by better technology; variations of the basic approach used must be considered. One possible avenue is holographic optics, and this is discussed in Chapter 11.

A second important characteristic is the time taken to change the state of a storage element. In principle this depends on the power required to change the state, and on the rate at which the writing mechanism (here the laser beam) can apply this power. Because the optical storage element is so small, the amount of power is also small; nevertheless it is significant, and the write data rates of optical stores are in practice limited by laser power and losses in the optical system.

A third vital characteristic of optical storage is that a light beam, unlike a magnetic field, can readily be focused from a distance. So there is no need for any part of the mechanism to be very close to the recording medium, and the problems found in magnetic recording with both 'flying' and 'in-contact' heads are largely avoided. It is also possible to protect the recording layer with a thick clear protective layer, or to use a clear substrate and read and write through this; either way the light beam is well out of focus at the outer surface and so is little affected by dust and minor scratches.

Another important group of characteristics is related to the way in which the medium is accessed. In this respect optical disks, tapes, and cards are not fundamentally different from magnetic devices; but, for technical reasons which will be discussed when we look at each type of store, the figures differ in detail.

Finally there are characteristics — such as the lifetime of recorded data — which depend on the specific type of medium, and these too will be discussed in later chapters. However, one very important characteristic must be mentioned here. It is impossible in practice to make recording media which are completely free from defects. This is true also of magnetic media, but in that case fairly simple methods of error management (such as discarding any disk sector or tape block which contains a defect) often suffice. However, the higher data density of most optical storage means that much smaller defects become significant; so it is found economically impossible to make media that can be treated in this simple way. For this reason, optical storage needs powerful error correction, based on redundant coding of the data, and error-correction methods are a very vital part of the technology.

THE TYPES OF OPTICAL STORE

There are two fundamental ways in which optical storage media, and the devices which handle them, can be classified; by the shape and size of the media unit (computer users often describe this unit as a *volume*), and by the recording technology. The first is mainly a property of the substrate, the second of the optically active recording layer.

Disk
Shapes and sizes closely match those of magnetic storage devices. By far the commonest form is the disk, where data is recorded on many concentric circular tracks, or turns of a spiral track (usually each turn is loosely described as a track). A single read/write station, or *head*, can be positioned on any track and data is read or written as the disk rotates past it. Unlike

most magnetic disk drives, current optical disk drives have a single head and each media volume is a single disk, or platter. The drive can access only one side of the disk. Double-sided disks are often used, but in such a drive only one side can be 'on line' at a time; the disk must be turned over, usually by the operator, to give access to the other side. There is no reason in principle why drives should not access both sides of the disk, or use multiple disks; but the weight and cost of the optical head are several times those of the magnetic equivalent, and the close track spacing means that each surface will need its own provision for track-following. This means that such devices, when they appear (and at least one is under development), will be expensive and used only in specialized applications.

Optical disks, like magnetic disks, come in a number of sizes. These are often formally specified in metric dimensions, but they are nearly always referred to in inch terms; so these will be used here, with the metric near-equivalents mentioned only initially (Fig. 1.2).

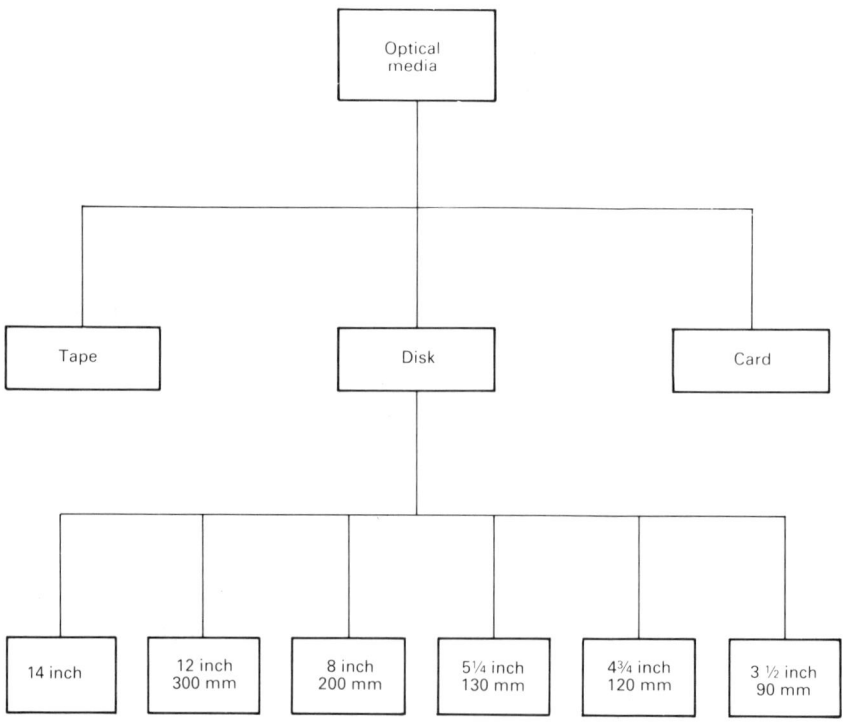

Fig. 1.2 — Media format.

The first disk size to be commercially available was 12 inch (300 mm) in diameter, no doubt because equipment for making videodisks in that size was readily available. The 8 inch disk (200 mm) was also introduced for the same reason. The 12 inch disk has been widely accepted and new products using this size continue to appear, but 8 inch has been very little used outside Japan and is now obsolescent.

The size which has become most popular is $5\frac{1}{4}$ inch (130 mm). Such a disk holds perhaps a quarter of the data that a 12 inch disk will take, but there is not much difference in the media cost per megabyte. This is partly because plastic substrates can readily be used for $5\frac{1}{4}$ inch disks; they are more difficult to use in the 12 inch size, several manufacturers preferring the more expensive glass substrates. $5\frac{1}{4}$ inch drives are also much cheaper than 12 inch drives, and faster access times can be achieved. Another attraction is that most $5\frac{1}{4}$ inch drives are designed to fit into the front-panel slot provided in many personal computers and workstations for $5\frac{1}{4}$ inch magnetic disk drives (this is often described as the '$5\frac{1}{4}$ inch footprint'). The importance of this is decreasing as such hosts turn to either half-height $5\frac{1}{4}$ inch or else $3\frac{1}{2}$ inch slots.

Very close to this size is the $4\frac{3}{4}$ inches (120 mm) of the Compact Audio entertainment product. This has been adopted by the computer world for CD-ROM and has become the dominant format for read-only optical storage.

Smaller disks than this are under development, particularly the $3\frac{1}{2}$ inch size, though none has yet reached the market. This size, together with $5\frac{1}{4}$ inch, are at present the favourites for rewritable disk drives.

At the other extreme, 14 inch diameter disks were used in one of the earliest systems to reach the market. This was soon withdrawn, but the same size of disk (though using very different technology) has been adopted for a new product. As this can hold three to four times the amount of data that the 12 inch disk will take, it is a useful alternative to 12 inch on large systems.

Tape
Another media format which follows magnetic precedents is tape. The attraction in both cases is that the thinness and flexibility of the substrate allow a very large area of the active coating to be stored in a small volume. However, the non-rigidity of the medium brings its own problems. The most serious is that precise location of the medium relative to the head is much harder to achieve, and this may limit the data density. Tape is essentially a serial access medium, and this is a disadvantage in many applications; and its flexible nature leads to stresses which can cause loss of data integrity in long-term storage. All these are problems shared with magnetic tape, but more significant in the type of application for which optical storage is usually seen as appropriate. For this reason, although some optical storage systems based on tape have been developed, few have reached the market.

Card
The third media format is the card, where the substrate is a rectangle of typically a few centimetres on each side. This has an optically active coating on one face — usually as a strip covering only part of the width of the card, similar to the magnetic stripe on the familiar credit card. The card format lends itself to a very simple mechanism, where the card is simply slid past a

stationary optical head. This can be done mechanically or by hand. Again problems of tolerance mean that the data density cannot match that used on disk; but it is not difficult to store a megabyte or more on such a card and this is ample for many applications. More complex mechanisms can be used where higher capacity is needed. Optical card, though a slow starter, thus looks to have considerable potential.

RECORDING METHODS

The other fundamental characteristic that distinguishes between various optical stores is the method of recording. The many methods available fall into three classes. The classes are in themselves quite distinct, but in practice it is not unusual for more than one class of recording to be included on one media volume — generally for different purposes, such as format information and user data. In addition, drives are being designed in which user data recorded by more than one method may be handled. These are known as 'multifunction' drives. These aspects of recording methods will be covered in the chapters on the various drive types; in the meantime the three classes will be discussed briefly (Fig. 1.3).

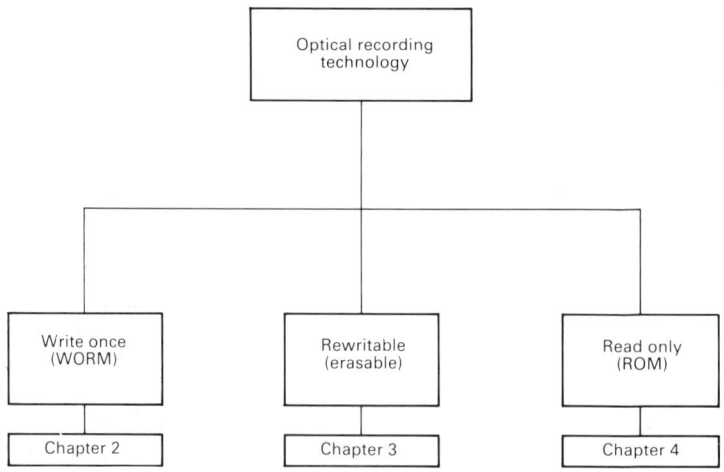

Fig. 1.3 — Recording technology.

Write-once

The first class of recording methods is generally referred to as WORM, which stands for 'write once, read many times' (some authorities prefer 'write once, read mostly'). The essential feature is that writing is not reversible; once the state of a storage element has been changed, it cannot be changed back to its original state. Data is always written in 'sectors', typically of a few kilobytes. These are indivisible units because of the coding methods used, which will be discussed later. It follows that any sector cannot be changed, but can only be superseded by a replacement sector located elsewhere. This has important implications for the host operating system. In theory data can be obliterated by setting any elements which were not set when originally written (in effect overwriting with an all-ones pattern), but drives do not normally provide this facility. The 'many' of 'read many' is in practice a very large number for modern media in a properly designed drive. The shelf life of recorded data is not infinite but all manufacturers will guarantee at least ten years and some promise thirty or more.

Read-only

Another class is read-only storage, which is often known as ROM (read-only memory). The most popular implementation of this in the computer field is CD-ROM, and this is sometimes taken to be synonymous with read-only optical storage. However, other formats do exist, including the videodisk; this is basically an entertainment product, but has some applications in the computer field, mainly as an interactive training medium.

Of course the data has to be written somehow in the first place. The implication of 'read-only' is that the disk is a copy which has been made in one operation, rather than sector by sector; its contents cannot thereafter be changed in any way. Again, there is no practical limit to the number of times the disk can be read.

There is an overlap between read-only and WORM technology; the disks used in WORM stores are often 'preformatted' with information (such as sector headers and synchronization signals) which is copied to the disk during manufacture and cannot be altered by the WORM drive.

Rewritable

The third class of recording methods is now usually described as 'rewritable', although the older term 'erasable' is still often used. This is much closer to magnetic store technology in that data written on the disk can be erased and replaced by fresh data. In principle the term would embrace media which could only be bulk-erased, as a complete volume ('reusable' might be a better term); but although such an arrangement might serve for some applications, such as back-up, it has not in fact been introduced. In all current systems, data is erased and rewritten a sector at a time; partial sectors cannot be changed, because of the coding methods used. In the earlier systems, separate passes (on successive disk revolutions) are needed to erase the old data and to replace it. Techniques which permit direct overwriting without a separate erase pass are now being developed.

While data can be read very many times, some media display 'fatigue' effects which limit the number of erase/rewrite cycles that can be performed on any sector. This was at first a serious obstacle to the development of rewritable storage, but more recently it has been possible to push up the limit. There is some disagreement among the experts as to whether an infinite number of erase/rewrite cycles is theoretically possible, or only a very large number. The difference is significant to the host, as in the latter case it may be necessary to monitor the system or (one may hope) just the media to see if the limit is being approached. A well-behaved program is unlikely to approach the limit, but a repetitive test program might do so.

The discussion of rewritable storage in this book is far from definitive: these systems are not yet established on the market, so it has still to be proved that all the problems have been solved.

DATA RECORDING FORMAT

A further, though less significant, classification of recording methods depends on the way in which data is represented (Fig. 1.4). This book will be

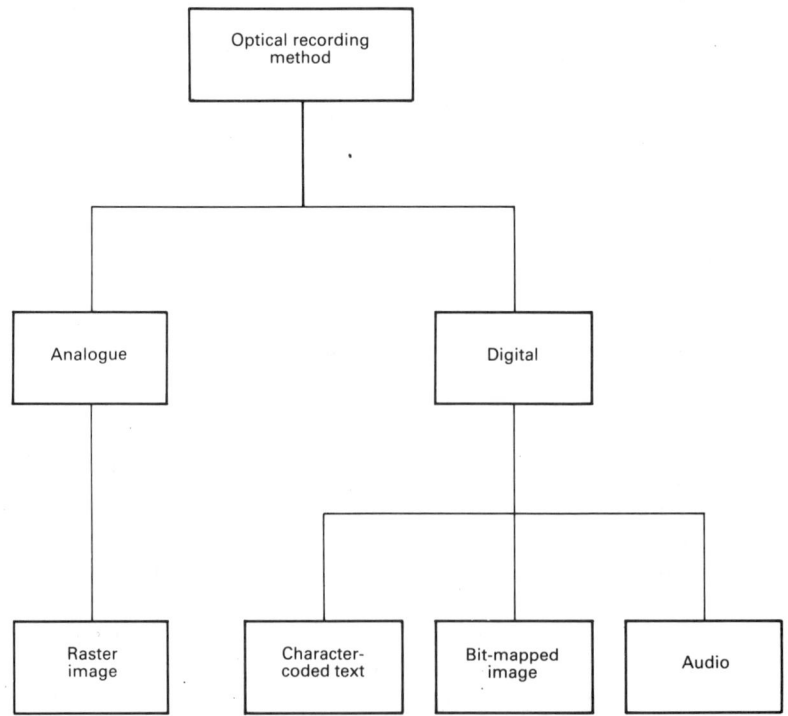

Fig. 1.4 — Recording method.

concerned primarily with digital data, but it should be noted that the standard videodisk records not digits but a video waveform, in analogue form. Videodisk was of course introduced, with little success, as an entertainment product. It has been adopted for training and demonstration;

sometimes as 'interactive videodisk' linked to a computer, which is used to control the selection of images from the disk and sometimes to overlay them with other forms of information. It is important to realize that that the digital computer cannot process the data, because it is in analogue form, but can only control the player. A variant of the videodisk format has been used to store character-coded data, but although a few read-only disks were issued in this format it has been made obsolescent by the success of CD-ROM.

There are two approaches to digital optical recording; with or without the use of error correction. It has already been said that powerful error-correction methods are needed if data is to be stored on imperfect media with an acceptable error rate; these involve redundant coding of the data. However, sometimes data is inherently so redundant that additional redundancy is not needed. The most important example is text stored as a bit-mapped image, rather than coded in ASCII or some other compact form. In this case the eye can compensate for quite major errors in reproduction. This approach has been used for some Japanese 'document storage systems'; in Japan, because of the nature of the script, more documents are handwritten than is common in the West, and these can only be stored conveniently as images. However, this approach limits the system to image storage only: it does not lend itself to data compression techniques, and so is extravagant in its use of disk capacity; and it is still necessary to have a means of handling errors in the 'housekeeping' information (sector/document headers, etc.). This approach has therefore not caught on in the West, and is becoming less popular in Japan; most image storage now uses the same error-correction methods that are used for text.

MEDIA MANAGEMENT

Practically all exchangeable *magnetic* media are loaded into their drives by hand, and much effort has been put into simplifying the process for the untrained operator. Automated tape libraries, storing a large number of specially designed tape cartridges which were mechanically loaded onto a drive, appeared in the 1970s but were never widely accepted. Hand-loading is simple and widely used for *optical* stores too, but automatic library mechanisms seem to be more acceptable than their magnetic counterparts. These mechanisms are invariably referred to as 'jukeboxes'; Chapter 5 of this book is devoted to them.

The fundamental characteristics shared by many forms of optical storage have been discussed in this chapter; in the next few chapters we shall look at particular classes of optical storage devices in more detail.

2
Write-once disks

In 1984 the first write-once, or WORM, optical disk drives went into full production; optical storage had at last broken out from a protracted development phase into the world of commerce. These were not the first optical devices on the market, as two were on sale in the 1970s. One was the IBM 'Photochip' store, a read-only store in which data was recorded photographically on plates which were then stored in magazines with a mechanical access mechanism. The other was the Precision Instruments 'Unicon', a write-once store using a wide short tape. Each of these had a limited success in a specialized market, but neither survived very long. Maybe it was partly because the Unicon failed to find a wider market that, for some years, most developers looked on write-once as a blind alley and concentrated on the difficult problems of rewritable media. However, a few companies persisted with WORM media, in disk form, taking advantage of the low-cost lasers and optical systems which were being made for the videodisk and Compact Audio market.

Once WORM storage was a reality, it became clear that it was more than just a stepping stone toward rewritable optical media. In some applications the permanence of a recorded WORM disk is a positive advantage. This is most obvious in archival storage, and also where there is a need to trace all the changes that the data has been through; for example in providing an audit trail for financial records. Thus WORM disk has become an important product in its own right, with a range of applications distinct from those of rewritable optical or magnetic stores, and has found a substantial market.

RECORDING TECHNOLOGY

Many recording technologies have been tried on write-once media, and several are still in use. Surprisingly, it turns out that it is not necessary to restrict a particular drive to media designed for one recording method; so long as its light beam can change the state of a storage element, and the change in state results in a change in reflectivity, any technology can be used. Optical disk drives usually have a laser rated at about 10 to 20 milliwatts, though higher powers are coming into use. The laser is used at full power for writing but at a lower power for reading, since reading must be non-destructive. The beam is focused to a spot about 1 micron (one thousandth of a millimetre) diameter at the surface of the active layer, and this defines the size of the storage element. Tape and card stores may use a larger focus spot.

Some examples of recording methods are described below, but the list is not comprehensive. Fig. 2.1 compares them diagrammatically; like other diagrams in this book, it is not to scale.

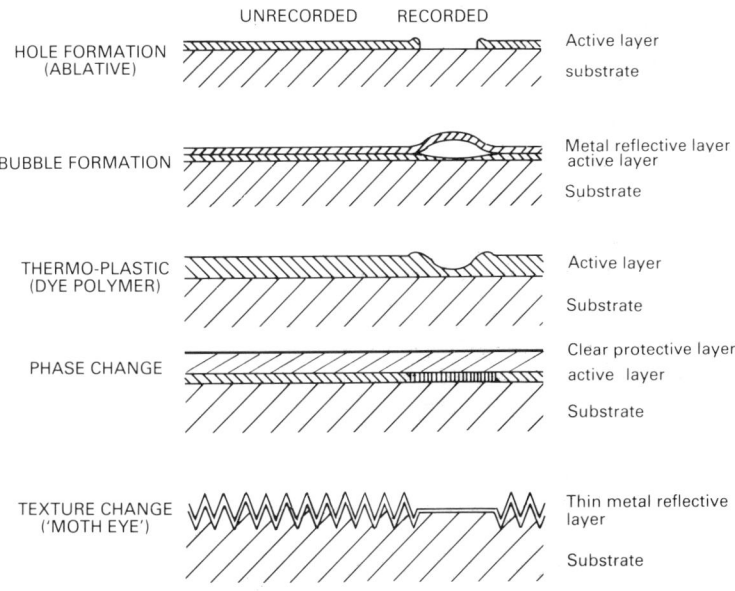

Fig. 2.1 — Some examples of WORM recording technology.

Ablative
In the simplest method, 'ablative' recording, the heat of the laser beam melts or vaporizes an area of the active layer corresponding to the focus spot. The active layer is usually a metal film, very thin to reduce the amount of energy required to heat it, since (with the limited power available from a semiconductor laser) this determines the write data rate of the store. If the metal is vaporized it may cause problems by being deposited on other signal elements, so melting is preferred. Surface tension draws the melted metal aside so that it solidifies with a crater-like rim round the hole. In a reflective system the metal layer may be backed by an inert layer which is dark, to increase the change in reflectivity. Ablative recording was used in the first commercial WORM store, the 'Unicon' already mentioned.

In a variation of this method, the active layer is vaporized by the heat of the laser beam but is contained by a plastic layer above it; this is deformed to form a 'bubble' which scatters the incident light. In some cases the bubble is designed to burst and leave a pit similar to that provided by ablative recording.

Another variation of the method is 'thermoplastic' recording. The laser beam softens the surface, and when it cools a depression is left which scatters the incident light; or again the depression may reach right through to the substrate to produce a similar effect to ablative recording. The sensitive film in this case is not metal but is a plastic layer containing organic dyes — usually called 'dye–polymer'. The dyes are chosen to absorb light at the wavelength produced by semiconductor lasers. Dye–polymer material is of particular interest because disks can be made more cheaply than with metal films.

Phase change
Another method of recording is based on a 'phase change' in the active layer. The change can be of various kinds but is most commonly a change between crystalline and amorphous or micro-crystalline states in a metal film. The film is initially crystalline, with a high reflectivity. A short pulse of power from the laser beam heats the signal element and allows it to cool very quickly, by conduction to the adjoining unheated parts of the film. It therefore cools with either much smaller crystals or in an amorphous form, which has a lower reflectivity. Unlike the previous method there is no change in the shape of the surface of the film, so a thick protective layer can be used over it. A related method uses two layers of different metals; the laser beam melts both layers, leaving a spot where the metals are alloyed together and the reflectivity is changed.

The last method that will be described here uses a substrate impressed with a relief pattern which repeats at an interval small compared to the size of the signal spot. Over this is deposited a very thin platinum coating. This reproduces the relief of the substrate surface, so it scatters light and appears dark. This relief pattern and its effect have been likened to the cornea of a moth's eye, so the material is often described by this term. The laser beam melts the surface of the substrate, which causes a smooth patch in the metal layer and thus a more reflective surface (Fig. 2.2).

Track format
Whatever the recording method, the signal elements are arranged serially along a 'track'; there are many tracks on the surface of the disk, arranged either as concentric circles or, more usually, as turns of a single continuous spiral. The tracks may be equally spaced throughout, or they may be grouped in 'bands' with a wider space between the bands. Along each track the data is divided into sectors, just as in magnetic disk practice, and each sector has a header which identifies it and also performs other functions such as synchronization.

Most, though not all, WORM disk drives require the disks to be 'preformatted'; this implies that the headers are placed on the disk in the course of manufacture (they are the same for all disks of one type). This is

Fig. 2.2 — Microphotograph showing 'moth-eye' recording. (Copyright Plasmon Data Systems.)

'read-only' information which cannot be changed in any way by the drive, and it will generally use a different technology from that recorded by the drive itself; however, the result is still a change in the reflectivity of some of the storage elements, so both header and data areas are read in the same way.

The drive needs further guidance in writing the data sectors between the headers. Firstly the spacing of the storage elements along the track must be defined; secondly the radial position of the track must be controlled. The latter is needed because it is impossible to make the axis of rotation exactly concentric with the header pattern, and the error is usually much greater than the track spacing. One way to take care of this is to extend the preformatting to include a continuous 'pre-groove', a groove which may be narrower than the laser spot. In some systems the laser follows the groove and the signal elements are recorded in it, often with an overlap at either side; in other systems the beam follows the 'land' between adjacent grooves. The pre-groove may include shallow modulation to serve as a 'clock' signal to indicate the storage element spacing. However, there are various other methods; most depend on the fact that it is only necessary to mark the required storage element position and spacing at intervals along the sector, not at every element.

Angular velocity

A factor which must be taken into account in the preformatting of the disk is the choice between 'constant angular velocity' (CAV) and 'constant linear velocity' (CLV) operation (Fig. 2.3). CAV simply means that the disk rotates at a fixed speed, just as a magnetic disk does. Data is written at a fixed rate, and consequently the spacing of signal elements, measured along the track, increases as the track radius increases. This means that only the innermost track is recorded at the highest density which the medium will take. It also means that the signal elements in the outer tracks are within the laser spot for a shorter time than those on inner tracks; if there is not a sufficiently wide tolerance on the amount of energy used to change a signal element, the write power may need to be varied according to the track radius. On CAV disks every track has the same number of sectors, and the sector boundaries can often be seen as radial lines on the disk.

CLV avoids these problems by varing the rotation rate of the disk according to the track radius, keeping the signal element spacing the same on every track. This typically increases the capacity of a disk by 50%. The penalties to be paid are an additional servo system to control disk rotation speed, and increased access time; this is because the speed of the disk, with its relatively high inertia, has to be changed as well as the position of the optical head. A compromise, MCLV (Modified CLV), groups the tracks into bands with the disk speed being the same for all tracks within a band but varying between bands. In yet another scheme, MCAV, the disk rotation speed is constant but the reading and writing data rates are varied with the track radius, so that the maximum density is always used. All these systems are in use, CAV being the most common; some drives are designed to operate in both CAV and CLV, although the preformatting of the disk will decide which is to be used for any media volume. It may be mentioned here that both Compact Audio and CD-ROM use CLV.

MEDIA

We have already seen that the first commercially successful WORM devices used 12 inch disks; this size was used for videodisks, so manufacturing plant for the disks and many parts for the drives were already available. There were also 8 inch videodisks, but for WORM this size never caught on in the West and it is becoming obsolete in Japan. $5\frac{1}{4}$ inch has become the next widely adopted size; in fact $5\frac{1}{4}$ inch drives have rapidly outstripped 12 inch, particularly in the number of interested manufacturers. $3\frac{1}{2}$ inch drives are just beginning to appear. 14 inch disks, used in an early product which had a very short market life, have now been revived in a different form and are likely to supplement and possibly supersede 12 inch on large systems. Other sizes have yet to emerge, although companies involved in the read-only CD-ROM product are developing a write-once version (which they call CD-PROM). This has the 120 mm ($4\frac{3}{4}$ inch) diameter used in the read-only version; an 80 mm version may follow.

Reflection and transmission
The optically active material takes the form of one or more thin layers on the surface of a rigid inert substrate, and is often protected by a further inert

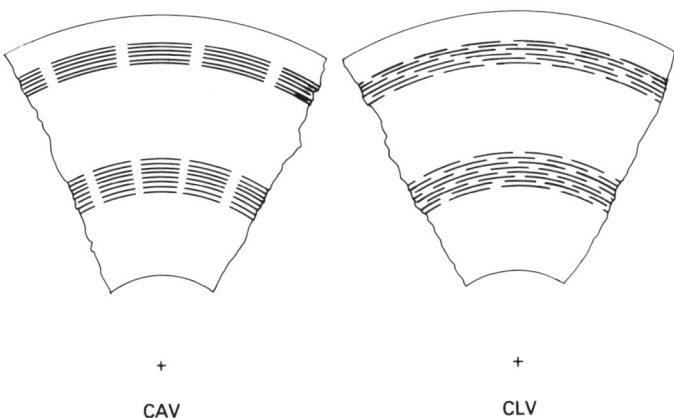

Fig. 2.3 — Sector layout for CAV and CLV.

layer. The state of the active layer may be detected either by transmission, in which case the light beam has to pass through the substrate and any protective layer as well as the active layer; or by reflection, in which case either the substrate or the protective layer can be opaque. In a reflective system, two active layers — one accessed from each side of the disk — can be used.

In practice, transmission is not now used in optical disk or card (although it was in some early prototypes) but may be used in optical tape systems.

Air incidence and substrate incidence
Reflective media can be arranged in two ways (Fig. 2.4). In the 'air-incident' layout the active layer is accessed by the light beam from the side opposite to the substrate; a tough transparent protective layer is therefore necessary (sometimes separated from the active layer by an air gap), but the substrate need not be transparent. In the 'substrate-incident' layout the active layer is accessed through the substrate, which must therefore be transparent while any protecting layer need not be. In either case the active layer is buried some distance below the surface on which the light beam is incident; consequently the beam is well out of focus at the surface, and covers a relatively large area, so dust particles or minor scratches have very little effect.

Substrate material
The substrate material for rigid disks must be very flat, and compatible with whatever further layers are to be placed on it. It must be fairly thin (typically 1 or 2 millimetres) to keep the size and weight of the disk within reasonable limits, but rigid enough to remain flat. In both transmission and substrate-incident-reflection layouts it must also be transparent. Suitable materials are toughened glass, plastic, and aluminium. Aluminium (which is obviously

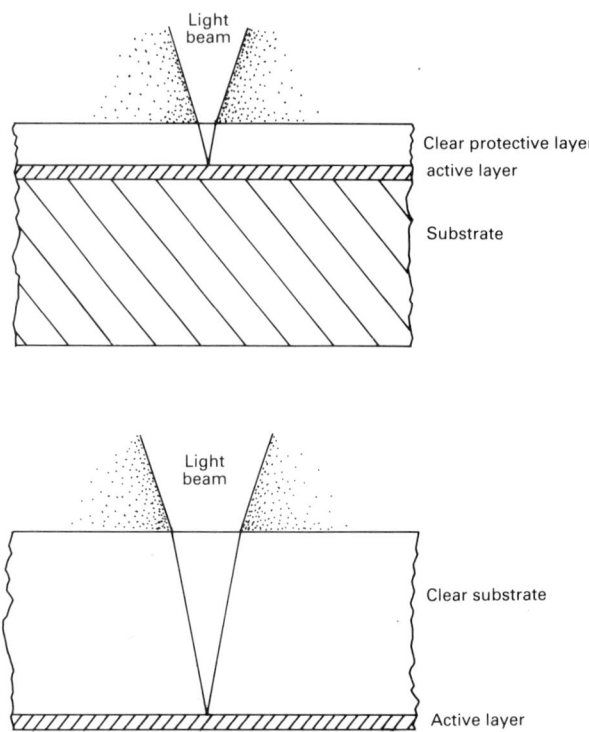

Fig. 2.4 — Disk layer structure for reflective media. Top: air incident. Bottom: substrate incident.

suitable only for the air-incident reflection layout) is favoured for 14 inch disks, substrates being available in this size from magnetic disk suppliers. For the 12 inch disk size, glass and plastic are favoured equally by different manufacturers; glass tends to be more expensive and to need more manufacturing steps but glass disks have a better manufacturing yield, so the final cost is not very different. The choice of a suitable plastic is fairly critical for large disks. Incidentally, toughened glass disks are at least as resistant to mechanical damage as plastic.

For smaller disks, plastic is now universally used. Polycarbonate, which is relatively cheap, is favourite; but in the substrate-incident layout it needs to be manufactured with care to avoid internal strains which can distort the light beam as it passes through.

Preformatting
Most WORM disks are partially preformatted in some way, and this information may be pressed onto the disk from a master (in the same way as will be described for read-only disks) before the active layer is applied. If the

substrate is plastic, the master may be one face of the mould in which the substrate is made, so no separate preformatting operation is necessary. This cannot be done with glass or metal disks, so the prepared substrate is coated with a layer of lacquer and the preformatting pattern is impressed into that. In the case of the 'moth eye' recording technology described above, the micro-relief pattern is formed in a similar way to that described for preformatting, and in the same operation.

Manufacture

The recording layer or layers are now deposited on the substrate. The composition of these layers depends on the recording method and the manufacturer. Often at least one of the layers is metal; the thermal properties of tellurium are particularly suitable, but as it is not chemically inert it is alloyed with other metals to reduce corrosion. Dye–polymer films are increasingly being used; they can be considerably cheaper to apply than metal.

Applying the active layers is one of the trickiest stages of manufacture, and each firm has its own approach. The aim of all of them is to achieve layers of uniform thickness, composition and surface relief which are nearly free from defects; nearly, because perfection cannot be economically achieved and the error-correction methods to be discussed later can cope with a certain level of defects. A protective layer is added if appropriate to the recording technology.

Disk structure

Most disks have a symmetrical construction (Fig. 2.5). Even if there are not two recording surfaces to make a double-sided medium, a dummy active layer is added at the back to reduce warping of the disk. Disks using air-incident recording methods have either a single substrate or two substrates cemented back-to-back. The active layers are outward, and a fairly thick transparent protective layer is deposited over each of them; alternatively a separate protective cover sheet may be attached on each side, leaving a small air gap, although this makes for a rather thick disk. Substrate-incident disks are made as a sandwich of two transparent substrates with the active layers inwards. If there is a protective layer at all it can be thin, and need not be transparent. There may be an air gap between the two halves of the sandwich, maintained by spacers at rim and hub. If so, the gap may be filled with dry air and sealed, or it may be left open to the atmosphere to prevent distortion of the disk if the external pressure changes.

Flexible media

Until now all optical disk drives have used rigid media, but a flexible medium has recently been announced under the trade name 'Digital Paper'. Disks based on this material differ in some details from the description above; in particular they do not need a balancing layer on the back of a single-sided disk, because symmetry is not necessary. The recording density is similar to that of rigid media. In spite of the name, the substrate is not paper but

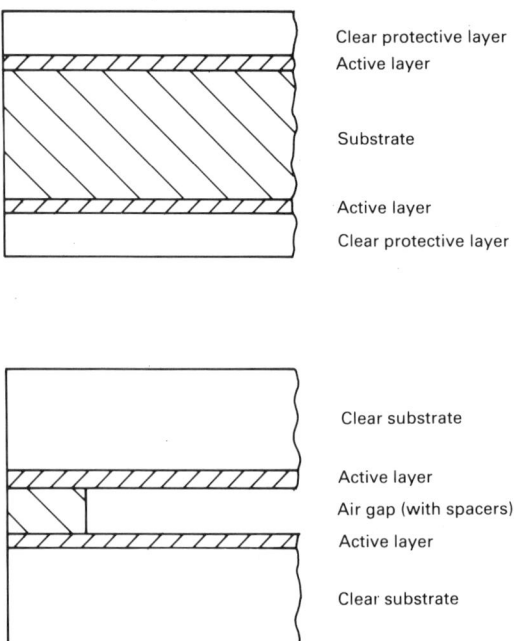

Fig. 2.5 — Typical double-sided disk structures. In the air-incident structure (top), the protective layers may be rigid sheets separated from the active layers by air gaps.

polyester plastic, only 25 to 100 microns thick; a dye–polymer active layer is used, with a thin protective coating over it. A completely new design of drive is needed. These disks should be cheaper to make than the rigid variety, and the drive may also be less expensive. However, some of the conventional medium's insensitivity to dust and surface contamination is lost because the active layer is buried less deeply, and so the light beam is spread over a smaller area at the outer surface; also the head-to-disk spacing is greatly reduced, to about 1 micron. Digital Paper disks are unlikely to be in commercial use before 1990.

Cartridges
Optical disks are much more rugged and resistant to dust or fingerprints than magnetic media. Nevertheless, WORM disks are always mounted within cartridges for protection and ease of handling. There are many designs of cartridge but the commonest arrangement (Fig. 2.6) is a plastic shell, with circular cutouts to allow the disk to be clamped to the drive hub. There are sliding shutters on each face: the appropriate set is opened automatically when the cartridge is loaded. This reveals a radial slot to allow the optical system access to the active part of the disk surface. The disk is so arranged that it can rotate freely within the cartridge when mounted in the drive, but is

Fig. 2.6 — 5¼ inch disk in cartridge. (Copyright Plasmon Data Systems.)

held by its rim when out of the drive. Precautions against the entry of dust are rudimentary, since dust is not a serious problem in optical storage (at least with rigid media). The cartridge includes a 'write-protect' device by which the operator can indicate that only read access is allowed; this is usually a plastic knob that is turned or slid to cover or uncover a slot in the cartridge edge, which can be sensed by a switch on the drive. The cartridge may have further slots or holes to tell the drive which side of the disk is presented for access, and possibly to identify a particular type of medium.

Stability
Archival storage is one of the most important applications of optical storage. Obviously it is essential that disks carrying data do not deteriorate after recording, even when stored — as is usual — in normal office conditions rather than in the controlled environment that is needed for magnetic tape archives. This stability depends mainly on the choice of materials. Since the substrate is inert it is not too difficult to find a suitable material. The active layers can be more of a problem. In particular, for ablative recording the best material from a recording point of view is the metal tellurium, but this is subject to slow corrosion if the atmosphere is moist. Ablative recording precludes the use of protective layers; sandwich construction, with the gap

filled with dry air, gives initial protection, but this is not now accepted as adequate because it is not easy to detect that a seal has become leaky in use. Tellurium is therefore alloyed with other materials, which have little effect on its recording properties but make it more resistant to corrosion.

An unlimited lifetime may or may not be attainable, but cannot be proved. However, there are techniques for accelerated life testing which allow fairly reliable predictions for a period several times the duration of the test. All makers now specify a life of at least 10 years for data recorded on WORM disks; one now says 30 years, another 100 years, and no doubt others will follow suit. It is not claimed that the media will not change at all during this time, but rather that the extent of deterioration will be limited, and the error-correction system has enough spare power to keep the error rate within the specified figure. In other words the 'raw' error rate of the data as read from the disk may worsen, but although the error rate seen by the user may also worsen slightly it will still be within specification. A shorter lifetime is sometimes specified for unrecorded disks; this is because slow changes may occur in the medium which increase the power needed to change the state of an element. A typical figure is four years.

It is usually assumed that reading the disk does not alter it in any way. There is evidence that this is not absolutely true, and that a very large number of read passes may cause some deterioration. The effect does, however, seem to be very small in all current media.

Defects

No manufacturing process will produce media completely free of defects; there is a trade-off between the manufacturing yield (and hence product cost) of media and the absence of defects. In the case of WORM disks, it is not economically practicable to make media free enough from defects to allow every sector containing a defect to be abandoned, as is often done with magnetic disks. Powerful error-correcting codes are therefore used, and a reasonable defect density can be tolerated. As the recording density is so high, a minor defect such as a pin-hole or foreign particle will often affect several consecutive storage elements; the error-correction method must allow for this. Error correction is discussed in more detail later in this chapter.

Testing is a problem with write-once media, since by definition it is not possible to test that the whole of the data area can be written. Besides sample tests, it is usual for a small part of the disk — not accessible to the user — to be reserved for manufacturing tests. Also non-destructive optical tests of the whole disk area pick up many of the defects that might cause writing errors.

Copying

The copying of preformat information from a master disk has already been discussed. Where WORM recording alters the surface profile of the medium, it is possible in principle to copy this to other disks (perhaps via intermediate disks) in a similar way. This was seriously proposed in connection with one of the first WORM media to use the 'bubble' recording method, but was not pursued and is not now regarded as practicable. However, it is of course possible to extend the preformatting data to include standard files — for example an operating system; the method of editing and mastering would be similar to that discussed in Chapter 4 for read-only disks.

ERROR MANAGEMENT

Error correction and detection are an essential part of any data storage device, since no storage method is perfect and yet the user requires something very close to perfection. The detection of errors is vital, since an undetected error can have very serious consequences. Once errors are detected it is desirable that they can be corrected; in this case failure is less serious, since the relevant part of the process can be repeated or the data recovered from some other source, but this can nevertheless be expensive. Small or non-critical computer systems rely on the storage peripheral itself to carry out error detection and correction (sometimes with the aid of the operating system). There is a limit to what can be achieved at a reasonable cost in this way, so where higher data integrity is required the host system will apply its own error detection and correction as well.

The following error rates, as seen by the application (i.e. after the device has corrected all the errors it can, with help from the operating system if necessary) are common, although there is always pressure for better figures:

Detected but uncorrected errors: not more than 1 in 10^{12} bits read;

Undetected errors: not more than 1 in 10^{14} bits read.

On a typical peripheral device in a typical application these figures correspond to something like one uncorrected error a year and one undetected error in 100 years.

Data coding and redundancy

The detection and correction of errors depends on the presence of redundancy in the coding of the data; in other words the number of storage elements used to store a given amount of data is not the smallest possible number. The proportion of errors that can be detected, and the extent to which they can be corrected, depend on the degree of redundancy — although not in a simple manner.

It is never practicable to eliminate all errors. The aim of the device designer is to use data-coding methods which are powerful enough to reduce the 'raw' error rate of the medium to a 'perceived' error rate which is acceptable to the user.

Detection of errors is achieved by redundant coding of the data, sometimes backed up by various tests within the disk drive to find marginal conditions such as low signal amplitude. *Correction* of errors can be done in two ways, on-the-fly or by re-try. On-the-fly correction needs more complex and more redundant data coding, allowing a defective data block to be corrected within the drive before it is passed to the host; as an alternative the block could be passed to the host together with enough information to allow host software to do the correction, but this is not normal practice with optical disk. Re-try simply requires the failed read transfer to be repeated, in the hope that the cause of the error will have gone away; the device may carry out the repeat on its own initiative, or it may need a fresh command from the host system. Re-try works very well with magnetic recording, where dust particles or (in the case of tape) misalignment of the medium are the commonest causes of error; it may be combined with the use of error-correcting codes to improve the unrecovered error rate further. Re-try is far less effective with optical recording, because this is intrinsically less sensitive to dust and uses more sophisticated methods to deal with misalignment.

Powerful error-correcting codes are therefore the rule on optical disk, including WORM. The codes are complex — so much so that their design and implementation is usually entrusted to one of the few specialist firms rather than done by the drive designer — and will not be discussed in detail here. The end result is that a 'raw' error rate (i.e. that seen if no error correction is used) such as one error in 10^5 bits is converted to a perceived error rate of 1 to 10^{12} or better. The price paid for the improved error rate is typically 20% to 50% data redundancy, and also some complex coding and decoding hardware. The coding involves treating a whole sector as a unit; within this, the order of the signal elements on the track may be quite different from that of the corresponding data bits at the interface of the disk drive.

Checking

As with magnetic disk storage, when data has been written to the disk it should be checked for correctness. Most optical disk drives do this automatically; some give the user the option of suppressing this read-after-write check, to improve performance at the expense of data integrity. One manufacturer claims that the check is not really necessary, because the read error correction on his drive will cope with any conceivable write errors; but few users would be willing to accept this proposition, so the option of checking is provided.

There are two approaches to read-after-write checking. The more common is that used with magnetic disk; a sector (or up to a whole track) is written during one revolution of the disk and then check-read during the next revolution. The check does not involve comparing the data read with that originally supplied by the host, but simply using the error-detection coding to test the sector for self-consistency. The disadvantage of this approach is that the time taken to write data is at least doubled, or more if whole tracks cannot be written.

The second approach is to read each storage element very soon after it has been written, checking at the end of each sector or block to see whether any errors are shown by the error-detection logic. This is called 'direct read after write' or DRAW, and is similar to the method used on most magnetic tape drives. One early drive, no longer available, achieved DRAW by having separate read and write laser systems; others do it with multiple beams derived from a single laser. In a few drives, each bit is actually checked while it is being written; this is called 'direct read during write' (DRDW), and in this case each bit is checked against the bit that should have been written at that location. DRDW requires a good deal more technical ingenuity than DRAW, and may in fact reduce the writing speed — although not as much as reading on a second revolution would.

Unfortunately a few manufacturers wrongly claim to use DRAW when in fact the check is made on a subsequent revolution (the term RAW, for 'read after write', would be valid). This is not deliberate misrepresentation, but rather an attempt to distinguish disks which are immediately readable from those which have to be processed (such as those which use photographic techniques, and which are normally regarded as 'read-only' disks).

Write error recovery

Write error recovery depends on the detection of an error by the read-after-write check. Unlike magnetic disks, the offending sector of an optical disk is not re-read if any error is detected; instead the error correction logic is used to see whether the write error can in fact be corrected in this way. It is usual to apply a stricter threshold (i.e. less powerful error correction) than is used for normal reading, to provide a margin for possible deterioration during the life of the disk. If the write error is found to be within this limit, no further action is taken. If it is not, the sector is rewritten. It cannot of course be rewritten in the same location, and (especially if checking is done a revolution after writing) the next consecutive location may not be available; it is therefore rewritten either in the next free location or in an area of the disk reserved for the purpose, according to the drive design. The sector allocation system needs to keep track of sectors that are relocated in this way; as we shall see later, optical disks usually have intelligent interfaces (such as SCSI) which take care of this problem and hide it from the host.

RECORDING FORMATS AND STANDARDS

If a disk is to be read on any other drive than the one which wrote it, it is obvious that the medium, recording method, storage element location and preformatting must be compatible — this is usually implicit in the choice of media. It is also necessary that the mapping of data onto the signal elements be compatible, and this is closely tied up with the error-detection/correction scheme used. Such details are of course defined by every manufacturer or media supplier for his own use; but if interchange of disks between drives of different makes is needed there must be a common acceptance of these definitions, which thus become formal or unofficial standards.

The establishment of data interchange standards for WORM optical disks has not yet made enough progress for WORM disk to be useful as a data interchange medium; it is to be hoped that things will improve. The first generation of disks, mostly in the 12 inch size, was designed with very little regard to data interchange; each manufacturer adopted his own format which was incompatible with all the others, apart from one pair who had a technology interchange agreement and adopted nominally the same definitions. This lack of standards was soon seen to be a deterrent to the wide adoption of optical storage; so when it became obvious that $5\frac{1}{4}$ inch media would be the next preferred size, the drive designers aimed for early agreement on a standard. They decided to do this through the official standards bodies, to get the widest acceptance. Much of the work was done in ECMA, the European Computer Manufacturers Association; not because many of the developers were European (they were mostly from the USA or Japan), but because this was thought to be the fastest way to a standard. This would then be passed on to ISO, the International Standards Organisation, for ratification as an ISO standard.

Unfortunately, agreement was harder to reach than had been expected, and after three years work the standard is still incomplete. A conclusion has been reached on most points, though at the cost of including some alternatives; this means that the standard will allow a set of slightly different and incompatible products. In the meantime, however, a number of manufacturers — now joined by IBM — have brought out products which do not take the standard into account. So, although the standard will certainly be issued, the extent of its adoption remains in doubt.

It is interesting to contrast these events with the development of standards for magnetic tape drives using the '3M' design of cartridge. In that case, a group of manufacturers set up informal working parties; these were able to reach agreement quite rapidly and to issue standards which were adopted by their own and other companies. These standards were then passed to the official standards bodies, which edited them before publication but made no significant technical change.

It is to be hoped that the standardization of future optical disk types will be more successful. There is a good chance that a single standard for 14 inch disks will emerge; one manufacturer has defined his product well in advance of any competition, so his specification is likely to be adopted as a *de-facto* standard.

One other format where a firm standard can be expected is the so-called 'CD-PROM', the WORM version of the CD-ROM. The latter is closely specified by a pair of manufacturers who can enforce standards through their control of patents; their standards for CD-PROM will also hold if this product is in fact a success.

MECHANISMS

So far in this chapter we have discussed the disk and the way in which data is arranged on it. We now turn to the mechanism which makes use of this medium, the write-once optical disk drive. It is appropriate to start at the point of contact between the two, the hub on which the disk is mounted.

Ideally, the axis of rotation of the disk would be precisely normal to the plane of the disk and concentric with the tracks on it. This depends on the design of the drive hub, the disk centre hole and the clamping mechanism. Perfection cannot be achieved, and the servo systems controlling the optical head are designed to handle eccentricity (or radial run-out) and deviation from the normal (axial run-out) of a fraction of a millimetre. These errors still need to be kept as small as possible, to ease the design of the servo systems.

Two clamping methods can be used; mechanical, where all the disk needs to have is an accurately cut centre hole, and magnetic, where it has a metal ring attached which is attracted by a magnet in the hub. In general the mechanical method is cheaper but allows greater errors. Both methods are used, and the selection of a method for the $5\frac{1}{4}$ inch disk was one of the causes of the delay to that standard.

Disk rotation
The spindle motor, which rotates the disk, must be controlled by a servo system if the drive rotates the disk at CLV (constant linear velocity). This servo system uses the servo information preformatted on the disk to match the data rate to a clock in the drive. CAV (constant angular velocity) drives may also use a servo-controlled motor, or alternatively a simpler constant-speed motor with the drive clock synchronized to the servo information. The inertia of a 12 inch disk is considerable, and the motor takes typically 10 seconds to spin the disk from rest to operating speed. When the drive is built into a library mechanism a more powerful spindle motor is often fitted to reduce the spin-up time.

Optical head
The optical head is the heart of the disk drive. Many of its components are derived from videodisk or Compact Audio technology, so they are relatively cheap. The essential parts (Fig. 2.7) are a laser to generate and modulate the light beam, one or more lenses to focus it on the active layer of the disk, a beam splitter (such as a half-silvered mirror) to deflect part of the reflected energy away from the outward path, and a detector to detect this reflected energy. There are often extra components to modify the beam for various purposes; in particular to allow it to be used to control the various servo systems, as well as for its primary purpose of reading and writing data.

In most WORM drives there is a mirror deflecting the beam through a right angle, so that most of the optical system lies on an axis parallel to the disk surface; only the objective lens (which focuses the parallel laser beam to a spot) comes between the mirror and the disk.

Gas lasers, sometimes more than one, were used in some early WORM disk drives. However, all commercial products now use a single semiconductor laser. A typical laser for this service is mounted in a can similar to that of a transistor, a few millimetres in each dimension. It has an optical output of 10 or 20 milliwatts at full power; the power can be modulated at the required data rate, which is necessary for writing, and reduced to a defined lower level for reading (Fig. 2.8). The light is emitted at a single wavelength. To obtain

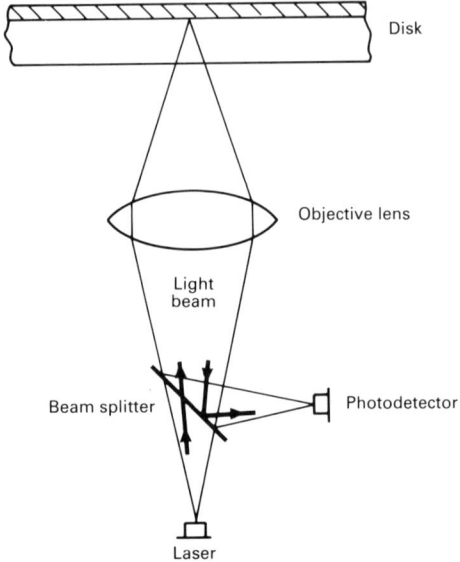

Fig. 2.7 — Basic optical system.

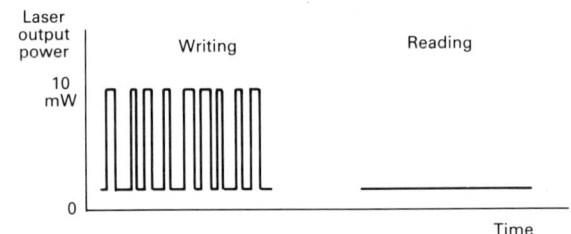

Fig. 2.8 — Laser output power waveform.

the highest data density we would like this to be a short wavelength; but the technology for manufacturing such lasers is not yet fully developed (although blue lasers of very low power have been made), so the lasers used are in the red or near-infrared area of the spectrum. The beam emitted is slightly divergent (unlike that of a gas laser which is very nearly parallel), but usually only by about 5°, so that a collimating lens is not essential. Early semiconductor lasers had a rather short lifetime; one spin-off from the entertainment field is better laser manufacturing technology, and the laser is now expected to last throughout the lifetime of the drive.

The reflected light beam is detected by a silicon photodetector, of similar dimensions to the laser and again owing much of its development to the entertainment field. It consists of several sections — in effect separate detectors, placed very close together. To sense the data represented by the light reflected from the storage elements on the disk, signals from these detectors are processed so as to sum the light falling on all of them.

Track following

The focus spot must be moved radially to whichever track is to be accessed, and kept on that track as the disk rotates even though the track may be eccentric. As electro-optic methods of deflecting the beam would be very expensive, the spot is moved by mechanical methods, under servo control. Most drives use two separate servomechanisms. Small radial movements are needed to follow the eccentricity of the disk, or to access another track close to the first (typically up to 20 tracks apart); for such movements the spot is moved by tilting the mirror which turns the beam through a right angle, as mentioned above. The mirror is very light so beam movement is fast, typically several track widths per millisecond. For larger movements, all or part of the optical system is moved radially (or sometimes in an arc which approximates to a radius). This movement is slower because of the greater inertia involved, but spans all the tracks on the disk. It is usual to mount the whole optical system on a carriage or arm and move it as a unit, which avoids any alignment problems within the head. Alternatively the laser can be mounted in a fixed position on the frame; in this case the light beam must be parallel where it passes between the moving and fixed parts of the optical system (Fig. 2.9). The fixed laser layout was used in some early drives which used gas rather than semiconductor lasers, since gas lasers are heavy, and is again becoming popular as shorter access times are sought.

Each of the two movements is controlled by a separate servo system. The mirror servo acts to keep the beam correctly located on the disk track; the carriage or arm servo acts to allow the oscillation of the mirror, as it follows the track, to be centred within its range of movement. The rate of response of the second servo is limited so that it does not attempt to follow the track eccentricity.

Focusing

It is very important that the laser beam is focused on the active layer of the disk; focusing must be dynamic, since the disk axis may not be precisely normal to its plane and the disk may not be perfectly flat. The beam is focused by moving the objective lens along an axis normal to the disk surface. The commonest way of providing this motion is to attach the lens to a coil working in the field of a permanent magnet, like the voice coil of a loudspeaker; the lens is moved by varying the coil current, under the control of yet another servo system (Fig. 2.10).

The focus servo and the fine track-following servo require as input a signal showing the deviation of the laser spot from the correct position, both in the plane of the disk and perpendicular to it. These are often derived from the same multi-segment photodetector that is used for the data signal, by

40 WRITE-ONCE DISKS

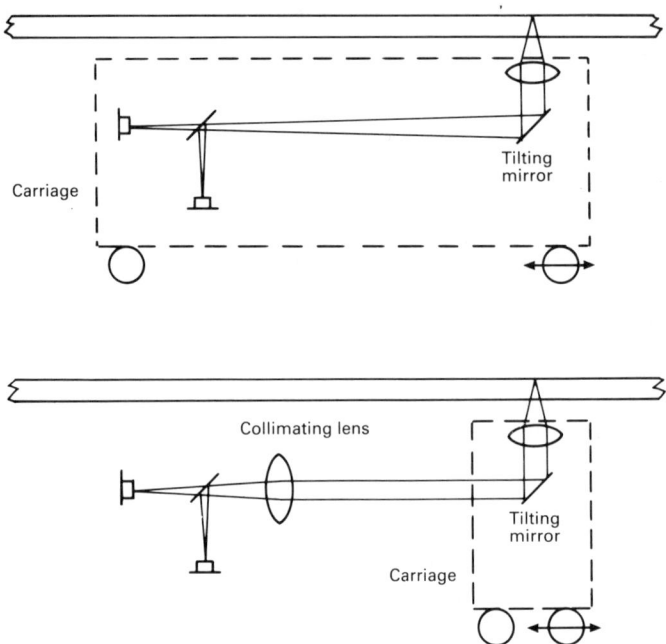

Fig. 2.9 — Alternative layouts for optical systems. Top: laser on head carriage. Bottom: laser fixed to frame.

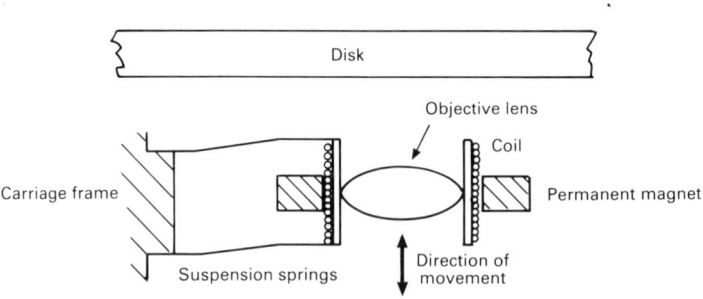

Fig. 2.10 — Method of focusing.

combining the signals from it in different ways. The details differ from drive to drive. In a typical example (Fig. 2.11) the track-following error is measured by dividing the four photodetector elements into two pairs, each pair collecting light from one side of where the track centre line should be

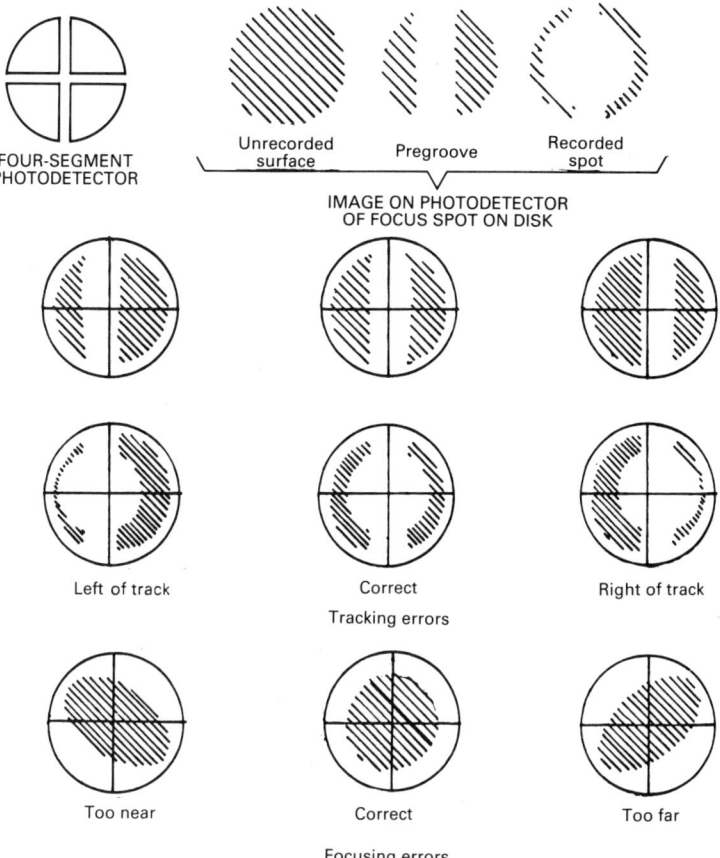

Fig. 2.11 — Use of photodetector to measure tracking and focusing errors.

(relative to the head). Their outputs are compared to find the difference between the amounts of light reflected onto each pair. The focus servo depends on additional optical components such as a knife-edge and cylindrical lens; if the beam is out of focus, the spot image reflected onto the photodetector is elongated in one direction if the beam focus is too high, and in a direction at right angles if it is too low. Using a four-quadrant detector, the light falling on one diagonally opposite pair of quadrants is compared with the other to obtain the error signal. Both error signals are filtered to remove the high frequencies representing the stored data.

Flexible disks
Flexible optical disks need rather different drives. These are at an early stage of development, but will probably reach the market in 1990. The most promising approach uses the 'Bernoulli effect', already exploited in a magnetic disk drive. When a flexible disk is rotated close to a stationary flat

plate, the disk is drawn towards the plate; it reaches a stable position parallel and very close to the plate, but kept out of contact by a thin air gap (Fig. 2.12). The gap is typically about one micron. The disk will rise over minor

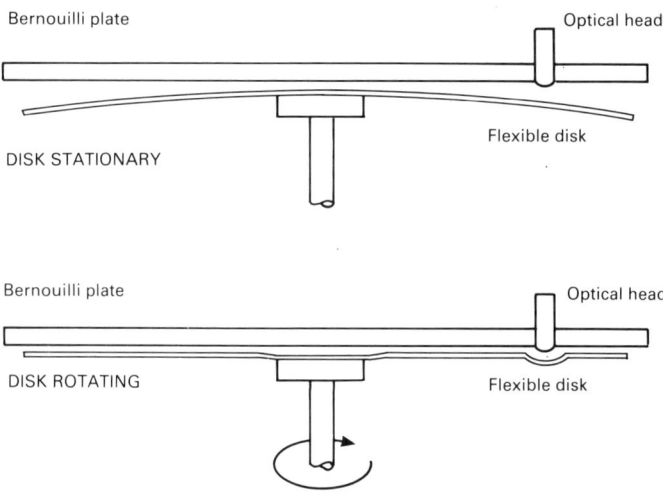

Fig. 2.12 — The Bernoulli effect.

protrusions without contact, developing a ripple rather like that of a stream flowing over a submerged rock.

The optical head is located in a radial slot in the plate; it carries only the objective lens and a mirror, with the laser and the rest of the optical components fixed to the chassis of the drive. The head-to-disk distance is very short, which allows a small lens to be used, and the distance varies so little that no focus-following mechanism is needed. This makes the optical head very light, so a single-stage track-following system can be used as in fast magnetic disk drives. The drive using flexible optical disks therefore has potential cost and performance advantages over rigid disk drives. Against this, the short head-to-disk distance brings with it some of the dust and surface contamination problems that are encountered with magnetic disks; more powerful error correction may be needed to take care of this.

DEVICE CHARACTERISTICS

The description in the preceding pages of the way the disk drive works will help to explain the characteristics which it displays when looked at as a 'black box'. We gave some general consideration to device characteristics in Chapter 1; we shall now take a closer look at them, noting those which have a particular bearing on the tasks for which WORM disks are suited, and comparing them with competing technologies. Of course characteristics vary in detail from one product to the next, and to assess any particular product the system designer needs at least a data sheet and, for a fuller appreciation, specifications. (He also needs to notice what is missing from these documents!)

A typical data sheet is given in Table 2.1. This is a fictitious example, though the figures are appropriate to a fairly early 12 inch WORM drive, and is introduced as a peg for the discussion which follows. (Appendix 3 includes typical data sheets for a range of drives now on the market.)

Some actual data sheets give more information than this, though this is enough for an initial assessment; others give less — the mean time between failures (MTBF) figure is often missing, with IBM one of the worst offenders. Sometimes more important characteristics are not shown at all in a data sheet, or buried in the descriptive text; for example that the disk is removable, and that only one side can be read at a time. The arrangement of the figures varies. Often those relating to the disk are separated from those relating to the drive (the disk need not be purchased from the drive supplier). In this example the items are listed in an order convenient for our discussion; performance characteristics first, reliability and environmental characteristics later. We shall discuss the items in Table 2.1 in the order in which they appear.

Capacity
The capacity specified is that guaranteed to the user, and declared at the interface if this is the Small Computer Systems Interface (SCSI) or some other intelligent interface; the space actually available for data is rather more than this to allow for bad sectors. There will usually be also a few test sectors which the user cannot see, although the service engineer may be able to reach them with diagnostic programs. The important figure is the capacity of one side, since this is all that will be on-line; two-sided disks may reduce the user's media bill but will do little else for him unless he has a jukebox. Unfortunately many suppliers quote only the total capacity of two sides, or at least give greater prominence to this. CLV disks usually have a capacity about 50% greater than CAV disks which are otherwise similar. Where a drive can use both CAV and CLV disks, the capacity and performance depend on the type of disk loaded.

The figures showing how the total capacity is divided into sectors and tracks are of no real interest to the user if the drive has an intelligent interface, as most do; in that case the disk structure is hidden from him. An exception to this is the sector length, which normally corresponds to the block length seen at the interface and so defines the unit of data transfer. The drive will keep a record of the mapping of the 'logical' blocks seen by the user onto the physical tracks and sectors of the disk. The disk space for this

Table 2.1 — Data sheet for a typical 12 inch WORM optical disk drive

Capacity per side	1 Gbyte (i.e. 1000 Mbytes)
Capacity per sector	1024 bytes
Sectors per track	32
Tracks* per side	32 000
Track format	Spiral
Data rate — continuous	256 kbyte/second
Data rate at interface — burst	2 Mbyte/second
Access time:	
Seek time (within 20 tracks)	1 ms per track
Seek time — average	200 ms
Seek time — maximum	500 ms
Latency — average	50 ms
Spindle run-up/run-down time	10 seconds
Write error checking	Next revolution
Disk life:	
Before writing	4 years
Recorded data	10 years
Error rate	1 in 10^{12} bits
Reliability — MTBF	10 000 hours power on
Power requirement	110 or 240 V, 50 or 60 cycles
Power consumption	400 watts
Drive dimensions	
(including SCSI controller)	
Height	8 inches
Width	19 inches
Depth	24 inches
Operating temperature range	10° to 40°C
Media storage:	
Temperature range	0° to 60°C
Relative humidity range	5% to 95%
Interface	SCSI

* 'Tracks' may be strictly turns of a continuous spiral.

record is not part of the user's allocation; but the directories recording the user's allocation of logical blocks to files (or anything else) are user data, and the user must decide where to put them. A simple but popular arrangement is to write the directories at the top end of the user's data area on the disk, starting with the highest numbered logical block (or sector) and working downwards; these directories are normally copied to magnetic disk when the optical disk is loaded into the system, and written to the optical disk only when it is about to be unloaded. This avoids using up disk space every time the directory is amended.

Performance

Two data rates are usually specified. The continuous data rate is the rate at which data is actually read from, or written to, the disk, allowing for headers and other housekeeping; in other words, averaged over a whole sector. This data rate can be kept up continuously, so long as the host can fill or empty the data buffers of the drive fast enough. If only one data rate is given, this will apply to reading. If DRDW or true DRAW is provided, the writing data rate will be the same; if not, it will normally be half the reading rate because each sector has to be checked a revolution after it was written. Note the warning in an earlier section of this chapter that some manufacturers' claims to provide DRAW are incorrect.

The burst data rate is the maximum rate at which data can be transferred across the interface to the host, and can only be kept up until the drive buffers are exhausted. The data sheet sometimes, but not always, quotes the buffer capacity; in most cases it will be at least the amount of data that can be held on one track of the disk — typically 32 kilobytes.

Access time has two components, just as in magnetic disks: 'seek time' and 'latency'. Seek time is the time taken for the access spot to reach the required track and stabilize there, so that the track can be read; latency is the time from this moment until the start of the required data reaches the head. Some data sheets quote these items separately, some only quote the total. The access time in any specific case depends on the number of tracks from the current head position to the new one, the rotational position of the disk, and whether the new track can be reached by a mirror movement alone or also requires a carriage movement. The figures quoted in the specification are therefore averages, usually based on a head movement across one third of the tracks. The average access time is greater than that for most magnetic disk drives; partly because of the greater inertia of the head, and partly because a lower disk rotation speed — and hence a greater average latency — is usual. $5\frac{1}{4}$ inch disks are faster than 12 inch disks as the head movement range is shorter and in most cases the disk speed is higher. As has been mentioned already, access times for CLV disks are considerably longer — typically one second — because of the need to change and stabilize the disk speed.

The spindle run-up and run-down times are not important if the drive is manually loaded; they are small compared with the time taken to replace one disk by another, and once loaded the disk is kept rotating constantly. They are more important in an automated disk library system, as we shall see in a later chapter.

The method of write error checking is important. Checking on a second revolution will double the number of revolutions needed; in other words the write data rate, averaged over a long transfer, will be half the read data rate.

Some data sheets do give separate write and read data rates to allow for this. It is also important to know whether the drive will automatically optimize write transfers by writing a whole track and then checking it before writing the next; this is not always clear from the data sheet. (The method is only sound when the whole track of data is presented at one time by the host. If data were retained in the drive buffers, rather than on disk, after the host had discarded it, it could be lost in the event of drive or power failure.)

Reliability and data integrity

The characteristics we have covered affect performance. Those that remain are concerned with reliability and environment, which are to some extent related. Disk life was discussed earlier in this chapter, but it should be noted that the specified figure is valid only if the disk is stored within the limits shown in the specification. In fact these limits are not onerous, and excursion beyond them for a short time (say days) will not have a drastic effect, so the average disk life will be well beyond the specified figure.

The error rate is that seen at the host interface, after the drive has done whatever error correction it can. It refers to the number of blocks which the drive passes to the host with a signal to show that the block contains at least one error (it may be totally corrupted). The rate is given as a proportion of the total number of bits transferred by the drive. The figure of 1 in 10^{12} is often specified, largely because this is typical of magnetic disk practice and so is acceptable to most users. It is not difficult to devise an error-correction scheme to give better results than this, though there will be some trade-off in cost and disk capacity. In any case the figure is chosen to allow for whatever deterioration is foreseen during the lifetime of the disk; in other words, in this example, the read error rate will be at least as good as the specified figure for ten years after the disk was recorded. In an earlier section we discussed the undetected error rate; this figure is very rarely given in manufacturers' data sheets or specifications.

The reliability of the drive is usually expressed as the MTBF in hours. It is of course a statistical average taken over a large number of drives and not a figure guaranteed for each one of them; there will be a substantial random variation between drives. The figure will be based on certain operating conditions which are often not spelt out in the data sheet, but which the drive manufacturer regards as typical; for example on operation under normal office environmental conditions, rather than at the limits of the specification, and on an 'average' number of read and write accesses rather than continuous access. The hours measured will be those for which the drive is powered up.

The reader is warned that the specification of reliability of optical disk drives, just as for any other electronic equipment in which there is no predictable 'wear-out' mechanism, is a contentious subject. To get a statistically valid figure from controlled tests would tie up many drives for a long time; few manufacturers will undertake this. Collecting data from drives in actual customer use is hard to do without gross errors. There are well-known methods of predicting MTBF figures by calculation based on the number and type of components used in the drive, but these can do no more than show what is likely to be achieved if the drive is well designed. As important as the average figure is the range of variation about it, and this is never specified; since the MTBF is usually greater than the time for which a drive is likely to be kept in service, if the range was small enough there would be no failures!

The specified reliability figures are thus no more than a rough guide to the reliability to be expected; it would be unwise to give them much weight, without other evidence, when selecting a drive.

Packaging
Most large drives, and other drives which are designed for 'external' use rather than building into the host, require AC power input. They are usually adjustable to a range of voltages and a choice of 50 or 60 Hz, though in some cases different versions of the drive may be needed for different supplies. $5\frac{1}{4}$ inch and smaller drives designed for building in need DC input from the host at the same voltages, and usually within the same current limits, as those magnetic disk drives that fit the same 'footprint'. Some specifications give 'average' and 'peak' figures for current and power consumption, as the demand is highest while the head is being moved; the difference is not usually great, so often only the maximum figure is given.

Drive dimensions of course depend on the drive type. 14 inch drives are often fitted in a waist-high cabinet, which may hold two drives and their auxiliaries. 12 inch drives are generally designed to fit a standard 19 inch wide mounting rack, taking up 6 or 8 inches of rack height; usually the controller and power supply unit are included within these dimensions, although in some cases they are separate items. Obviously such drives can be mounted in a desktop box instead of a rack if preferred. A typical 12 inch WORM drive is illustrated in Fig. 2.13 and 2.14.

Most smaller drives are designed to fit into the standard slots provided for 'internal' peripherals in PCs and many other small computers. Many $5\frac{1}{4}$ inch drives fit the '$5\frac{1}{4}$ inch footprint'; newer ones may fit the 'half-height $5\frac{1}{4}$ inch footprint'. $3\frac{1}{2}$ inch drives, and those using the 80 mm version of 'CD-PROM', will be designed for the '$3\frac{1}{2}$ inch footprint', which also allows them (with an extended front bezel) to fit $5\frac{1}{4}$ inch half-height slots. These internally mounted drives may include a controller, but sometimes this is a separate item for which additional space must be found — often a single circuit board. Again, such drives can also be fitted into desktop boxes; in this case the box is usually large enough to hold the drive, its controller if appropriate, and an AC power supply unit.

A typical $5\frac{1}{4}$ inch drive is illustrated in Fig. 2.15.

Environment
The operating temperature range (like other environmental constraints, such as humidity and dust concentration) corresponds to a normal office environment; there is nothing about optical disk systems that calls for special precautions.

48 WRITE-ONCE DISKS

Fig. 2.13 — 12 inch WORM optical disk drive. (Copyright Laser Magnetic Storage International.)

The storage temperature and humidity ranges for the media are of some importance, since ease of storage is claimed as a major advantage of optical disk. The figures given in the example are typical, but there is a surprisingly wide variation between suppliers. Some quote only the same temperature range as for operation; at the other extreme, a storage temperature range of $-40°$ to $+90°C$ has been specified for 'moth-eye' media.

Interface
The final item in our data sheet is the interface. Interfaces are discussed in detail in Chapter 7, but the norm for WORM drives is SCSI. This is a high-level (or intelligent) interface that hides most of the details of data layout and error recovery from the host. Other interfaces may be available as options; on the one hand interfaces to suit specific computers (most often the IBM PC and some DEC machines), and on the other simpler interfaces, often proprietary. Lower (or mechanism level) interfaces allow drive and controller to be designed and bought separately; they are not widely used, because of the importance of correct co-operation between drive and controller in error management.

Price
One figure which never appears in a data sheet or specification is the price of the product. This obviously varies with the manufacturer, the specification, the size of the order, and the level of support provided (not to mention the strength of the buyer's bargaining position). As a very rough guide, in 1988 a

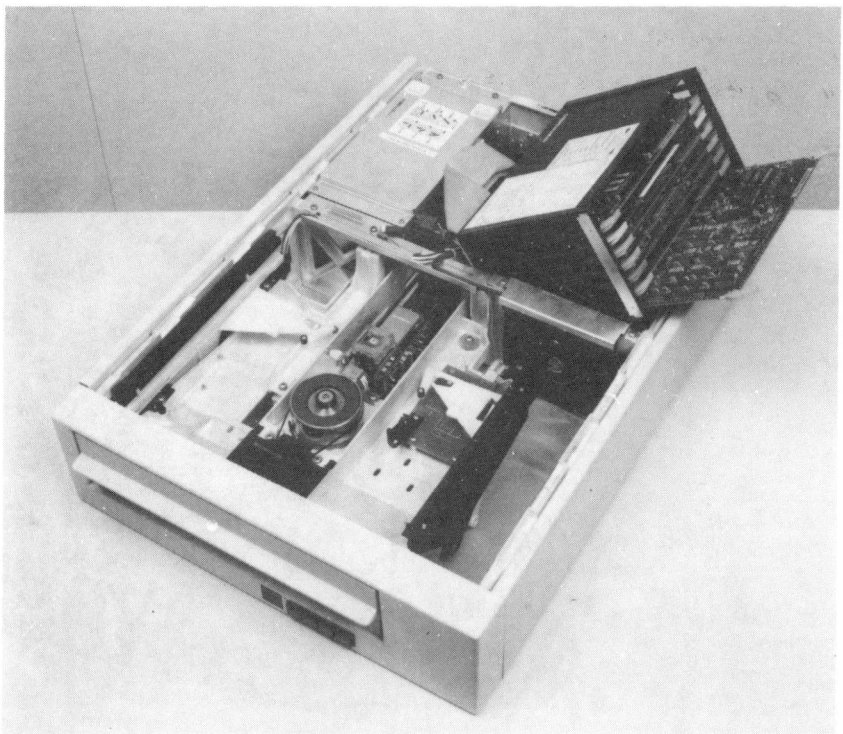

Fig. 2.14 — The drive shown in Fig. 2.13 with top cover removed, and no disk in the drive. The hub is towards the front (lower left) of the drive; the optical head, which accesses the underside of the disk, moves on slides between the hub and the back of the drive. (Copyright Laser Magnetic Storage International.)

12 inch WORM drive, in large quantities, costs $6000 to $10 000 and a $5\frac{1}{4}$ inch drive $2000 to $3000. Media cost is even more variable, but typically $400 for a 12 inch disk and $60 to $120 for a $5\frac{1}{4}$ inch disk; this works out at about 10 to 20 cents per megabyte. (Dollar prices are generally quoted since these are relatively stable, most manufacturers being in the USA or Japan.) As with all computer equipment, prices tend to fall over the years; in particular the price of disks is as yet far from stable.

Ruggedized drives
As well as standard drives, there are a few ruggedized drives on the market. These are intended mainly for military or mobile use. The medium is inherently rugged, and the head-to-disk spacing is relatively large, so it is much easier to ruggedize an optical disk drive than the magnetic equivalent. Even so, ruggedized drives are heavier and more expensive than the standard types.

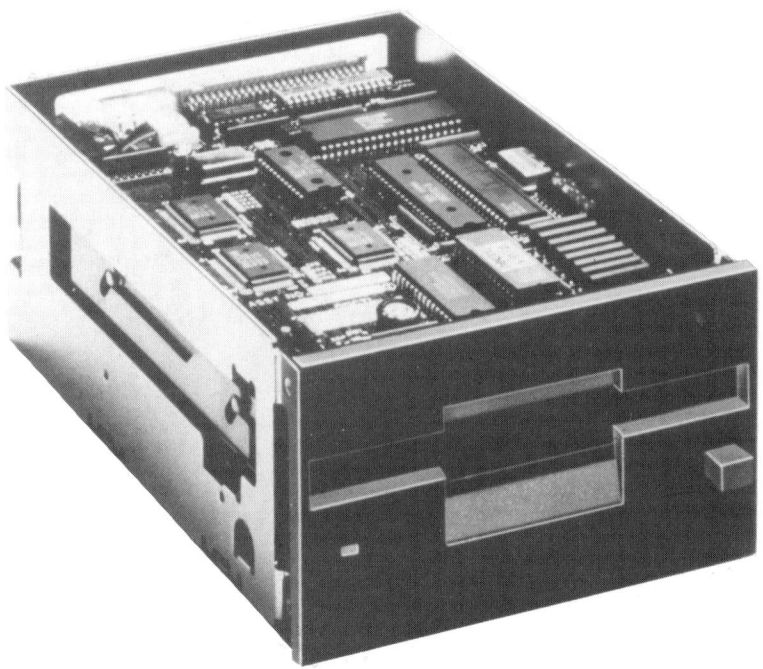

Fig. 2.15 — 5¼ inch WORM optical disk drive. (Copyright Maxtor Europe.)

STRENGTHS AND WEAKNESSES

Having looked at the characteristics of WORM optical stores in isolation, we can now compare them with competing technologies to see where their strengths and weaknesses lie. In practice this means comparing them with magnetic tape and disk stores.

Comparison with magnetic disk

Strong points of WORM storage are the ruggedness of the medium, its tolerance of climatic variations, and the wide head-to-disk spacing. These features make it easy to design the drive so that the disks can be removed, and they make the disks easy to handle and store when removed. In contrast, the only magnetic disk drives with removable media are those with relatively low data density and hence high media cost; and disk packs or cartridges need careful handling and storage (less so, of course, for extremely low data densities as on floppy disks).

The high data density achieved by WORM disk storage is also a major strength. One side of a WORM disk can hold as much data as a multi-platter magnetic disk drive, and this directly reduces the size of the drive and (in the case of removable media) the disk pack or cartridge.

The non-erasability of WORM storage can be either a strength or a weakness depending on the application. In comparison with magnetic disk it is mainly a weakness, since re-usable media have an obvious cost advantage where disks are used only for transient storage. Magnetic disks are not often used for long-term storage; they are less suitable than WORM because magnetic disks need environmental control, are inherently less permanent, and (even when removable) have a higher media cost per megabyte.

Magnetic disks have the edge over optical disks of comparable price when performance is compared; it is not obvious how long this difference will persist. It has been claimed that WORM drives using flexible media will approach the performance of magnetic disk drives.

In terms of data integrity there is little to choose between optical and magnetic media; in fact the hard (i.e. uncorrectable) error rate is a trade-off between user requirements and cost, and both kinds of disk could use more powerful error correction to produce a better figure.

Finally, there is no clear advantage either way in terms of mechanism cost; the single head requirement of the optical drive is offset by its more complex head, additional servo systems, and error-correction logic.

Comparison with magnetic tape

The comparison with magnetic tape brings in different criteria. Tape is cheaper than magnetic disk; the cost per byte of WORM is not significantly different from that of conventional magnetic tape if used once, so obviously in favour of tape if the medium is re-used. Helical-scan magnetic tape is considerably cheaper than WORM disk. Optical disks have some advantage over tape reels in terms of volume capacity and storage space; they are obviously easier to handle than open-reel tape but very similar in this respect to tape cartridges.

A major strength of WORM disks is their long life and environmental tolerance. Even the latest tape cartridges have a lower maximum temperature (32°C) than the standard office environment; and where tape is used for archiving it needs regular attention and environmental control, which makes it expensive to store.

Again, non-erasability can count either way. It makes magnetic tape the better medium for backup, but worse for archiving.

WORM storage has an obvious advantage over tape in respect of access time; but its data rate falls within the range available from various tape systems.

WORM also offers better error rates than most magnetic tape units. This is not an inherent advantage, however, but a result of the more powerful error correction used in WORM stores. Magnetic tape systems can be built with more error correction if required, and some such products exist — notably helical-scan devices using the DAT (digital audio tape) cartridge.

WORM stores are more expensive than comparable tape stores — though of course deciding what is comparable is somewhat arbitrary when the products differ so much.

Software support

Both magnetic disk and tape are long-established products, and software for their management is universally available. For optical disk the choice is not yet so wide, and may involve an addition to the basic operating system.

APPLICATIONS

The characteristics of any product, not least the price, decide the applications for which it will be considered. In this case the characteristics are similar in many ways to those of magnetic disk and tape, so clearly the same applications are potentially suitable; which technology will be preferred depends on a detailed comparison such as we made in the last section.

Archiving

The application where WORM storage offers most benefit is data archiving. For this purpose removable magnetic disk media are much more expensive, in dollars per megabyte, than WORM disks. Most types of magnetic tape cost about the same per megabyte as WORM disk for the initial purchase, although helical-scan tapes (such as those based on digital audio tape) are much cheaper; but magnetic tape needs regular attention and a controlled environment, and this adds to its cost. Archiving on WORM therefore has a cost advantage over most magnetic media, besides offering a guaranteed life of at least 10 years and a likely life which is much longer. For archival applications access time is likely to be unimportant; the only disadvantages of WORM will be the need to introduce supporting software to the host operating system, and (probably) higher mechanism cost.

Image storage

Another application for which WORM storage is popular is image storage. Bit-mapped images are rarely changed in detail rather than replaced, and they are very hungry for storage (especially if in colour), so the high data density of WORM storage suits this application well. Whether it is economical in comparison with magnetic storage depends, to a large extent, on the length of time for which the images are to be stored; in the extreme this application merges into archiving.

Transaction records

WORM disks are also used for transaction records, and here the attraction is that they provide a clear and almost tamper-proof audit trail, as any record that is changed is replaced but not overwritten.

Data interchange

In principle data interchange between sites, or between separate systems on the same site, is a suitable application for WORM disk; the ruggedness and high data density of the medium may offset its inability to be re-used. However, physical data interchange is becoming less important with the spread of networking; in any case the lack of established standards for optical disk hinders this use. Data interchange on WORM will probably not extend far beyond moving disks from systems recording current transactions to related systems giving access to archives.

Several successful implementations of WORM optical disk systems are discussed in Chapter 9.

CURRENT STATUS

A book of this kind, which takes many months to reach the bookshop and then remains in print for years, is not the place for up-to-the-minute information on the state of development of a product. The next few paragraphs summarize how things stand at the start of 1989. The reader may supplement them by following the monthly and weekly technical press; if he is seriously interested in using WORM storage he will seek further information from product suppliers or from a consultant.

12 inch and 8 inch drives

In 1989, then, the 12 inch drive — which was the first to appear — is well established. About eight manufacturers are concerned, most of whom have been reasonably successful; one failed, but has been resurrected in a new guise, and some of the others have changed hands. One of these manufacturers is European, one is in joint Europe/USA ownership, one is fully USA owned and the rest are Japanese. The first-generation products from these manufacturers all use different formats and media; there is one exception, where interchange of recorded media is theoretically possible but not done in practice. All these products store between 1 and 2 gigabytes per side, with a single exception which uses modified CAV (with a variable data rate) to store 2.5 gigabytes. Enhanced products are now appearing, but no progress towards data interchange can be seen. No new companies have entered the field for some years. Some of the drive manufacturers make their own disks, but there is a trend towards the use of the independent media manufacturers which exist in the USA, Europe and Japan; disks from more than one manufacturer are available for many of the drives.

Some of the Japanese manufacturers also introduced 8 inch disks, which could be used either in their 12 inch drives or in more compact mechanisms. These were scarcely used outside Japan, and are becoming obsolete.

$5\frac{1}{4}$ inch drives

Development of $5\frac{1}{4}$ inch drives began two or three years later than 12 inch. Many more manufacturers are interested — over 30 at the last count, fairly equally shared between Japan and the USA. Nearly all disks come from independent suppliers in each of these regions and in Europe. However relatively few products are yet on the market. This is partly due to the slow progress towards a data interchange standard. Many manufacturers chose not to announce a product until there was a standard to follow: it has been hinted that some companies whose development started late were happy to see the standard fall behind schedule.

Nevertheless a number of companies have announced products, and several have delivered in quantity. They fall into two groups. The first group is committed to the standard, and has introduced products which conform to what they guess it will be; when the standard is complete these companies are likely to offer products which conform to it, and which will probably read disks from their earlier drives as well. The second group has chosen to ignore the standard; some because they foresaw the delay and were not prepared to wait so long, some because they regard standards as irrelevant to a substantial sector of the market. IBM has recently joined this group by introducing a WORM drive (in fact made by a Japanese company) which does not attempt to conform to what exists of the standard. It seems, therefore, that although many products meeting the standard will eventually be on sale, probably a larger share of the market will remain with non-standard designs.

14 inch drives
One of the first WORM products to be announced used 14 inch disks; these had aluminium substrates and the drive used three separate lasers, two of them gas lasers. The drive had a very high performance and capacity, but was extremely expensive. It was a commercial failure, and the firm abandoned it and withdrew from this market, although there is still some US Government interest in the design.

However, the 14 inch size has recently been adopted by another manufacturer, using different technology; a product with 3.6 gigabytes per side capacity has been announced. This is likely to be popular for very large systems as an alternative to 12 inch drives. As yet no other manufacturers have declared an interest in this disk size; if and when they do, there is a good chance that they will accept the first manufacturer's specification as a *de facto* interchange standard.

Future products
No other write-once devices are in or near production at present. When rewritable disks (discussed in a later chapter) are established, many drives will be designed to accept both WORM and rewritable media, and possibly read-only media as well; these are described as multi-function drives. Since much work on rewritable drives is based on 3½ inch disks, WORM disks of this size will be introduced too.

Two other WORM products which are on the way are the flexible disk drive, already discussed, and the so-called 'CD-PROM'. This is a write-once product which will conform, so far as is applicable, to the standards defining the CD-ROM read-only disk and some of its future variants; it will therefore be 120 mm (4¾ inch) diameter, and incompatible with other WORM drives because of its very different error-correction system.

In the next two chapters we will look in detail at rewritable and read-only optical disks and drives.

3
Rewritable disks

Most of the early research into optical storage aimed at a storage system in which data could be written, read and replaced at will; in other words, at something very like the familiar magnetic tape and disk systems. In the event, good rewritable media were found very difficult to make. Write-once media were easier, and so attention was switched to these, but rewritable storage remained the target for many companies; and now at last it is on the threshold of commercial use, with several products announced although none is yet in full production. Meanwhile, as we saw in the last chapter, users have found that write-once storage is not just a step towards the rewritable store; it is a valuable product in its own right.

Rewritable storage builds to a great extent on techniques which have been developed for write-once storage; much that was said in the last chapter applies also to this one and will not be repeated. Indeed, many manufacturers plan 'multifunction' drives which can handle both write-once and rewritable media, although the first few products announced cannot do this. As we saw in the last chapter, read-only data can be placed on WORM disks during manufacture as an extension of the pre-format information, so multifunction drives will be able to handle read-only disks as well; whether read-only disks will in fact be made in the appropriate formats is another question.

RECORDING TECHNOLOGY

The recording technology used in rewritable disk stores is basically the same as in WORM stores. A laser beam, focused to a spot of about one micron diameter, heats up an area corresponding to one storage element; when the area cools its state has been changed in some way that can be detected optically. However, some addition is needed so that the change in the storage element can be reversed, erasing the data stored so that the element can be re-used. There are several ways in which this can be done, and three will now be discussed; these are the ones which now attract most attention, but others may be used in the future.

First, however, we must consider how much of the content of a disk will be rewritten at a time. In principle a disk would be rewritable even if it could only be bulk erased (as is sometimes done with magnetic tape) to leave a completely blank disk. This would give some saving on media cost but would not be very useful, and in fact no manufacturer has proposed such a disk. On the other hand, the coding methods used make it impossible to replace a unit smaller than a disk sector. This is therefore normally the unit of rewritability, though if the drive has an intelligent interface it will itself do whatever is necessary to make the logical block appear to be the unit.

Phase change

The first recording method to be considered is phase change; the method has already been discussed in connection with WORM storage, but now has to be extended to allow data to be erased. This can be done by heating the signal element above its melting point, just as for recording, but allowing it to cool more slowly so that a crystalline structure can develop. One way to do this is to heat a larger area, for example by defocusing the laser spot slightly and increasing the laser power; this prevents heat being conducted away from the storage element as fast as if it were immediately surrounded by a cold area. Reading is exactly as for WORM disks using the phase-change method, which makes the design of multifunction drives simple.

Dye–polymer

The second method uses dye-polymer media. These too have been discussed in connection with write-once storage, as the 'thermoplastic' method of recording. When writing data, the laser beam softens the material and leaves a pit, which in rewritable practice does not reach through to the substrate; by heating a larger area, the pit is smoothed out and the stored data is thus erased.

Magneto-optical

The third method — which has been the object of much research, because the media proved easier to make — is magneto-optical recording, usually shortened to M/O. This (as the name implies) is actually a hybrid between magnetic and optical recording; the material of the active layer is one which retains magnetism, as in a magnetic disk, and it is the magnetic state of the storage element that is changed. The laser beam heats the focus spot, as usual (Fig. 3.1); but in this case it is not heated to the melting point of the active layer. Instead it is heated only to a critical temperature at which the medium no longer retains magnetism. When the spot cools it becomes magnetized again, in a direction which depends on the external magnetic field. That field is produced by current in a coil, or by a permanent magnet, and it is now in the opposite direction to that in which the disk was originally magnetized. Thus those signal elements which have been heated by the laser beam end up magnetized in the opposite direction from those which have not been heated.

To erase a recorded element, the same process is repeated but with the external magnetic field reversed so that the element is returned to its original state. In principle the coil current could be reversed as the laser beam passed from one element to the next, and so existing data could simply be

Ch. 3]   REWRITABLE DISKS   57

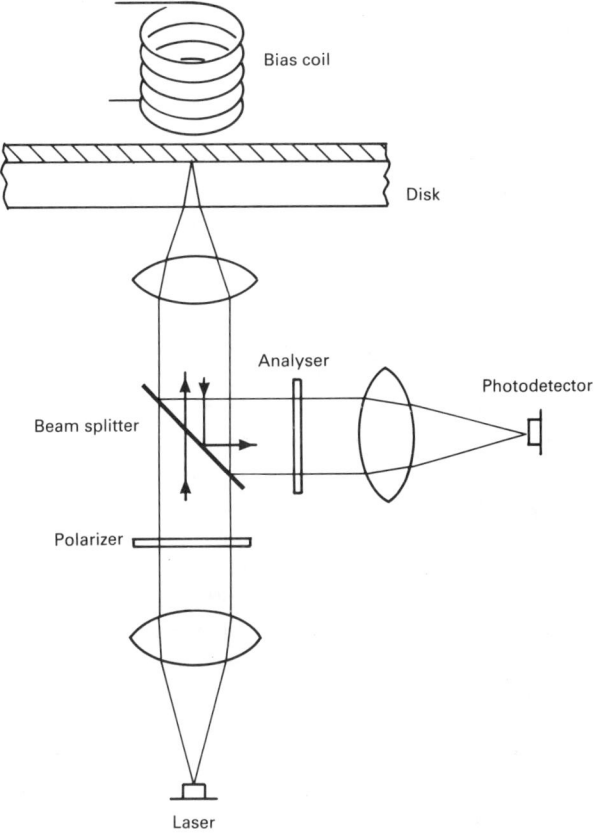

Fig. 3.1 — Optical system for magneto-optical recording.

overwritten just as is done on magnetic disks. In practice it is difficult to reverse the current so rapidly (and quite impossible to turn a permanent magnet round in this time), so a disk sector is totally erased during one revolution of the disk; with the external field in one direction all signal elements are heated by the laser beam to return them to the zero state. During the next revolution the field is reversed and data written by modulating the laser beam as the disk passes under it.

Reading the data on an M/O disk depends on a physical effect known as the 'Kerr' effect. When polarized light is reflected from a magnetized surface, the direction of polarization is turned through a small angle; clockwise if the surface is magnetized in one direction, anticlockwise if the surface is magnetized the other way. By introducing extra components into the optical system, this change in polarization can be converted into a change in the amount of light reaching the photodetector, and detected in the usual way.

In other respects, rewritable disks are very similar to WORM disks; preformatting, pregrooves and clock signals can be used and either constant angular velocity (CAV) or constant linear velocity (CLV) can be chosen.

MEDIA

Erasable media have proved considerably harder to make than WORM media. For this reason, and others, attention has been concentrated on the smaller disk diameters; particularly on $5\frac{1}{4}$ inch disks, but also on $3\frac{1}{2}$ inch, and in fact the first group of products to be announced included both these sizes. Most manufacturers intend to produce multifunction drives. Erasable disks and their cartridges are usually identical, so far as is possible, with their WORM counterparts. A draft standard for $5\frac{1}{4}$ inch WORM disks was discussed in the last chapter; this has been drawn up with extension to erasable media in mind. As in the WORM field, some manufacturers choose to ignore this standard. There is no corresponding standard for $3\frac{1}{2}$ inch WORM disks, and so in this field the erasable media standard will come first; the standards bodies are considering such a standard but it will doubtless be some time coming.

While rewritable stores have been under development, there has been much concern about fatigue effects; it seemed that these might limit the number of times any storage element could be erased and rewritten. These effects were very marked on earlier disks, limiting re-use to a few hundred cycles. As media improved this limit was progressively increased. The experts still do not agree whether media can be made to stand a truly infinite number of rewrite cycles, or only a very large number. The question is rather more than academic. No application is likely to perform a very large number of cycles, even in disk sectors storing directories; but a badly designed test program could soon clock up this many accesses to a few sectors. However, the fatigue effect leads to difficulty in recording data rather than the loss of data already recorded; so the usual read-after-write checks should give sufficient protection to data.

It is because of this cycling problem that only M/O disks are on the market at present. These have been developed to the point where a life of over a million rewrite cycles can be specified. The alternative materials, using phase-change and dye–polymer techniques, are limited at present to a few thousand cycles. Although this is enough for some purposes, the supporting system needs to prevent the limit being exceeded accidentally by an unexpected program loop or a test program. (This problem is not serious in audio recording, and a 'rewritable Compact Audio' disk will soon be on sale.) Other technologies which may have less stringent cycling limits are the subject of research.

The lifetime of recorded data has also been under debate. For some time it was thought that this would be shorter than that of data on WORM disk, perhaps only two or three years; however, some manufacturers are now predicting that data recorded on rewritable disk is safe for ten years.

Disk manufacturers hope to achieve the same defect level on rewritable as on WORM disks, so that they can use the same error-correction schemes. As disks are not yet in full commercial production, this has yet to be demonstrated; if it does prove difficult, it will tend to make rewritable disks dearer than WORM disks.

ERROR MANAGEMENT

The management of read errors on rewritable disks is exactly the same as on WORM disks; the error-correcting code in which the data is recorded recovers errors on-the-fly, throughout the specified life of the data, to the same error rates that are specified for WORM storage.

Write errors are detected in the same way as for WORM disks; no drive using direct read during write (DRDW) has yet been announced, so a check-read of each newly written sector on a subsequent revolution is the rule. However, as it is now possible to rewrite the faulty sector, fewer substitute sectors are needed; in fact exactly the same methods can be used as for magnetic disks.

RECORDING FORMATS AND STANDARDS

The intention of most manufacturers to offer multifunction drives means that formats and standards will be the same whichever type of media is in use. Since formats are established for $5\frac{1}{4}$ inch WORM drives, we may expect most rewritable drives to adopt these. Some manufacturers, however, do not conform to the forthcoming international standard for these WORM disks; their rewritable disks will presumably not conform either.

There are no standards for $3\frac{1}{2}$ inch WORM drives — and in fact no WORM drives yet available in this size. The formats will therefore be decided by the rewritable disk and drive manufacturers, and WORM disks will follow suit. Although the various standards bodies are proposing work in this field, it remains to be seen whether they are any more successful than they have been with $5\frac{1}{4}$ inch WORM disks; they already have several incompatible proposals in front of them. It has been suggested that the $3\frac{1}{2}$ inch rewritable disk is the 'floppy disk' of the future; if so, standardization is essential whether it comes about by agreement or through the commercial dominance of one maker's ideas.

MECHANISMS

The rewritable disk drive is basically the same as the WORM drive but with some additional features to allow data to be erased. Where phase-change or dye–polymer media are used, these changes are very minor; the use of a higher-powered laser (or possibly a second laser) and some modifications to the control of focusing and laser power may be all that is needed. This makes it easy to design the drive to handle both rewritable and WORM disks.

More changes are necessary to produce a drive for magneto-optical media. The first is the introduction of a coil or permanent magnet to produce a magnetic field at the focus spot. This can be very small, and can be placed on the opposite side of the disk to the optical head, though it must move with it. Interaction with the coil which moves the objective lens has to be avoided. Some extra parts are needed in the optical system, to convert the small change in direction of polarization into a change in the amount of light reaching the photodetector. The laser power has to be higher than that used in WORM devices, typically 50 milliwatts: even so, the polarization change is very small, so it is hard to distinguish the signal from the various sorts of noise in the system.

In either case, if the drive has an intelligent interface there will be changes in its internal logic to provide for the different approach to write error management. And if the drive is to be multifunctional, it must be able to distinguish between WORM and rewritable disks — there will be coded holes in the disk cartridge to make this possible.

DEVICE CHARACTERISTICS

The first rewritable drives to be commercially available were delivered at the end of 1988. It is thus too soon to discuss the full range of characteristics. However, it seems safe to predict that $5\frac{1}{4}$ inch drives will have very similar characteristics to their WORM equivalents. There will also be a trend towards shorter access times and, to a lesser extent, higher data rates, since rewritable drives are seen as competing more directly with magnetic disks than are WORM drives. One of the first $5\frac{1}{4}$ inch rewritable drives to be announced uses disks to the proposed ISO standard, with about 300 megabytes per side; it has an average access time of about 50 milliseconds. It also supports a non-standard format in which the capacity is about 50% higher with a similar access time. The proposed retail price is $6000 with disks at $250.

In the $3\frac{1}{2}$ inch size, two groups of designs are emerging; on the one hand, drives aiming for high performance, to compete with hard magnetic disk drives in the same size; on the other, drives designed for low cost to win maximum sales in the personal computer market — these may be seen as in some ways an alternative to the floppy disk. One $3\frac{1}{2}$ inch rewritable drive which has been announced uses CLV and holds about 160 megabytes per side with average access time about 150 milliseconds. Another, using CAV, holds 64 megabytes on a single-sided disk with average access time under 50 milliseconds. Likely prices are $2000 to $3000 for the drive and $80 to $100 for the disk.

The prices mentioned above suggest that rewritable (and presumably, in due course, multifunction) drives will not cost a lot more than their WORM equivalents, but disks will be perhaps twice the price; however disk prices in particular are difficult to forecast in the longer term.

STRENGTHS AND WEAKNESSES

By and large the strengths and weaknesses of erasable optical disk stores are the same as those of their WORM counterparts. They offer high volume capacity (although there are no 12 inch or 14 inch erasable disks in sight); performance which is modest in magnetic disk terms; media cost per megabyte which compares with magnetic tape; a rugged removable medium with an excellent storage life; and error rates similar to magnetic disk.

The major difference, of course, is that the medium is now rewritable, without any compensating loss except for an increase of price. This immediately puts rewritable disk on the same footing as magnetic tape for applications where the medium can be re-used. At the same time it compares in functionality, if not yet quite in performance, with magnetic disk.

Unlike WORM disks, rewritable drives can rewrite data without moving it to another sector. There is also no need to handle directories off the disk, to avoid waste of disk capacity by very frequent rewriting. As a result, erasable optical disks will usually use the same software as magnetic disks (although excessive read-rewrite cycles may have to be prevented), so availability of software should not be a problem. This contrasts with WORM storage, whose introduction has been delayed by the lack of suitable software.

APPLICATIONS

Rewritable disks could be used for all the applications that have been described for WORM disks; but it is obvious that they are less attractive than WORM for archival applications and wherever the integrity of an audit trail is important. The higher price of rewritable disks will also discourage their use where rewritability is not essential. This price difference may disappear if rewritable disks sell in greater quantities than WORM disks.

However, the ability to rewrite opens up two major application areas. The first of these is on-line storage, where the magnetic disk is at present supreme. Rewritable disk drives do not yet match the more advanced magnetic disks in performance; they are at present fairly evenly matched in capacity and price. In this application, the ability to exchange disk cartridges is not always of major importance, although it does have some value in improving resilience where drive or system faults occur. While it is a little early to predict a landslide, it does look as if rewritable optical disks will take an important place in this application area once their reliability has been proved. Already a small computer has been announced in which magnetic disk is completely replaced by rewritable optical disk.

The other area in which erasable disks have a lot to offer is that of backing up data for security purposes. At present back-up most often uses magnetic tape; this is mainly because of the low cost, compactness, and easy handling (at least in cartridge form) of the media and the fairly low cost of the drive. Back-up to fixed or cartridge disk is sometimes used for performance reasons, and back-up to floppy disk is used on personal computers because of the very low cost of the drive. Rewritable optical disks are likely to be comparable with magnetic tape in most of these respects. Mechanism cost is relatively high, however; so optical back-up is most likely to be used on systems which already need an erasable or multifunction drive for other applications.

CURRENT STATUS

A great deal of development effort has been applied to the erasable optical disk, but the problems have been formidable. The first commercial products were delivered at the end of 1988; it is too early to be sure that they will be commercially and technically successful. In the previous section of this chapter we saw that there are major areas of application to which rewritable storage looks well suited; the question, therefore, is how soon the manufacturers can convince their customers that they have a reliable product at a competitive price.

Once the last technical and production problems have been solved, rewritable optical disks are likely to overtake both WORM and read-only disks (discussed in the next chapter) as the leading sector of the optical storage industry. A large number of suppliers can be expected to appear. WORM and read-only products will not be superseded, however; they have their own application areas where they will continue to be of value.

4
Read-only disks

Write-once and rewritable storage share the same ancestry, as we saw in the last two chapters. They have their origin in the search for cheap and compact data storage; they do the same job, in principle, as magnetic disk and tape. Read-only storage has a different purpose. In fact it is only 'storage' by courtesy; its function is the *distribution* of information from one originator to a number of users. The users may be within the same organization as the originator, or linked to it — for example as agents. The greatest impact of read-only storage, however, is in the wider field of publishing. Read-only disks can supplement and sometimes replace both on-line databases and the printed page in a wide range of commercial, administrative, and scientific applications.

CD-ROM (which stands for compact disk read-only memory) is by far the most important form of read-only optical disk, although not the only one. It is a very close derivative of the Compact Audio disk which has been so successful in the entertainment field. Thus the effort needed to bring CD-ROM drives and disks into production was much less than that for WORM and erasable disks; Compact Audio disks were on the market in 1983 and CD-ROM demonstration disks only two years later. On the other hand, additional factors were needed to make read-only disks a success; the availability of 'program material' — the information on disk without which the hardware would be pointless — and of methods of access to that material.

CD-ROM has no writable direct equivalent, although one is under development (CD-PROM). Read-only disks equivalent to various existing WORM drives have been proposed, one under the trade name OROM. The idea is that these could be read by the same drives that write and read WORM (and perhaps also rewritable) media; however none is on or near the market now. One other type of read-only disk exists that can store data; the videodisk. This was designed as a medium for video films, in the entertainment field. As such it was a commercial failure, but it has found a niche in the educational and training market; its prime purpose is to store images, but it can also be used to store data. However, it is not likely to succeed in the computer industry in view of the competition from CD-ROM and its derivatives. It will therefore not be described in detail in this book; for more information see the appendix on 'Further reading'.

MEDIA AND RECORDING METHODS

The CD-ROM disk is identical in construction to the Compact Audio disk; only the information carried on it is different. The resemblance is so close that CD-ROM disks can be made on the same production lines as audio disks.

The disk is 120 millimetres in diameter and 1.2 millimetres thick. The information on the disk — whether data or music — is carried as a relief pattern on a surface buried within the disk. This pattern takes the form of a sequence of 'pits' separated by gaps, which together form a continuous spiral path; the information is represented by variations in the length of the pits and the gaps. The pits are 0.5 micron wide and 0.1 micron deep, and the turns of the spiral are spaced by 1.6 micron; the length of pits and of gaps varies from 0.8 to 3.6 microns.

Manufacturing details vary from one maker to another, but the basic construction of a compact disk consists of a clear plastic substrate, a metal film, and a protective layer (Fig. 4.1). The substrate is most often polycarbonate. It is pressed to shape in a mould, one face of which is flat while the

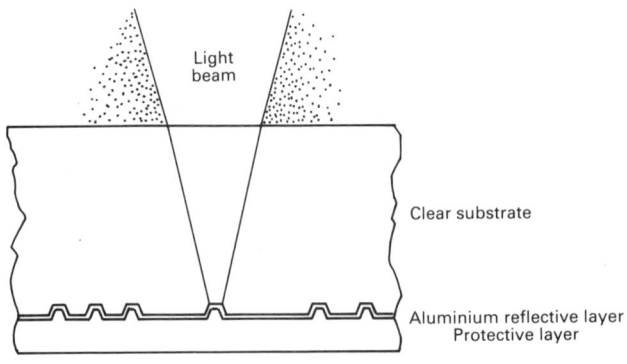

Fig. 4.1 — Compact Disk layer structure.

other is a 'stamper'; this carries (in reverse) the information pattern which is to appear on the disk. Thus the substrate itself, rather than an added layer, is the carrier of the data. The metal film is added to the substrate, on the surface carrying the information, to ensure that light is totally reflected at this surface; the metal is usually aluminium and the film is very thin (a small fraction of a micron). An inert plastic layer a few microns thick, applied as a lacquer, prevents damage to the metal film. The disk label is printed directly onto this protective layer.

CD-ROM disks are invariably single-sided, and are not fitted in cartridges. They are usually sold in the same simple plastic boxes as compact audio disks. As the use of 'caddies' (discussed later) for loading disks into drives becomes more common, disks may be supplied in these instead.

The construction of videodisks is very similar to that of CD-ROM disks, apart from their size; videodisks are 12 inches, or occasionally 8 inches, in diameter. Other forms of read-only disk, if introduced, will be similar in principle; in detail they will be designed to be compatible with whatever WORM or erasable disks are to be used on the same drive.

Like all optical media, read-only disks are very rugged. All the materials used are inert, so there is no reason to predict any limit on their life. Certainly there have been very few such problems with either CD-ROM or Compact Audio disks; in the one case widely reported, an unsuitable ink was used for the labels and it attacked the protective lacquer and the metal film below.

In an earlier chapter we saw that it is not economical to make WORM media completely free of defects. The same applies to read-only disks. The solution, once more, is to code the data in a form which provides error detection and correction; this is discussed later.

DISK MASTERING AND MANUFACTURE

There are two stages in the production of a read-only disk; the preparation of the data which the disk is to carry, and the actual manufacture of the disk as one of a batch of identical disks. The link between the two stages is the 'master'. This is a disk which is produced by a one-off method, but which is identical as far as its data pattern is concerned with the desired end product. The steps which lead up to this master disk are collectively known as 'mastering' (Fig. 4.2).

The first step is the collection and editing of the data to be placed on the disk, and this will be discussed in the section on 'Access methods and file structures'. At present the disk manufacturers require the information to be presented on magnetic tape, in the sequence in which it is to appear on the disk and in a precisely defined format; this tape is the 'master tape' (usually in several volumes). In the future, WORM or erasable disks may be used instead of tape. The manufacturer processes the master tape in a standard way, regardless of its contents. The processing consists mainly of dividing the data into sections corresponding to disk sectors, and coding each sector to provide for error correction and detection. The result is a 'pre-master'; this is often also on tape, although some manufacturers retain it in magnetic disk storage.

The final step in mastering is the production of the master disk itself from the pre-master. This is done in real time, with the pre-master data presented to the mastering machine is in a continuous stream at a constant rate. The mastering machine is similar to a WORM drive, using a modulated laser beam to write the information pattern (translated into varying pit and gap lengths) onto the master disk; however, beam position and disk speed are controlled externally to produce the required layout, since there is no preformat on the disk to be followed.

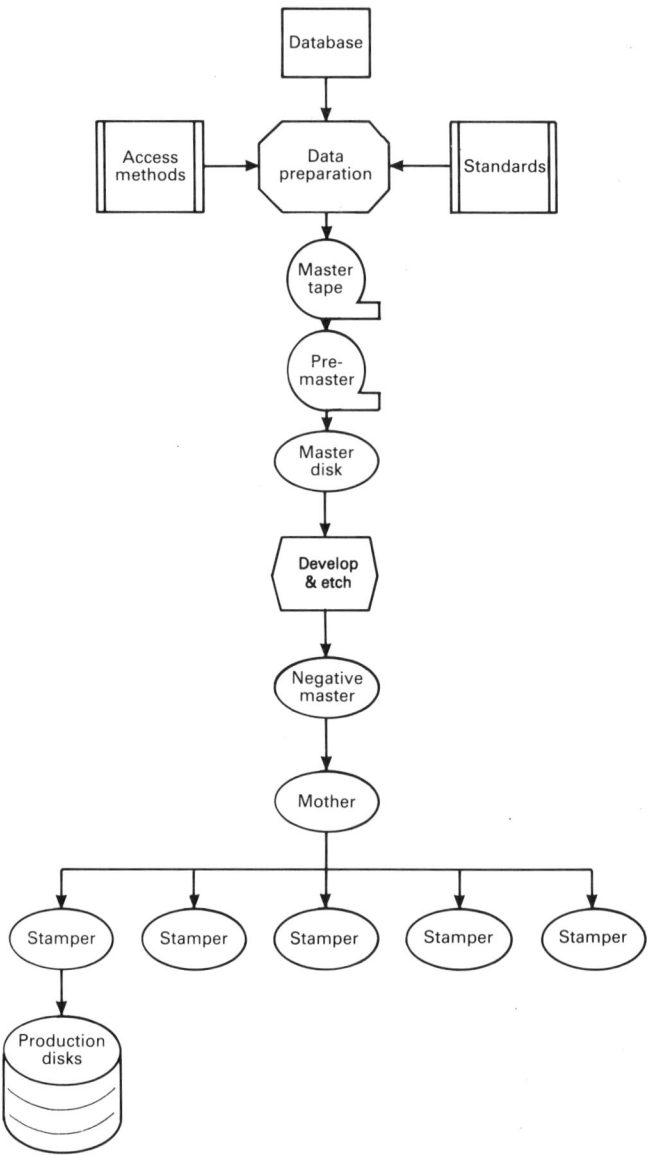

Fig. 4.2 — CD-ROM manufacturing process.

The mastering machine could use any recording technology that produced a relief pattern on the master; the method normally used, since it gives the most precise control over the shape and size of the pits, is a photographic one. The master disk is a glass plate coated with a thin layer of photoresist (a form of photographic emulsion). The photoresist is exposed, wherever a pit is required, by the laser beam. When the whole disk has been recorded, it is developed by treating it with a chemical which dissolves the resist only where it has been exposed. The disk is then etched to a carefully controlled depth, and the remaining resist removed to leave a surface pattern which is precisely that wanted on the production disks; in this state it is known as a 'positive master'. This completes the mastering process.

The rest of the manufacturing process for CD-ROM disks is the same as for Compact Audio disks, and is often done on the same production line; the process for other read-only disks is similar. First a thick metal layer is plated onto the surface of the positive master, and then separated from it to become a 'negative master'. The form of this is precisely that required for the stamper from which the production disks will be made; however, because it is the only copy (and the positive master may have been damaged when separated) it is not used in this way, except possibly to produce a single proof disk for the customer to check. Instead, the same process is repeated twice to produce, first, a 'mother' disk and then from this as many stampers as required. These stampers are used in moulding presses to make the production disks.

Inspection and testing is carried out at several points in this process, and is more rigorous than it would be for audio disks. Nevertheless it is not economically practical to check the whole of the data on every disk produced; nor is it necessary, since the disk is not unique but can easily be replaced.

RECORDING FORMATS AND STANDARDS

CD-ROM is by far the most important form of read-only optical disk. One of the reasons for its success is its precise specification; every CD-ROM disk can be read on every CD-ROM drive. (Whether the system supporting the drive can support every disk is another matter, discussed later.)

Tracks and paths

We saw in the last section that data is represented as a sequence of pits and spaces forming a continuous spiral path. The observant may have wondered why the word 'path' has been used rather than 'track'. The reason is that in the entertainment industry a 'track' is a logical rather than physical section of the disk contents, of varying size; the close relation between Compact Audio and CD-ROM has led to the word being used in this sense in the context of CD-ROM. This is not a problem, because 'track' in the sense of 'path' is not an important concept in CD-ROM, but it can cause confusion to those dealing with both CD-ROM and WORM disks — beware! For the rest of this chapter, 'track' refers to a logical division rather than to the spiral path or a turn of it.

Disk layout

CD-ROM disks use the constant linear velocity (CLV) format. The spacing of signal elements along the spiral path is constant; the rate of rotation of the disk is varied to match the path radius, so that data is read at a constant rate. The spiral path (which runs outwards) is divided into sectors of equal length, and hence equal data capacity. Sector boundaries therefore do not line up along radii of the disk, and the sector structure cannot be seen by looking at the disk. Sectors are identified solely by their sector number. The turns of the spiral are not numbered. The sector number is in fact compound, made up of 'minutes', 'seconds' and sectors; this scheme has been carried over unchanged from Compact Audio technology.

Each sector can hold 2048 bytes of data; these are coded in a complex way to provide for error correction and detection. An alternative coding method allows 2336 bytes of data with no error correction; this is not used for normal data, but is sometimes appropriate to image storage. Tracks, but not individual sectors, in the two coding methods may be carried on the same disk.

The disk is normally limited to 270 000 sectors, which at 2048 bytes per sector can hold 552 960 000 bytes. If the convention that 1 megabyte is 1024×1024 bytes is followed this is 527 megabytes. If, rather illogically, we define a megabyte as 1000×1024 bytes, the capacity becomes 540 megabytes; for some reason this is the figure usually quoted. Just to confuse matters further, it is possible to get 330 000 sectors onto the disk, giving a capacity of over 600 megabytes; disk manufacturers discourage this at present, because they find the outer 5 millimetres of the disk are particularly liable to defects.

Data retrieval

Data is normally retrieved by its sector number. However, there is provision for the contents of the disk to be divided arbitrarily into up to 99 tracks. Tracks can be of any length, and the contents of a track can be retrieved by specifying its track number instead of the address of the first sector. This can make data retrieval easier; however, 99 data units are too few for many purposes, so this facility is not often used on CD-ROM (it is of course used on Compact Audio disks).

Standards

All the features of CD-ROM which have been discussed — and many more — are defined by a specification known as the *Yellow Book*. This was drawn up by Philips and Sony, the companies which jointly developed CD-ROM; a corresponding *Red Book* from the same source defines Compact Audio. The use of CD-ROM is permitted only by licence from these companies, and it is a condition of the licence that these specifications are observed. They have therefore the force of international standards, even though they have not been endorsed by external standards bodies. The *Red Book* and *Yellow Book* are available only to licensees, although their contents are by now fairly well known; for example see the book by Buddine and Young listed under 'Further reading'. However, an edited version of the *Yellow Book* has now been released to the standards bodies and will shortly be published as ISO 10149 and ECMA-130.

The assignment of data to particular sectors is implicitly defined by the master tape, since the disk manufacturer places data on the disk in precisely the order in which it is found on that tape. The *Yellow Book* does not define this order; nor indeed does it control the data content of the tape in any way. This has important implications for compatibility of disks with applications, as will be discussed in the section on access methods and file structures.

CD-I, CD-ROM XA and DVI

A further specification issued by Sony and Philips is the *Green Book*, which defines a compact disk format known as compact disk interactive (CD-I). CD-I is in effect a subset of the possible applications of CD-ROM (see Fig. 4.3); where the *Yellow Book* leaves the content of the data sectors

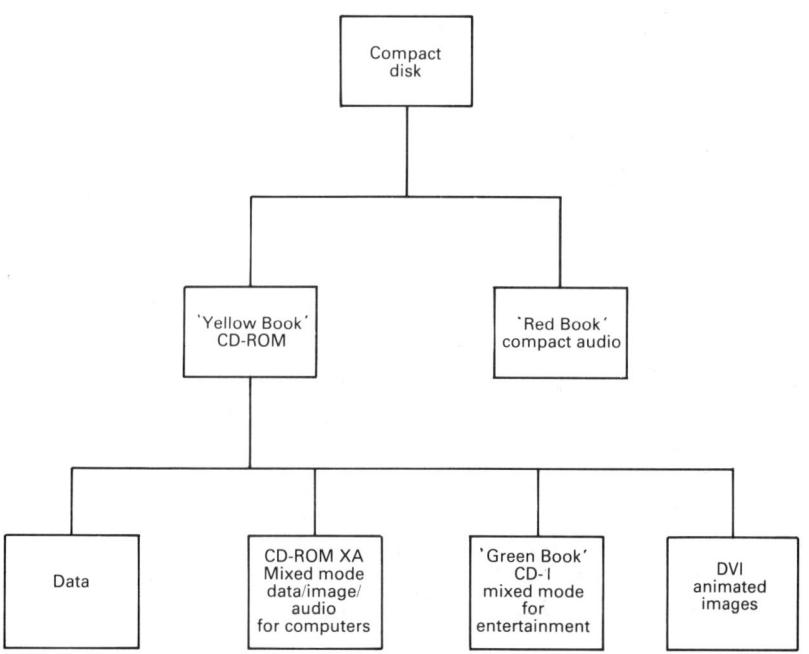

Fig. 4.3 — Compact Disk specifications.

undefined, the *Green Book* defines a number of specific ways in which sector contents can be used to carry data, sound (at several fidelity levels, offering various compromises between sound quality and playing time), pictures, or software. The *Green Book* also defines a particular set of hardware on which CD-I disks are to be read, and requires that software to drive it is carried on the CD-I disk. The intention is that, as with Compact Audio, every CD-I system will be able to use every CD-I disk.

CD-I is aimed squarely at the home entertainment/education market, and so is not of direct concern to the computer industry. However, the CD-I data format is so defined that, subject to certain constraints, data tracks on CD-I disks may be read and interpreted by computer systems; likewise data prepared for CD-ROM may be included in CD-I disks. Philips and Sony have announced that they will develop a standard for the application of CD-I data formats to CD-ROM, but the details are not yet known. It will be called CD-ROM XA.

Another format which extends the definition of CD-ROM is digital video interactive (DVI). This also defines a specific use of the data in the CD-ROM sectors; in this case with a single purpose, the presentation of images (including animated images). DVI is not a Philips/Sony development, although it builds upon the *Yellow Book* standard and so requires the usual licence. Unlike CD-I, DVI is designed for use in computer systems and does not define the supporting hardware. At the time of writing the DVI specification is not final, but it does appear to handle animated images better than CD-I.

Other read-only disks
There are few defined formats for read-only disks outside the CD-ROM group. Videodisk is not widely used for storage of computer data; it can be quite effective when the data represents mainly images, but suffers from lack of standards and from poor economics in comparison with CD-ROM. WORM videodisk media and mechanisms are also available although not widely used.

Other read-only disks are not at present on the market; those most likely to appear are direct equivalents of WORM disks, designed to be read on the same drives. In these cases the format will follow the WORM equivalents exactly.

A development which has recently been announced is a disk the same size as CD-ROM and similar in most respects, but with four times the capacity. This will have applications in both entertainment and computer fields. Whether such a product will succeed, in an industry which has adopted CD-ROM as a universal standard, is open to some doubt.

ERROR MANAGEMENT
As in WORM drives, read error management depends on the use of error-correcting codes; any sector found to be in error is corrected without interruption to the data flow. In the case of CD-ROM there is no provision for re-reading a sector; this is a result of its derivation from Compact Audio, where re-reading is obviously impracticable. Because of this, and because a user encountering an error has no back-up to fall back on (though he could order a replacement disk), the error correction scheme is more powerful than is usual on WORM drives; it is capable of reducing hard errors to

1 in 10^{14} rather than the usual 1 in 10^{12}. However, some drive manufacturers think such high data integrity is not necessary, and so keep their prices down by implementing only part of the possible error correction; they usually quote 1 in 10^{12}.

The Compact Audio coding scheme itself includes fairly powerful error correction, and this is carried over into the CD-ROM format. However, this is not sufficient to achieve the error rates required for computer applications. A further level of error correction is therefore superimposed on the first. The actual coding scheme is very complex; readers wanting to study it are referred to the book by Buddine and Young, or that by Bouwhuis *et al.*, listed under 'Further Reading'.

Write error correction is of course not an issue as far as the CD-ROM user is concerned. The disk manufacturer has to ensure that the master disk is free from errors that are beyond the power of the error-correction code to handle; in doing so he leaves an ample margin for defects arising during the production process. This checking has to be done after the master has been developed and etched, and the only remedy for a defective sector is to make a new master disk. As mastering is done under very carefully controlled conditions, this is not often necessary.

The error-correction coding used on CD-ROM is very different from that used on write-once and rewritable disks. Where read-only disks are designed to be compatible with writable disks, they will of course use the same error-correction coding as those disks. There is no standard error-correcting scheme for data recorded as such on videodisks; where data is recorded as an image of the text, error correction is usually unnecessary because of the redundancy of text stored in this form — in other words, text is readable even if considerably distorted.

VOLUME AND FILE STRUCTURES

In the chapters on WORM and rewritable disks we did not discuss the content of the data recorded on the disk. It can be assumed that the system that reads the data is the one that recorded it, or at least one co-operating closely with it, so the system understands the content of the data. The disk drive itself is completely transparent to data, treating it simply as a bit stream (though divided into blocks of a specified length). Thus standards for data content are not important to users of these disks.

While read-only disk drives are also transparent to the data stream, the relation between the writer and the reader of the disk is far more remote. The disk publisher — and particularly the CD-ROM publisher — may aim to sell disks to a wide range of users with an equally wide range of equipment. The user may want to use his equipment to read disks from several sources; he will certainly not want to use different equipment, and preferably not even different software, for each disk. For CD-ROM to become a universal medium, therefore, it is not enough to have standards at the disk and drive level; there must also be standards for the structure of the data on the disk.

Proprietary data structures
In view of the completeness of the standards laid down by Philips and Sony for Compact Audio and CD-I, ensuring that every disk can be used on every system, it may seem surprising that their CD-ROM standard (the *Yellow Book*) stops at a much lower level. The explanation given is that these companies did not know how users would want to organize data on CD-ROM, and did not want to restrict their choice. Be that as it may, the consequence was that early CD-ROM disks could be used only on the 'delivery systems' for which they were designed, since other delivery systems could not interpret the data on the disk. ('Delivery system' is a clumsy but useful term which describes the application software and the system on which it runs.) The user had to choose his disk first and then buy the delivery system that suited it; if he bought another disk he might need to buy another delivery system, sometimes even if the disks came from the same manufacturer.

In practice, of course, things were not quite as bad as this. MS-DOS was soon accepted as the standard operating system for CD-ROM delivery systems, and hence the IBM PC or its equivalent as the standard hardware. An extension to MS-DOS, and drivers to suit all the available CD-ROM drive mechanisms, were made available. Only the application software was undefined, and this could be carried by the CD-ROM disk itself or a floppy disk accompanying it. Thus although the user might not be able to switch disks at a stroke, at least he need not duplicate anything.

This situation was good enough for freestanding systems, where the data had only to be displayed on a screen. Even so, it meant that the user was tied to the software selected by the disk manufacturer, when another software package might have suited his needs better; and changing from one disk to another could still be tedious. It was not satisfactory where the user wanted to integrate CD-ROM with an existing system; even if this used the IBM PC, the software to link the CD-ROM to his other applications was probably not available, and if he used other hardware he had greater problems (although a few CD-ROM disks were produced for use on DEC systems, using the 'Uni-file' structure which is proprietary to DEC).

High Sierra
CD-ROM developers realized that this lack of compatibility would deter potential users. A number of them therefore met as an informal working group to produce a standard for the structure of data published on CD-ROM. The group called itself the 'High Sierra' group, from the place where it met, and the standard it produced in 1986 was the 'High Sierra Standard'. This was passed to the official standards bodies, who adopted it and issued it with minor revisions; it is now published as ECMA standard ECMA-119, 'Volume and file structure of CD-ROM for information interchange' and as ISO 9660, which is technically identical with the ECMA document (see Fig. 4.4).

The standard has two aims. The first is to enable the user to run any disk on his existing system, or whatever delivery system best meets his needs, and

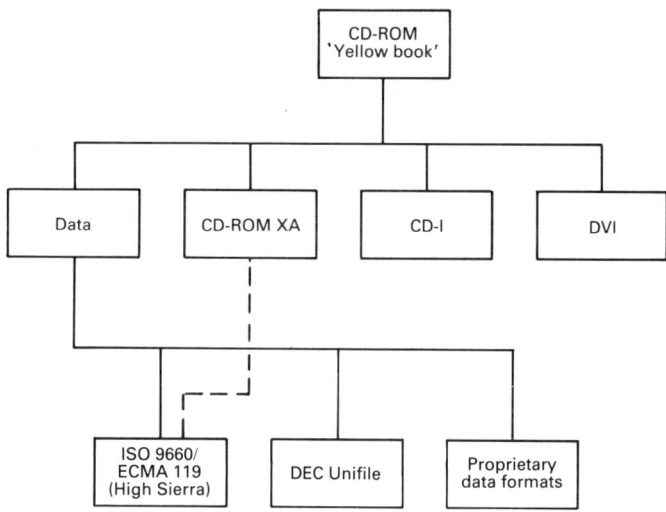

Fig. 4.4 — CD-ROM data standards.

to select the access software most suitable for his application. The second is to do this in a way that does not hinder future developments, such as the exchange of disks between CD-ROM and CD-I systems or the introduction of write-once and rewritable equivalents of CD-ROM.

Disk publishers and software developers have accepted the 'High Sierra' standard with enthusiasm. Most new disks follow the standard, and a choice of access software is available. System manufacturers (more specifically, operating system suppliers) are also taking advantage of the standard; the range of hardware that can support CD-ROM has extended well beyond the IBM PC area. This has brought CD-ROM a good deal closer to achieving its potential as a near-universal means of publishing digital data.

The standard defines CD-ROM data structures at several levels; logical sector and block, record, file, volume (i.e. the complete disk), and volume set. The details are complex, but the most important points can be summarized as follows (see Fig. 4.5).

Firstly, the data space on the disk is divided into logical blocks of fixed length, which may be grouped into logical sectors also of fixed length. Although the relation between logical and physical sectors is deliberately left flexible, in practice the two will usually correspond; the sector length will be 2048 bytes and the logical block 512, 1024 or 2048 bytes.

Secondly, logical blocks are grouped into named files of any length, in the same way as in most operating systems. A file may be subdivided into file sections, which need not be contiguous nor even on the same volume (disk). This allows file sections to be located for optimum performance, or data to be appended to a file when an additional disk is issued (and is also necessary to allow for the future extension of the standard to writable disks).

74 READ-ONLY DISKS [Ch. 4

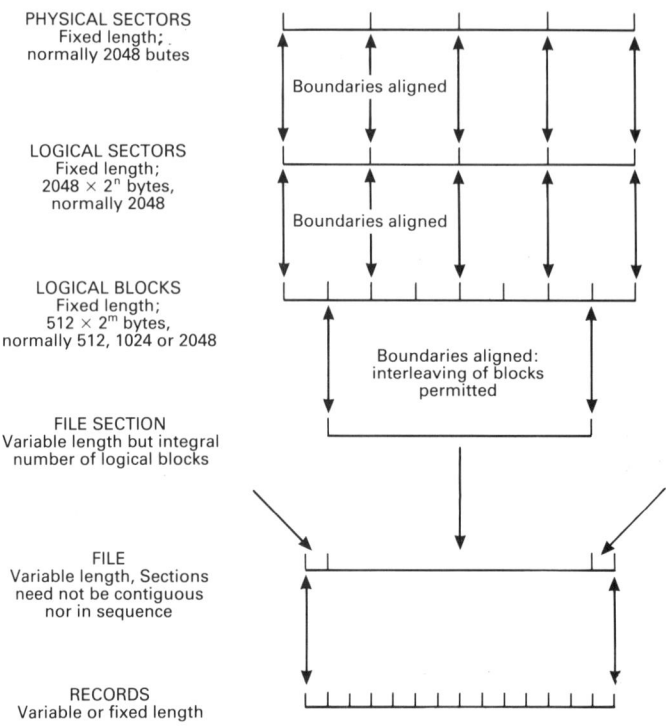

Fig. 4.5 — High Sierra file structure.

However, within a file section the logical blocks are contiguous, except that there is provision for regular interleaving if required.

Thirdly, the contents of a file may (optionally) also be subdivided into records, which may be either fixed-length or variable length; the two forms cannot be mixed within a file. Record lengths need not be related to logical blocks.

Fourthly, directories (which may be structured as a hierarchy) are specified to describe the files and the location of their sections. These are similar to the directories of MS-DOS and other common operating systems. Additional descriptors are used where necessary to describe the data structure of a particular disk to the delivery system.

Finally, volume descriptors are specified which describe each volume and its contents, and its relation to other volumes in the set. It is recognized that a set may grow after initial issue. Each volume descriptor therefore states the number of volumes in the set at the time, and their contents; the system can then scan all the volumes known to it to find the one giving the largest set size, and take the description of the set from that volume. The volume descriptors contain other information by which the delivery system can check that it is capable of handling the disk; in particular, the standard defines levels of compatibility, each a subset of the next, so that simple data structures and delivery systems need not be burdened with all the paraphernalia of more complex systems.

Although the standard is primarily a specification of the disk contents, it also specifies those characteristics which the delivery system must have in order to be compatible with all disks conforming to the specification.

One feature of the disk is not defined; this is the content of a 15-sector 'system area' at the beginning of the disk. This may be used at the disk maker's discretion. Obviously if used it may restrict compatibility — this could be deliberate, as part of a security system, or for the purpose of charging for access.

An alternative file structure, 'Uni-file', has been used on CD-ROM disks designed for use with DEC computers; it is proprietary to DEC.

There are no recognized standards for other types of read-only disk.

ACCESS SOFTWARE

The majority of read-only disks contain information which is intended to be read by a human reader, just like information in print. However the volume of data that a disk can hold is vast — equal to several hundred books of typical size; it would be practically impossible for the reader to find the particular item he wanted by reading a conventional index or contents list. So to make access manageable, disks are invariably associated with access systems, which are simply application software designed to present a friendly interface to the user and enable him to find what he wants simply and quickly.

As we saw in the last chapter, lack of standards meant that early CD-ROM disks were each associated with specific access software, either carried on the disk or on an associated floppy disk. With the adoption of the 'High Sierra' standard it became possible to mix disks and software more freely. It is still necessary to choose access software which is appropriate to the disk contents, of course, but most disks fall into one of a few fairly general classes — for example abstracts, bibliographic citations, statistical tables — and so relatively few varieties of software are needed to suit them all. This leaves software designers free to design access systems more closely matched to the needs of specific users.

Detailed discussion of access systems would not be appropriate to this book. Indeed the systems now available are still relatively simple, most of them being based on systems originally written for access to on-line databases; several are described in detail in the book by Buddine and Young listed under 'Further reading'. Now that 'High Sierra' has been accepted, leading to freer competition, we can expect considerable development.

However, to describe briefly a typical system, the user will be presented with a menu inviting him to select a particular topic and browse through it, or else to enter a word or combination of words which identify the item of interest. Typically a search of this kind will find many items which include these words, and the access system reports how many are found. The user can then, if he chooses, narrow his search by entering additional words. For instance, if he started by entering 'cow' and the system reported 97 entries, he could add 'brown' and might find the list reduced to 26 items. He can refine his definition further if he chooses; or he can call for a list of the items. He can then either select a particular item from the list, or scan through them; in either case he will be shown more of the item — perhaps the complete entry, if short enough, or maybe an abstract.

This is the basis of an access system; there is often the choice of control by menu, which suits those who only use the system occasionally, or by command line which is faster for the regular user. Many refinements are possible. For example, in a system which displays encyclopaedia entries, moving the cursor to a word and pressing a key could take the reader directly to the entry under that word; pressing another key would return him to the original article. It is in the provision of such refinements that access systems are likely to develop. (The term 'hypertext' has been used in this connection).

Where the disk contains images as well as text, a more sophisticated access system is needed. In a typical case, text is displayed with a symbol (or icon) to show that an illustration is available, and a keystroke causes this to replace the text on the screen. It may be possible to make cross-references from the image — for example to point at a part of it with the cursor to call up an enlargement, or a text description of the part. An example on these lines will be described in a later chapter.

MECHANISMS

As CD-ROM predominates in the read-only field, the CD-ROM drive will be described in some detail. Fundamentally it is similar to WORM and erasable disk drives; the absence of a write function only eliminates some of the electronics, removes the need to modulate the laser beam, and reduces the power required from the laser to about 1 milliwatt. It is still necessary to control the disk speed (at constant linear velocity in this case), follow the data path with the laser beam, and detect the information carried by the disk. It is also necessary to control beam location, focus, and disk rotation speed by servo systems. However, there are some simplifications. CD-ROM drives rotate their disks much more slowly than WORM or rewritable drives. Also less laser power is needed at the disk so a simpler, lighter optical system can be used. Consequently most manufacturers consider that a single-stage tracking system is sufficient; the whole optical system is moved to follow the eccentricity of the track, and the mirror is not tilted. The mirror may be omitted altogether, so that the main axis of the optical system is perpendicular to the disk (Fig. 4.6).

A recent development is the integration of laser and photodetector in a single unit, using a diffraction grating as a beam splitter. This considerably reduces the size and weight of the optical system, and also reduces its cost. It is likely to be in wide use from 1990. The term 'holographic head' has been

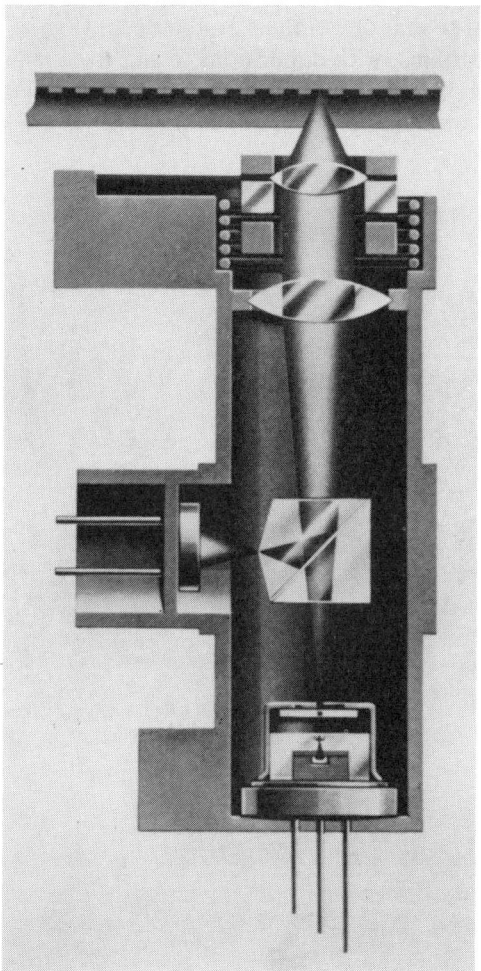

Fig. 4.6 — CD-ROM drive optical head. (Copyright Laser Magnetic Storage International.)

used, although it does not form a holographic image on the disk (holography is discussed in Chapter 11 and Appendix 2).

Using a single-stage tracking system does mean that access to nearby tracks is slower than with a two-stage system, but this is unimportant in most CD-ROM applications. For movements over a larger number of tracks the access time depends mainly on the time taken to adjust the disk speed, since a relatively low-power (and therefore cheap) motor is used.

In nearly all respects the CD-ROM drive is optically and mechanically similar to the Compact Audio disk drive, although built to a higher standard. Much of the electronics is also the same, only the additional error correction and the interface being different. Indeed, some CD-ROM drives have an audio output which allows them to be used to play Compact Audio disks.

Early CD-ROM drives were designed as freestanding units, in casing very similar to that of Compact Audio decks (Fig. 4.7). Drives for building in to host systems, with dimensions to suit the $5\frac{1}{4}$ inch footprint, followed; half-height $5\frac{1}{4}$ inch drives are now appearing (Fig. 4.8). Fig. 4.9 shows such a drive installed in a personal computer.

Fig. 4.7 — Desktop CD-ROM drive. (Copyright Hitachi UK.)

Fig. 4.8 — CD-ROM drive in half-height $5\frac{1}{4}$ inch format. (Copyright Laser Magnetic Storage International.)

The original CD-ROM drives were very closely modelled on Compact Audio decks, and disks were loaded in the same way — by lowering the bare disk into a drawer or a compartment under a hinged lid; the disk was

Fig. 4.9 — CD-ROM drive installed in a personal computer. The CD-ROM drive is below a 5¼ inch floppy disk drive at the right of the front panel. The picture also shows a disk in its caddy. (Copyright Hitachi UK.)

clamped (mechanically) when the drawer was closed or the lid lowered. This is satisfactory when the drive stands on a desk top. However, built-in drives may be mounted vertically; the simple method of loading the disk is then impracticable, and so the 'caddy' has been introduced. This is a form of cartridge, but the disk is not fixed into it; it can be dropped in before loading in the drive and removed afterwards so that only one caddy is needed. At first each manufacturer used a different caddy. A common design is now emerging; when this is sufficiently established, disk manufacturers are likely to supply disks in these caddies rather than in Compact Audio boxes. (A CD-ROM disk in a caddy can be seen in Fig. 4.9.)

Videodisk drives are similar in principle to CD-ROM drives, although information is stored in a format which is based on that of a television frame. However the disk is larger and rotates faster, so a two-stage tracking system is always necessary. Although videodisks are normally read-only, write-once media and drives are also available.

The only other read-only disks that are likely to be used will be designed to be compatible with specific write-once or rewritable disks. The drives will therefore be WORM or erasable drives without significant modification (probably described as 'multifunction' drives), and no further description is needed here. It is unlikely that drives capable of playing both standard WORM or erasable disks and CD-ROM will be designed, because the difference in standards and particularly in error-correction coding would make them almost as expensive as two separate drives.

DEVICE CHARACTERISTICS

A typical data sheet for a CD-ROM drive is given in Table 4.1. This is a

Table 4.1 — Data sheet for a typical CD-ROM drive

Capacity	600 Mbytes
Data rate — continuous	153 kbytes per second
Access time — average	500 milliseconds
— maximum	1000 milliseconds
Error rate	1 in 10^{12} bits
Reliability — MTBF	10 000 hours
Power requirements	+12 V 0.25 A (average) 1.3 A (max)
	+5 V 0.45 A (average) 0.7 A (max)
Drive dimensions	41 mm high ⎫
	146 mm wide ⎬ Half-height 5¼ inch footprint
	206 mm deep ⎭
Mounting position	Horizontal or vertical
Disk loading	Caddy
Operating temperature	5° to 40°C
Interface	SCSI

fictitious example rather than a specification of an actual drive, though as we shall see there is relatively little difference between drives.

Some actual data sheets will give more information than this; far too many will give less. In particular, the MTBF figure is very rarely given. Let us look at each characteristic in more detail.

Capacity

The capacity of all CD-ROM disks is the same (although it may not all be used). Where different drive specifications give different figures this is because they have defined the capacity in a different way, as discussed in an earlier section; there is no difference between the drives themselves.

Performance

The data rate is always shown as 153 kilobytes per second; the corresponding disk rotation rate is rarely shown, but it varies from 200 rpm for the innermost turn of the spiral to 530 for the outermost. In principle there is no reason why disks should not be run at a higher speed (although ultimately the strength of the disk will set a limit); in practice all disks are run at the speed originally chosen for Compact Audio disks.

Access time does vary from drive to drive. It is affected by the design of the tracking system and by the power of the motor, since the latter determines the time taken to change the disk speed. Early drives had average access times around 1 second; faster drives are now available, but as faster access tends to increase cost there are still slow drives on the market.

Data integrity

Error rate was discussed in an earlier section. The error-correcting code on the disk enables the drive to reduce errors at the drive interface to less than 1 in 10^{16} bits. However, many drive manufacturers choose not to implement all the possible error-correction measures and so quote 1 in 10^{12} bits. This is more than ample for most purposes, especially where the data on the disk is text which is to be read from a screen. In a few cases, such as where the disk carries critical figures or software, the higher level of 1 in 10^{16} may be desirable, and drives are available which specify this figure. It should be noted that error rate is not the only criterion of a drive's ability to read information correctly; drives vary in their ability to cope with dirty or damaged disks, but this information will not be found in the data sheet.

Reliability

Reliability is hardly ever specified on a CD-ROM data sheet. The figure in the table is the only one found, and refers to an early drive; it is likely that current drives average around 20 000 hours. The absence of the figure from the data sheet is of little importance, since as we saw in Chapter 2 such figures are of doubtful value.

Power

The power requirements shown are those for a drive designed to be built into a system; there is some variation between drives, but not very much. Drives designed with their own cabinets to stand on a desktop require AC mains power instead, typically about 25 watts.

Packaging

The dimensions shown also refer to a drive for building in; they correspond to the half-height $5\frac{1}{4}$ inch footprint. An increasing number of drives is appearing in this size; earlier drives for building in were full-height. Many drives are also, or only, available in self-contained cases, and are larger because the case also holds a mains power supply. The size of the disk itself makes it impossible to fit a CD-ROM drive into a $3\frac{1}{2}$ inch footprint.

Mounting position and disk loading are related. Where the drive is mounted vertically the disk cannot be just dropped into a drawer or onto a spindle, so a 'caddy' is necessary. Where there is no provision for a caddy the drive can only be mounted horizontally. At first each drive maker designed his own caddy, but now a single design is widely accepted. The use of caddies is therefore spreading, and may become universal.

Environment
The operating temperature range is sometimes stated (and in some cases also the humidity range); in other cases simply 'office environment'. The latter is ambiguous because US offices generally have tighter temperature control than others, but in fact CD-ROM drives have few environmental problems.

Interface
The last item in the table is interface. Most drives are available with a choice of interface, implemented either within the drive or by a separate controller card. As we have seen, most delivery systems at present use IBM personal computers or compatible machines; to suit these, nearly all drives are available with a suitable interface, using a separate controller card which plugs into one of the PC's expansion slots. As the use of CD-ROM spreads to larger systems the SCSI interface is expected to become popular, since this is an intelligent interface and also allows the drive to share a port with other peripherals. Many drives are therefore available with SCSI interface. In the case of desktop drives and those fitting the full-height $5\frac{1}{4}$ inch footprint, the SCSI controller is usually integral with the drive; this is not always possible with half-height drives and the controller may be a separate board.

Price
Prices do not appear on data sheets, but a typical one-off price in 1988 is around £900. Desktop drives cost a little more because they include a case and power-supply unit. This price may be expected to drop by maybe a third as production volumes grow.

The manufacturing cost of the disk itself is usually only a small fraction of its price, since the value lies in the information carried on it. Typically there is a one-off charge of two or three thousand pounds for the preparation of the master disk and stampers; thereafter the price ranges from about £25 per disk for a quantity of 100 to around £5 for quantities above 1000. However, this varies with the manufacturer and also with the delivery time; three or four weeks is typical, but most manufacturers can achieve three days for an extra charge, and some offer a 24 hour turnaround.

Other types of read-only disk
When read-only disks designed for use on WORM or erasable disk drives come on the market, the drive characteristics will obviously be those specified for their original use. For comparable disk sizes the capacity will be much the same as CD-ROM. In general these drives offer higher performance than CD-ROM drives, and in particular shorter access times. The ability to handle read-only disks will add nothing to the cost of such a drive,

which of course is much higher than that of a CD-ROM drive. Read-only disks to these specifications will be a lot more expensive to make, since they cannot be made on Compact Audio production lines, but this cost is still likely to be small in relation to the value of the information carried.

Videodisk drives designed for the entertainment market may be adequate for data held in image form, but not for applications associated with computers. For these a professional machine which can be controlled by a computer is normally used. One such machine will store 55 000 full-screen images and 30 megabytes of data, with average access time 5 seconds, in a mains-powered desktop unit about 20 inches by 16 inches and 5 inches high, and costs around £1000. Drives which support write-once media are a good deal more expensive. The manufacturing cost of read-only videodisks is about twice that of CD-ROM disks.

STRENGTH AND WEAKNESSES

As a computer peripheral, CD-ROM competes with magnetic media where these are used for the distribution of data and software. However, its main significance is as a competitor to more diverse methods of publishing; in particular to printed paper, microfiche, and on-line computer databases. We shall consider the applications of CD-ROM, and how it competes with these alternatives, in the next section and in Chapter 10. First we shall review those characteristics which determine the choice.

The greatest strength of CD-ROM is its high data density; this allows the equivalent of hundreds of printed books or floppy disks to be carried by a single disk. CD-ROMs are made by a mastering process, so the cost is high for a single copy, but falls rapidly with quantity. In consequence, the cost per megabyte is very low when many copies of large quantities of information are wanted; conversely it is high for a few copies of a limited amount of data.

A further strength of CD-ROM is its resistance to damage and wear and its high data integrity. We have seen that an error rate of 1 in 10^{16} can be achieved. This is far better than is economically possible for any other publishing medium, and will be valuable for some applications such as software distribution. However, the widest use of CD-ROM is to carry data which will be read from a screen, and for this purpose such high integrity is not really needed.

In comparison with the non-electronic publishing media CD-ROM offers fast random access and high data rate. CD-ROM data can be manipulated by computer. This does not necessarily mean that the computer can understand and act upon the contents of the data itself; this is unlikely to be possible if the data is in image form, whether representing text or graphics. However, it does mean that extensive indexing and very powerful access methods can be used.

All the above advantages are shared by other types of read-only optical disk. CD-ROM has the particular advantage of very effective standardization, at least at the physical level; when the 'High Sierra' standards are also followed, CD-ROM becomes a very widely acceptable medium. It seems doubtful that any other read-only disk will approach this position for some years.

To offset these strengths, CD-ROM is incompatible with the normal types of WORM and rewritable drives; it is compatible with the forthcoming CD-PROM write-once disks and drives, but it remains to be seen whether these will have a real impact on the market. Consequently CD-ROM is attractive only where it will be used extensively. In contrast, distribution of data on magnetic media uses drives which are already included in computer systems for other purposes; thus there is no extra equipment cost.

The same point applies more forcibly where the data is to be read by the human eye, and the user does not already have a computer. In this case the comparison is not between the cost of different peripheral devices but between complete 'delivery systems'. Since every human is equipped with a delivery system for printed text at no cost, CD-ROM has to offer considerable advantages in other directions (such as ease of access or cost of media) to offset the cost of even the simplest delivery system.

Finally, a word about read-only disks designed to be read on multifunction drives designed for standard writable disks. Many of the above points apply, except of course that of drive compatibility. In general, these drives offer higher performance than CD-ROM drives, but at a substantially higher cost. There is likely to be a limited market for such disks where high performance — and especially fast access — is important. They may also be used for distributing software to systems which already have this type of drive for other purposes. However, the lack of universality of these types of disk will prevent their wide use.

APPLICATIONS

Read-only disks are reproduced at low cost from a master which itself is expensive to make. Disks are therefore expensive if only a few are made, but cheap in large numbers. This makes read-only disks very suitable for publishing. They are particularly well suited where the data published needs to be read into a computer system; for example numerical material that can be analysed in a spreadsheet, or program code. Even so, read-only disks are most widely used for text which is simply displayed on a screen for a human reader. CD-ROM is the dominant format; other read-only optical media can be used for publishing, but at present the only one in use is videodisk. However, this is not often used as part of a computer system; most videodisk players have their own output channels (video screens) which do not depend on a host computer, although in some cases a host is able to control the selection and display of images from the disk.

The use of read-only disk for data publishing, and its pros and cons in relation to other media, are discussed at length in Chapter 10. That chapter also covers the type of information that is published, and the sources it comes from.

The only applications that fall outside the publishing field are those where a firm uses read-only disk to distribute data within its own organization — for example, copying service manuals or price lists to branch offices. Although the data is not made public, in all other respects it is equivalent to publishing. It hardly needs special consideration, except to point out that in this case the issuer of the disks has closer control over the users than any publisher has; so compatibility of disks with different hardware and software is rarely a problem.

CURRENT STATUS

At present (1989), read-only disk is practically synonymous with CD-ROM. Very few data-carrying videodisks have been published, other than those designed for use on videodisk players which may be independent or interactive (under computer control) but are not really computer peripherals. Read-only disks compatible with WORM drives have been proposed but are not on the market. CD-ROM, however, has become an established product. About half-a-dozen manufacturers have drives on the market, and over 100 companies have published disks or announced plans to do so. However, the number of disks and drives sold is not yet very great. This is largely due to the lack of standards for data structure, which has meant that most installations were dedicated to a single publisher's disks. With the adoption of the 'High Sierra' standard, users can now install drives and access software in the knowledge that most future disks will run on them; similarly, publishers can produce disks knowing that a wider market can be reached.

Some drives of the early type, based directly on Compact Audio players, are still available. These are built into desktop boxes, and are loaded by placing the bare disk in a drawer or in a compartment under a hinged lid. Most later drives are designed to fit the $5\frac{1}{4}$ inch footprint, either full or half height. These can be built into the host computer, or supplied in a free-standing case including a mains power supply. Some are still loaded with bare disks, and so must be mounted horizontally, but caddy loading is becoming the norm and this allows horizontal or vertical mounting.

There are manufacturers in Japan, Europe and the USA. The tight standards situation means that there is relatively little difference between drives. However, as we saw earlier, access time does vary, and there is also a difference in error rates depending on how much of the possible error correction is actually implemented. Prices reflect these differences.

Philips and Sony have recently issued a provisional specification for an 80 mm version of the CD-ROM disk, to hold 200 megabytes. The specification also defines a cartridge to contain the disk, and is intended to enable drives to fit within a $3\frac{1}{2}$ inch footprint.

Videodisk players have been available for several years; although most of these are free-standing, some allow a computer to select and control the images displayed. WORM media are available as well as read-only. However videodisk has not been developed as a true computer storage medium.

Read-only disks can be made to fit drives designed primarily for use with WORM disks, but there has been very little demand for them.

For some purposes, optical card is an alternative to CD-ROM, although it has not yet made an impact on the market. Optical card is discussed in Chapter 6.

In summary, CD-ROM is now an established technology; other forms of read-only disk do not show much promise at present; and optical card is technically feasible, but has not yet found a full-scale application.

5
Automated disk libraries

The user with a couple of optical disk drives has access to a gigabyte or more of data. For many this is enough, but some have databases which are much larger than this. In a lot of them the latest data is used frequently, while older data is used less often. All the disks, regardless of age, can be kept on line; this keeps the access time down to a fraction of a second, but it needs many drives and these are expensive. Alternatively, all but the most recent disks can be kept on the shelf in a disk library, with one or two drives and operators to load disks on demand. This needs fewer drives but more staff, and the access time becomes minutes or even hours. This is often too long — when a client is on the other end of a telephone, for example. Many users find a better answer to this problem in the *automated disk library*. This gives them access within a few seconds to all their disks, without extra drives or staff; what it does add is a fairly complex piece of machinery for moving disks from a storage rack to the disk drives.

In fact, everyone now refers to an automated disk library as a *jukebox*. This started off as technical jargon, because some early types worked like the coin-operated record players found in bars. However, it is now so widely used that we must accept it as a respectable technical term, and some manufacturers use no other. (On the other hand, one of them prefers to use 'optical storage and retrieval unit'!)

TECHNOLOGY

Disks for use in a jukebox are no different from those for manually loaded drives, and can be exchanged between the two. Usually the disks are in the same cartridges that are used for ordinary drives, though as we shall see there are exceptions. Those readers who have met automated tape libraries will notice the difference here — most tape libraries used special tapes and cartridges, which could not be used anywhere else. The size of the disk has a major effect on the design of the jukebox. To a lesser extent the type of drive and cartridge does too, although many jukeboxes are made in more than one version so that different drives can be used.

The jukebox comes in several forms, but all have the same basic parts (Fig. 5.1). Firstly there is a rack (or 'storage matrix') which holds a number of disks, each in a separate slot; secondly one or more disk drives; thirdly a

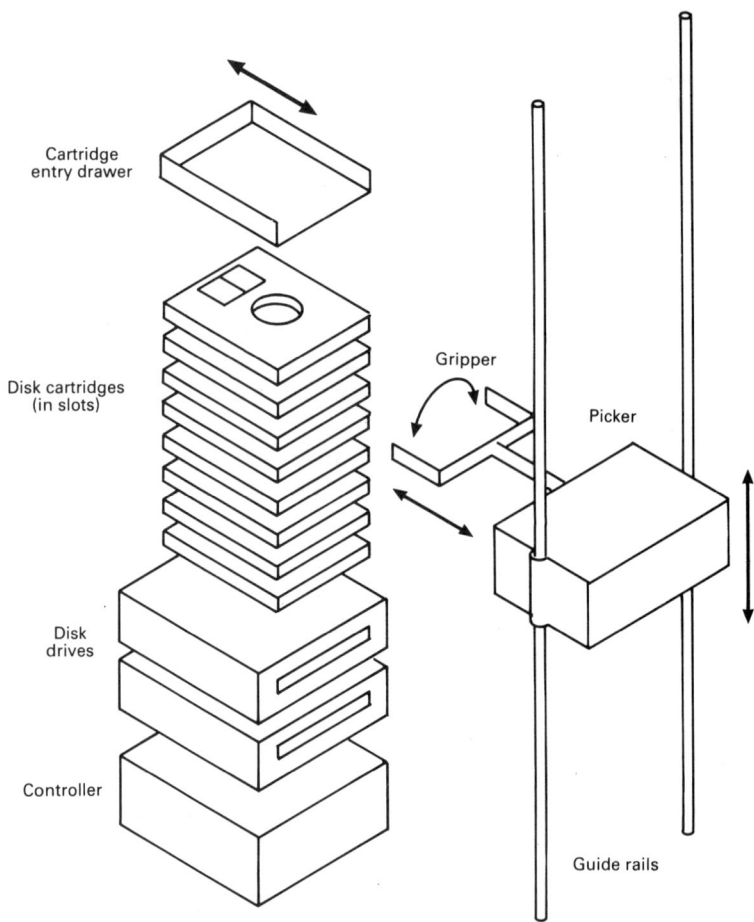

Fig. 5.1 — Simplified schematic of jukebox.

mechanism (the 'picker') which can take any disk from the rack and load it on a drive, or return it from the drive to the rack; and fourthly a controller, which takes orders from the host computer and uses the other three parts to carry them out. Most jukeboxes also have an entry slot or drawer (Fig. 5.2), where the operator puts a disk so that the picker can place it in the rack or a drive. In a few cases there is no input slot; then the jukebox has to be stopped and opened up, and the disk put straight into the rack. Disks are taken out of the jukebox in the same way that they are put in.

Most jukeboxes now use disks in cartridges, as we have seen, but a few use bare disks. Disks in cartridges are less likely to be damaged, and can be used in free-standing drives as well as in the jukebox. On the other hand, bare disks take up less space; also some types of cartridge are not suitable for

Fig. 5.2 — The entry drawer of a jukebox, with a 12 inch disk in its cartridge. (Copyright Laser Magnetic Storage International.)

use in a jukebox. The disk drives used in jukeboxes are very similar to those designed to be loaded by hand. They often have sensors added to help the controller to keep the various parts of the jukebox in step, and sometimes a more powerful motor is fitted to the jukebox version of a drive; then less time is needed to spin the drive up to its working speed. This improves performance, since the spin-up time is quite a large part of the access time.

In the most common design of storage rack (Fig. 5.3), the disks are held horizontally in slots one above another to form a vertical stack. This can hold anything from 16 to 80 or so disks. One or more drives are mounted in the same stack, above or below the disk slots. The picker mechanism is next to the stack. One part of the picker moves up and down, so that it can be brought level with any disk slot or drive. An arm is then extended from the picker, and this arm grips the disk cartridge and draws it out of the slot or drive. The picker then moves to another slot or drive, and the arm pushes the cartridge into this. Jukeboxes nearly always use double-sided disks, and the arm can turn the cartridge over while the picker is moving to the drive.

Operation
The sequence of actions in loading a disk begins with the picker moving level with the slot that holds the disk. The arm extends, grips the disk cartridge

Fig. 5.3 — Interior of LMSI jukebox. The disk drive is at bottom left, with the storage rack above it and the picker mechanism to the right. (Copyright Laser Magnetic Storage International.)

and pulls it into the picker. The picker then moves to the level of the disk drive, turning the cartridge over if this is necessary. The arm extends again to push the disk into the drive, releases it, and is withdrawn. The drive then clamps the disk to its hub, just as if it had been manually loaded, and spins it up to working speed. The whole process takes a few seconds. However, as soon as the picker has put the disk in the drive it is free to fetch a disk for another drive; therefore two or three drives can share a picker mechanism without having to wait for it too much.

The same sequence is followed in reverse when a disk is unloaded. Some jukeboxes have a picker arm which can hold two disks; then when the disk in a drive is to be replaced by another, the picker starts by fetching the second disk. It then goes to the drive and exchanges disks, and finally puts the first disk away in its slot. This allows the second disk to be be spun up while the first is being put away, so the access time is shortened.

A large jukebox may have a second storage rack on the other side of the picker mechanism; the storage racks may be horizontal (Fig. 5.4). In other designs the picker does not move but the storage rack moves instead. The

Fig. 5.4 — Interior of Filenet jukebox. There are two horizontal storage racks with a drive below them; the picker mechanism moves in front. (Copyright British Olivetti.)

rack may move up and down (or sideways), if the number of disks is small; alternatively it may move in a circle, with the disks held in radial slots like slides in the carousel of a video slide projector.

Types of jukebox

Jukeboxes appeal to users with very large databases, and these users are most likely to choose 12 inch disks so that they need fewer volumes. For this reason the first jukebox designs, and most of those which have been sold up to now, are designed for 12 inch disks. One or two Japanese firms have 8 inch versions. However, there is also a market for jukeboxes which hold $5\frac{1}{4}$ inch disks; these are less expensive and more compact than 12 inch jukeboxes, and have shorter access times. In some circumstances a $5\frac{1}{4}$ inch juke box with two drives may be more cost-effective than a few 12 inch drives without a jukebox.

Jukeboxes are available to suit most 12 inch disks and cartridges, and also 5¼ inch disks using the ISO standard cartridge or one or two of the proprietary cartridges. It does not, of course, matter to the jukebox what class of medium the cartridges contain. So far this has invariably been WORM, but if the drive can handle rewritable and read-only disks, the jukebox will deal with them equally well.

CD-ROM disks can be handled by a jukebox, though the lack of a permanently fitted cartridge calls for a different design. Jukeboxes have been designed to take Compact Audio disks, and CD-ROM jukeboxes will be based on these; none is on sale yet, but at least one is on the way. Probably a fairly small number of disks — say ten or twenty — will meet most needs.

CONTROL

The simplest application of a jukebox is as a peripheral to a host computer. The controller takes orders from the host computer and uses the picker to carry them out. Usually the connection between the controller and the host is independent of that between the drives and the host. When a disk is loaded, the controller's job is complete as soon as the picker arm has placed the disk on the drive and withdrawn; the controller then signals the host, and the host instructs the drive to clamp the disk and run it up to speed. The intelligence of the system can be divided in various ways between the host software and the controller. For example, one or other of these must know which slot each disk is in, but it does not matter whether this is the host or the controller.

When the jukebox acts a server to a host or a network of hosts, the interface will be some kind of local area network. If the intelligence of the server is in a separate unit, this is in effect the host to the jukebox, and the interfaces between them are the same as in the last case. Otherwise the jukebox controller and the server intelligence are combined in a single unit; in this case the drives will be connected to the controller directly, and it will be the controller that keeps track of where all the disks are.

A third possibility is that there may be no host computer; the jukebox itself may be the core of a free-standing system, which will usually serve a number of terminals. As far as the jukebox is concerned this is very similar to the integrated server case, though now the controller itself, rather than the host, will run the applications needed to serve the users at their terminals. An example of such a system is described in Chapter 9.

CHARACTERISTICS

We shall only look at the characteristics of the jukebox as a computer peripheral, under the direct control of a host. Servers and free-standing systems are outside the scope of this chapter; there will be some discussion of them in Chapter 8.

To a large extent the characteristics of a jukebox are those of the drives installed in it. As we have seen, these are very similar to manually loaded drives, although the spin-up time may be reduced by fitting a more powerful motor. Many jukeboxes can take a choice of drives, so the data sheet is often in two sections — one referring to the drives, the other to the controller, picker and storage rack; sometimes the jukebox data sheet does no more than say which types of drive can be used.

The data sheet in Table 5.1 refers to a hypothetical, but typical, jukebox for 12 inch drives.

Table 5.1 — Data sheet for a typical jukebox

Number of drives	2
Number of disks	30
Average cartridge exchange time	10 seconds
Reliability — MTBF	7000 hours
Power requirements (mains voltage AC)	2 kVA peak
Temperature range	50°–100° F
Noise level	60 dba
Dimensions	60 inches high
	60 inches long
	30 inches wide
Interface	RS232

In this case the jukebox data sheet does not include details of the disk drive, so the text would say which drives can be used. Their characteristics can then be found from their data sheets.

We shall look at each item in more detail.

Capacity
Most jukeboxes have spaces for one or two drives; some allow up to five. A second drive may be fitted just to give a margin of safety in case the first breaks down. Performance, in terms of the amount of data transferred in a given time, goes up as more drives are fitted, but not in proportion; the results obtained depend very much on the way the jukebox is used. Many users find two drives are enough, some use three; only a few users fit more. Jukeboxes for $5\frac{1}{4}$ inch disks rarely allow more than two drives.

The number of disk slots varies very much between designs. Often there is more than one version of a design, with different numbers of disk slots. For 12 inch disk jukeboxes, models now on sale take from 16 to 141 disks; $5\frac{1}{4}$ inch jukeboxes go up to 32 disks. Sometimes disk drives and disk slots compete for the same space; then the limit on the number of disks is reduced, by perhaps five or ten disks, for each drive added.

Performance
Disk exchange time is the most usual measure of performance, but sometimes load and unload times are given separately. The figure may or may not include the time it takes to spin the disk up to its working speed. The data sheet should say whether it does; if in doubt, spin-up time had better be

added to the figure that is shown. A standard 12 inch drive spins up in eight to ten seconds, while a drive modified for use in a jukebox will often spin up in four or five seconds. Jukeboxes for 5¼ inch disks are faster than their 12 inch cousins — typically twice as fast.

System performance will depend very much on the way the jukebox is used, and also on the number of drives fitted; the figures in the data sheet should be taken only as a guide.

Reliability
Reliability, as we saw in earlier chapters, is not at all easy to predict. Data sheet figures are only a very rough guide. However, jukeboxes do have a lot of mechanical parts and these are more likely to give trouble than electronics. The MTBF quoted for a jukebox will, as a result, be lower than that for most other peripherals. We shall see what this implies later in the chapter. The figure in the data sheet usually refers to failures of the jukebox mechanism and controller only, not to drive faults, but this should be made clear in the text.

Environment
Jukeboxes use quite a lot of power when they are in motion, less when waiting for orders. They are designed to work in normal office conditions, but a large jukebox in heavy use can give out three kilowatts in the form of heat, so air conditioning may be needed. Noise may also be a problem. Figures in data sheets vary between 55 and 65 dba; the lower level may be tolerable in a large office, but the noise tends to come in thumps and buzzes which are more distracting than a steady hum.

Size and shape vary very much between designs, and of course the more disks that can be held, the bigger the jukebox will be. Some 12 inch jukeboxes are tall and narrow, up to 80 inches high, but the lower, longer form is more usual (Fig. 5.5). 5¼ inch jukeboxes are much smaller, a typical 32-disk unit is about 20 inches square and 30 inches high.

Interface
As we have seen, most jukebox controllers have an interface to the host which is quite separate from that of the disk drives. Traffic over the jukebox interface is very light, since the controller takes several seconds to carry out a command from the host. The interface is usually RS232, which is fast enough and cheap to implement. However, a few jukeboxes use SCSI, since this is the interface used by nearly all disk drives, so jukebox and drives can share the same port on the host.

Price
Price is not shown on data sheets, and it varies very much with the capacity of the jukebox. At present a small 12 inch jukebox costs about $30 000 and a large one $100 000. 5¼ inch jukeboxes are a good deal cheaper — typically $15 000. The price is usually given for the jukebox alone, without disk drives or disks.

Fig. 5.5 — Exterior view of the jukebox shown in Fig. 5.3. (Copyright Laser Magnetic Storage International.)

Jukeboxes for CD-ROM

Jukeboxes for CD-ROM disks will have rather different characteristics. One which has been announced, though not yet sold, holds 240 bare disks in a circular magazine, with the drive in the centre. Disks are exchanged in not more than seven seconds. The whole unit is 6 inches high and about 16 inches square and will probably cost about $12 000. This is obviously a spin-off from the entertainment world; few computer users are likely to want such a large number of disks.

STRENGTHS AND WEAKNESSES

The great strength of the jukebox is, of course, that it gives access to a large number of optical disks. We could do this in two other ways, and we shall compare the jukebox with these.

On the one hand we could put each disk on a separate drive. This would give an access time of a fraction of a second, which compares to several seconds for the jukebox. It would avoid the high cost of the jukebox, but at the expense of using more disk drives. The cost of the two approaches will be similar when five to ten disks are in use, and for more disks than this the library will certainly cost less to buy.

On the other hand we could keep the disks on a shelf, with an operator to load them onto a drive. The access time would become minutes rather than seconds. The cost of the jukebox would be saved, but the cost of staff time would have to be set against the saving. In this case it is much harder to compare costs, because extra staff may or may not be taken on. If the shelved disks are only needed occasionally, this is the most economical approach; if they are in constant use, so that full time staff are needed, the jukebox is probably cheaper in the long run. The jukebox is much less likely to make mistakes, and will work long hours without extra cost.

The jukebox does not take sick leave either. Nevertheless, one of the weaknesses of the jukebox is that its reliability is poorer than that of most peripheral devices. The system designer has to give careful thought to the effects of a breakdown; in some cases he may need a second library as a standby. Some jukebox manufacturers claim that disks can be loaded by hand if the picker mechanism breaks down, but experience shows that this is not always successful.

APPLICATIONS

Jukeboxes are useful where there is a lot of data which is not used often, but which must be reached quickly when it is needed. For some applications a jukebox is the obvious solution. In other cases the choice between this and other solutions will need a detailed study of their cost and performance. In general, a jukebox will not be cheapest if there are only a few disks, and will not be suitable if access times of a few seconds are too long. It will also not be the cheapest solution if the total database, however many disks there are, is used only a few times a day; even so it may be chosen because it gives faster access and fewer errors than a human operator. In between these two limits, many applications will be better served by a jukebox than by one drive per disk or by loading disks by hand.

In many organizations the most recent data is used much more often than older data, although the latter is still needed at times. A common arrangement is to keep the recent disks on separate drives and older ones in a jukebox.

There are other circumstances in which hand-loaded drives and a jukebox can complement each other. An example is a user with a number of branch offices. Each of these can have a couple of disk drives, so that transactions can be recorded and recent transactions consulted. Older disks, which are consulted less often, can be transferred to a jukebox in the head office and accessed over a communications link.

If a jukebox is heavily used for reading records, it may be best to avoid writing new records at the same time because this affects performance. One solution is to have a separate, hand-loaded, drive for the disk to which new records are written. However, if only some times of the day are busy, it may be better to record new records temporarily on a magnetic disk; they can be copied to an optical disk in the jukebox at a quieter time.

Jukeboxes are mechanically complicated, and as a result their failure rate is rather high in comparison with other parts of a computer system; the mean time between failures will probably be between 5000 and 10 000 hours. Where the jukebox is used to retrieve old records, a few hours without it may not matter; for example, it may be a replacement for a paper system where retrieval of data took days. If regular service is more critical, the system designer needs to provide for at least a reduced service if the picker fails. Jukebox suppliers sometimes claim that disks can be loaded by hand if the picker fails; this is far from easy, and is a job for an engineer rather than office staff. Assuming that a separate set of disks is kept somewhere as backup, it may be easier to load these into a separate drive. However where something near full service is needed, the only satisfactory solution is to duplicate the jukebox as well as the disks.

CURRENT STATUS

There are about a dozen jukeboxes for 12 inch disks on the market. Most of these have been developed by specialist firms in the USA, who have designed their products so that disk drives from several different makers can be used. In Japan, on the other hand, jukeboxes have been designed by (or for) the same companies as disk drives; these take only the one make of drive. Just about every 12 inch drive on the market can now be fitted into one jukebox or another. There is also a jukebox to fit the one 14 inch drive on the market.

12 inch jukeboxes have sold well, particularly in the larger sizes, and it has been predicted that more than half of the 12 inch WORM drives sold will go into jukeboxes.

Jukeboxes for $5\frac{1}{4}$ inch drives came later; few are yet on the market but a number are on the way. The specialist manufacturers are responsible for some of these too, but more drive manufacturers are developing their own jukeboxes. The proportion of $5\frac{1}{4}$ inch drives used in jukeboxes may be fairly small. However, a lot of these drives will be sold so there will still be a good market for $5\frac{1}{4}$ inch jukeboxes.

CD-ROM jukeboxes are not yet on the market, but they can easily be adapted from versions designed for Compact Audio disks. They will be attractive where one CD-ROM server is connected to a number of enquiry terminals, as might be the case in a large library. Their use will increase as the number of CD-ROM databases in a particular field grows. However, most CD-ROM systems will have only one screen, and manual disk loading will suffice for these.

The reliability of the present generation of jukeboxes is poorer than that of most other storage peripherals; this is inevitable, because their mechanical parts are complex. We can expect a good deal of effort to go into making jukeboxes more reliable, but they are never likely to be as reliable as disk or tape drives.

6
Optical tape and card

All the devices we have discussed so far use media in disk form. The disk combines random access with high data density; it is the favourite format for optical storage, as it is for magnetic storage. However, in both cases, other formats exist. In this chapter we shall look at some optical storage media other than disk, and at devices that use them; these are tape and card. Several early developments of optical storage, which are not now on the market, used these forms of media; they are discussed briefly in the last chapter of this book.

OPTICAL TAPE

Interest in optical storage devices using tape media has continued, in spite of the limited success of earlier tape devices. The principal attraction is the thinness of the substrate. If the same area density can be achieved as on disk, the volume density can be several times higher. This makes it practicable to store hundreds of gigabytes on a single volume of manageable size, and hence to have this much data on line for the cost of a single drive. Media costs are also substantially lower. Access times to tape are always much longer than to disk, but for some applications this is acceptable.

In practice it is not easy to use as high an area density as on disk. The main problem is that tape is not a rigid medium, so it is harder to locate it precisely. However this can be overcome by track-seeking techniques where the data track is searched for and followed using servo techniques. A number of companies have tried to develop systems. Most of these have fallen by the wayside, but a Canadian company, Creo, has demonstrated advanced prototypes at several trade exhibitions. Creo intends to be in full production by the end of 1989.

The Creo machine looks very much like an open-reel magnetic tape drive (Fig. 6.1). Each tape is 880 metres long and 35 millimetres wide, and one terabyte of data (1000 gigabytes — one million megabytes) can be stored on each reel. 33 tracks (including a clock track) are recorded in parallel; however the tracks are not written along the tape but across it, using an oscillating optical head. When a set of 33 tracks has been written right across the tape, the tape is stepped forwards to allow the next set to be written. The bit spacing is 1.5 microns in each direction, and the laser focus spot is about

Fig. 6.1 — Optical tape drive. (Copyright Creo Electronics Corporation.)

1 micron across — similar figures to those used on optical disk. The data rate is 3 megabytes per second and the average access time 28 seconds. To allow fast access, an address track is written along the tape, near one edge, and read by a separate stationary head. The machine is expensive — around $200 000 — and a reel of tape will initially cost $10 000, which works out as 1 cent per megabyte. This figure is expected to drop by about half in two or three years. It compares with a current figure of around 10 cents per megabyte for most WORM disks, which is also likely to fall.

This drive can be used with various types of media. At present only WORM tapes are available, using dye–polymer sensitive layers; 40 milliwatt lasers are used for writing, and a separate low-power laser is used for reading. Rewritable media are likely to be developed if there is a demand for them. They may need higher-power lasers. The archival properties of all media depend on the substrate as well as the sensitive layer; it remains to be seen whether this tape-based medium can achieve the long data life offered by optical disk. At the moment the suppliers guarantee a 20-year data life, but this depends on the tape being stored in suitable conditions.

Another manufacturer is developing a system using shorter lengths of optical tape in cartridges, with a mechanism allowing any cartridge to be loaded automatically into the drive: a set of 128 cartridges will store 750 gigabytes of data and the average access time is 10 seconds.

OPTICAL CARD

Media for optical storage can also be used in the form of cards. A number of companies are working in this field and various field trials are going on, although there is not yet any full-scale application. The favourite card size and shape is that of the familiar credit card, but with the magnetic stripe at the back replaced by a coating carrying data which can be read optically. Where the magnetic stripe card can hold a few hundred bytes of data, an optical card of the same size can hold several megabytes. The hunt is on for applications where this sort of data capacity is wanted on a card which can be carried in the wallet or sent through the post without any special packing. One that looks attractive is the storage of personal medical records. The idea is that anyone can carry his complete record around with him on an optical card; whenever he visits a doctor or a hospital, this can be put into a device and read instantly. At least one large medical insurance company in the USA is planning to use this scheme, and there are smaller trials elsewhere. Amongst the many other uses that have been proposed are EFT (electronic funds transmission) and the distribution of computer software.

Media technology is much the same as for disks. There seems little call for a rewritable card; read-only media are useful for data and software publishing, but WORM media will be needed where data has to be added from time to time. The most active media company uses a proprietary material in which silver particles are carried in a gelatine film, and writing with a laser beam produces pits in the surface; other companies prefer dye–polymer media. Read-only cards can be reproduced very cheaply by a printing process; WORM cards are expected to cost a few dollars each.

In most parts of the optical storage field, mechanism development has been delayed by the lack of satisfactory media. In the optical card field, on the other hand, cards are widely available but devices to write and read them are not. Indeed, one of the media companies has found it necessary to sponsor the development of basic designs for these devices. These are then licensed to prospective manufacturers. Very few such products are on the market at present, but one company will offer a reader for read-only cards at a quantity price of $600; they also offer a reader/writer for WORM cards at $800. The latter device stores up to 1 megabyte. Track spacing is 15 microns and bit spacing 10 microns; the laser spot diameter is about 5 microns. The data rate is 12 kilobytes per second when reading and a tenth of this when writing. The optical head moves along the card to write a track, and the card itself is moved sideways to position it for the next track. The current design is intended to stand on a desk, but a 5¼ inch footprint version is proposed, and devices with two or four times the capacity are also on the way.

Another company has shown prototypes of a much more ambitious drive. This uses an optical head with multiple lenses on a rotating disk (Fig. 6.2) to store 24 megabytes on credit card sized media, with the prospect of

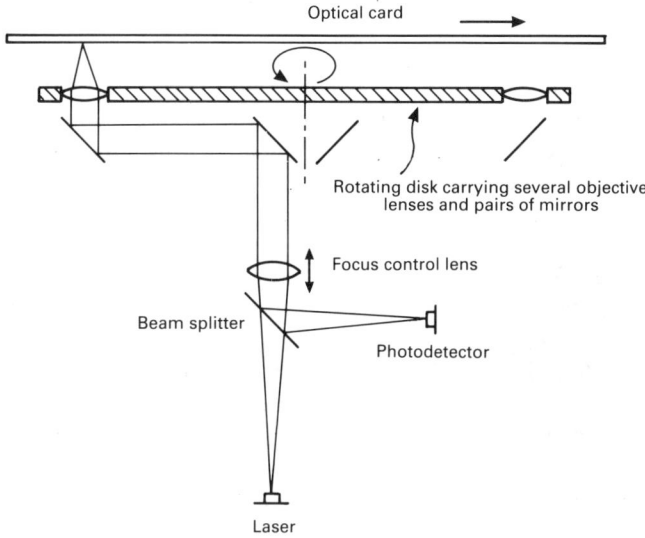

Fig. 6.2 — Optical system for rotating-head card drive (simplified).

increasing this to 200 megabytes. There are 24 000 tracks at 3 micron pitch and the spot diameter is about 1 micron. Read data rate is 125 kilobytes per second, and write data rate is half this. The company has not predicted the production cost; it is likely to be in the thousands of dollars range.

Development work on optical card media and devices is concentrated in North America and Japan. There has been no contribution from Europe, although some application studies have been begun.

The 'smart card' should be mentioned here, if only to make it clear that this is neither an optical card nor a magnetic stripe card. Instead it contains a fairly small amount of non-volatile semiconductor storage (typically 16 kilobytes) and also a simple microprocessor. The card is connected to a host either through contacts on the face of the card or else by inductive coupling. Smart cards are not in competition with optical cards for storing large amounts of data, though they will compete with magnetic stripe cards in applications such as cash and credit management, and access control.

7

Controllers, interfaces and standards

In the last five chapters we have looked at the different devices that can be used to store computer data in optical form. However, no peripheral device is of use on its own; we must be able to attach it to a host of some kind. The host may be anything from a mainframe computer down to a dedicated microprocessor. Whatever it is, there is a *peripheral interface* which links the host to the peripheral. Most device makers would like their product to be used with a range of hosts; so they follow one or other of the various standards which exist to define peripheral interfaces.

A peripheral device consists, in general, of a *mechanism* and a *controller*. Sometimes these are built into the same package, so that the interface between them is not visible to the system designer. In other cases the two parts can be bought separately, even from separate suppliers. To make this practicable the interface between the two parts — the *mechanism interface* — must also be defined. Usually it will be defined in terms of a standard, although sometimes the controller manufacturer will design to suit whatever the maker of the mechanism chose to use.

The standards we have been talking about are both *interface standards*. They aim to allow hosts, controllers and mechanisms to be connected without the need to design special hardware and software for every combination; they also make it possible for a system designer to replace one peripheral device by another without too much difficulty. Completely separate from these are *interchange standards*. These define the form which a volume of the optical medium, and the information recorded on it, should take. The aim is to allow media recorded on one device to be read on another, which may not be identical in design with the first. Interchange standards let the user move volumes from one system to another; this may or may not be important to him. They also let the user replace one device by another of a different design without the need to transcribe all the data he already has. Many device manufacturers choose to ignore interchange standards; they often have good technical reasons for doing this, but the user must recognize that he will be 'locked in' to that supplier.

The unrecorded medium — a blank disk or tape, for example — is often defined in the interchange standard. However, it is perfectly possible for data to be recorded in different ways on volumes which, when blank, were identical. For this reason a separate *unrecorded media* standard often exists. In some cases, one of the international standards bodies has chosen to combine the two standards while another has issued them separately, though remaining compatible with the first.

In this book, when we talk about a controller we always mean a *device controller* — the controller which links a mechanism to the peripheral interface of the host. This must not be confused with a peripheral controller, which is part of the host and links its internal bus to its peripheral interface. Because of this risk of confusion the term peripheral controller is now not widely used. On small systems the term 'interface adaptor' is general; on a larger system it may be a 'channel' or 'I/O processor'.

PERIPHERAL INTERFACES

The peripheral interface to be used will depend on the design of the host, though it may be possible to add an interface adaptor to the host if it does not already have one that is suitable. In the past, peripheral interfaces have been very diverse and often designed for a particular class of peripheral. Recently there has been a trend to more general interfaces. The most relevant of these are the IBM expansion card bus, used on personal computers, and SCSI — the small computer systems interface — which is used mostly on larger systems, although it can also be used on PCs (see Fig. 7.1).

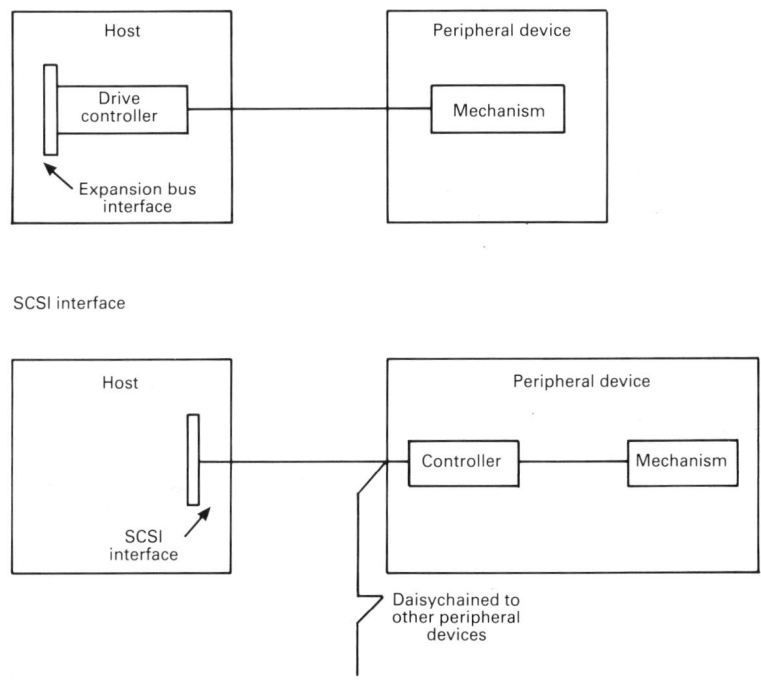

Fig. 7.1 — Interface configurations.

IBM expansion card bus

The connectors carrying the IBM expansion card bus are normally on the mother board of the PC; each has a card slot so that controllers or complete peripherals can be mounted inside the PC cabinet. The bus connectors include power rails, and the cards use the PC's power supply. In fact the slots can be used for other purposes than supporting peripherals, and the bus itself is completely general. The cards may carry RAM or ROM memory which can be used as if it were part of the PC's memory, and programs controlling the card can be run in the PC itself. This allows peripheral controllers to be simple and cheap, although there is no reason why they should not also carry their own microprocessors and firmware, and thus be largely autonomous. The interface is of course defined by IBM, and it is accepted as an industry standard although it has not been adopted by the independent standards bodies. IBM's PS/2 range of PCs has introduced a different expansion card bus, the 'microchannel interface', which is much the same in principle although more powerful.

SCSI interface

In contrast, SCSI is designed specifically to lift the burden of peripheral control from the host, as far as this is possible. It is a generalized interface, like the IBM one, in that it is intended to support many types of peripheral. In fact it has also been used for other purposes than peripheral connection, though this was not the original plan. SCSI is often described as an 'intelligent' interface; what that means is that much of the intelligence needed to control the peripheral device is in the peripheral controller rather than in the host. In particular, in a storage device such as an optical disk, the host need know nothing at all about the method of error management; all error correction and detection is done by the controller. Sometimes the host may notice a hesitation in the data flow, but that is all, except in the rare case (maybe once a year in a typical device) where the error cannot be recovered. Of course, statistics on recovered errors are available to the host so that it can monitor the behaviour of the device.

The SCSI standard has to be used with caution, just because it is so general. The standard defines the physical and electrical requirements of the interface precisely, though it does allow some options such as a choice between single-ended and balanced cable drivers. However, the logical requirements are far more open. Several 'command sets' are defined, each of which covers a specific class of peripheral — disks, tape, printers and so on. But within each set, very few commands are 'mandatory' — usually two or three. A larger number, typically a dozen, are 'optional'; this means that the designer need not use them, but if he does he must use them as defined in the standard. Many more command codes are assigned to 'vendor defined' commands, which the designer can use if and how he chooses. Also the standard does very little to define the status information which is returned by the peripheral to the host in response to various commands and conditions. It follows that specifying that a device shall use the SCSI interface is by no means enough to make sure that it is compatible with a host that supports

SCSI. In practice, an SCSI peripheral will be compatible with an SCSI host as far as physical equipment is concerned (though the options need to be watched); but the host software that drives the interface, forming and sending commands and making sense of the responses, often has to be written specially for each peripheral.

Two measures are bringing some relief from this problem. Firstly, 'common command sets' now exist for most classes of peripheral. These have usually been put together by an *ad hoc* committee of device manufacturers; they have then been assimilated, as recommended options, into the SCSI standard by the independent bodies which control it. Each common command set lists a subset of the 'optional' commands which must be implemented, and which is sufficient for all the normal functions of the device. Other commands, optional or vendor-defined, can be used in addition by any designer to provide extra functions. The use of the common command set means that standard host software can make use of any peripheral which conforms, but it may not be able to take full advantage of all the features of the peripheral; in particular, status responses are still largely undefined.

The other way in which the compatibility problem can be eased is for the supplier of the peripheral to provide the necessary driver software to run in the host. Many device manufacturers have found they have to do this in order to sell their products; so drivers for the more common hosts are now quite widely available. This means, in theory, that if a user wants to replace one SCSI device by another, he only has to replace the software driver. Of course it is rarely as simple as that: one device may offer a rather different set of facilities from the other, and each device supplier will make sure that his driver uses the features of his device to the full.

MS-DOS extensions
A similar case is the attachment of CD-ROM drives to personal computers which use the MS-DOS operating system. Microsoft, the designer of MS-DOS, has not only modified the operating system to take CD-ROM, but has also written a set of drivers to suit most of the available mechanisms. This should make it easy for the user to change from one design of CD-ROM drive to another.

Acceptance of standards
SCSI and the IBM expansion card bus have been adopted throughout the optical disk industry. Every drive is now available with a controller to suit one or other of these standards, and often both versions are on offer. A few early drives did not support either of these interfaces, but all those that are still on the market have come into line. In some cases other interfaces are available as well, usually to suit particular hosts such as DEC.

Neither of the two popular interfaces we have looked at will handle very high data rates. If and when very fast optical disk drives come along they may have to use some faster interface. A standard for a faster version of SCSI is being discussed, under the provisional name SCSI 2. Another intelligent interface which may be used is called IPI-3: at present it is used mainly for fast magnetic disks.

Much the same applies to optical tape; but optical card has much lower performance and so a slower and cheaper interface can be used. This is often RS232. Most optical disk libraries also use RS232 for their host connection, as we saw earlier, although a few use SCSI.

CONTROLLERS

For many types of peripheral device, it is usual to make the controller quite separate from the mechanism. There are various reasons for this. The controller may support a number of mechanisms — which need not all be of the same type; device and controller may come from different suppliers; or the system designer may want to mount the controller and the mechanism away from one another. Various standards for mechanism interfaces are used where controller and mechanism are separate. Many of these standards suit only one type of device: for example the 'ST412' interface which is widely used for small magnetic disk drives, or the 'Pertec' interface used for open reel tape drives. Some standards were written by committees; others started out as the specification of a single manufacturer and have been followed by competitors, thus becoming 'industry standards'. In either case, the standard may have been taken up and formally issued by a national or international standards body.

More recently there has been a move towards the use of mechanism interfaces which can support more than one kind of mechanism, so that a more general design of device controller can be used. The best-known standard of this kind is ESDI — 'enhanced small device interface'.

Optical storage practice

Optical storage does not follow this trend towards separating the controller from the mechanism. In optical storage devices the controller and mechanism are usually combined as one unit. If they are separate, the interface between them is often not a standard one, and is not visible to the system designer. The main reason for this is the complexity of the error management methods which are needed in optical storage, as we have already seen. Each manufacturer makes his own choice of the way he will handle this; the controller must be designed to suit whatever method is used in a particular drive. Controller and mechanism designers have to work very closely together, and so the company that makes the drive will usually make the controller too. There are exceptions, however; in the USA a few mechanism designers have chosen to leave the design of the controller to one of the firms which specialize in this field. In this case a standard mechanism interface may be used, and ESDI seems to be the favourite. The controller still needs to know what the drive does about errors, but as and when recording formats become standard, some compatibility between drives will come about.

Packaging

The controller may be built into the same package as the mechanism, or it may be a separate unit. The choice depends on several factors — in particular on the type of peripheral interface and on the amount of space available. Some peripheral interfaces, such as SCSI, are intended for use with controllers which are separate from the host; others, such as the IBM expansion card bus, require that the controller — or at least some part of it — is plugged into the mother board of the host PC. In the latter case the mechanism may be mounted in the PC as well, though this is usually possible only if it fits the standard slot (or 'footprint').

The space problem arises mainly where the mechanism is designed down to a particular size. At the moment this is most likely to be the standard $5\frac{1}{4}$ inch footprint (either full or half height) used for peripherals on PCs; the $3\frac{1}{2}$ inch footprint will be even more of a challenge. If the peripheral interface is to be the PC's expansion card bus, there is no problem; the controller is simply built as an expansion card, and linked to the mechanism by an interface which need not conform to any standard. On the other hand, if the peripheral interface is not associated with a card slot, the most convenient place for the controller is in the same package as the mechanism. Some optical disk drive manufacturers have been able to fit an SCSI controller as well as a drive into the standard footprint, but others have not. In this case, the system designer has the problem of finding somewhere else to put the controller.

There is less problem where the device is designed to stand apart from the host, usually on a desktop, although sometimes two or more devices may be brought together in a floor-standing cabinet. In this case it is easy to make the box large enough to take both mechanism and drive, and normally a power supply unit as well. This arrangement lends itself well to peripheral interfaces, like SCSI, which do not provide card slots in the host. Where the device is connected to a PC there may be another problem: since the cable from the controller (in the PC) to the mechanism is not entirely enclosed, it may need to be shielded and therefore to have special circuitry at each end. For this reason, a controller designed for a drive mounted inside a PC may be unsuitable when the drive is mounted elsewhere.

Sharing of controllers

When the controller is mounted apart from the drive, there is no problem in making it control several drives (Fig. 7.2) — many controllers support up to four. There may be a separate cable from the controller to each mechanism; more often the connection is a bus, in the form of a daisy chain. If the controller is packaged within the drive things are not quite so simple. In this case two types of drive have to be supplied (Fig. 7.3); 'master' drives with the controller, and 'slave' drives without. It is not always desirable to share a controller between drives, since most controllers can handle only one data transfer at a time. Using a controller for every drive also gives some protection against failure of the controller.

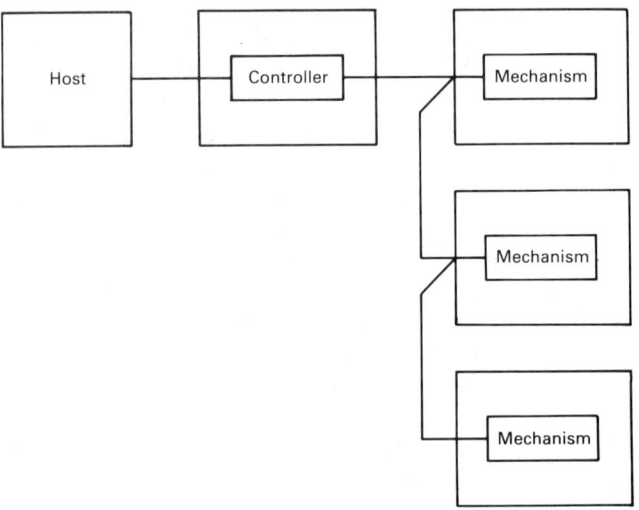

Fig. 7.2 — Shared controller configuration.

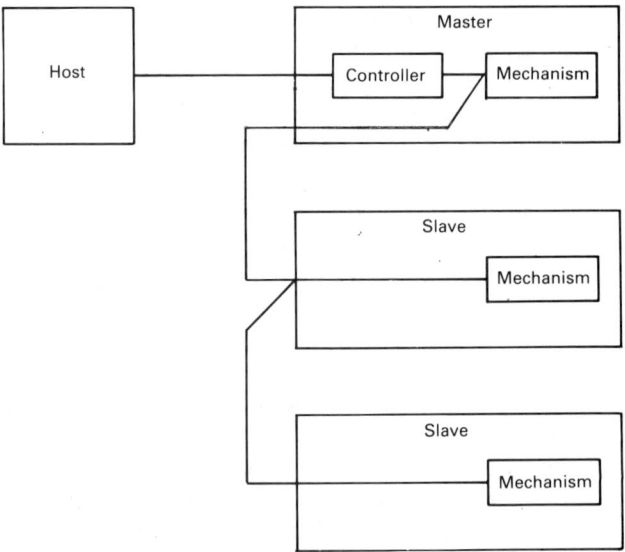

Fig. 7.3 — Master and slave configuration.

INTERCHANGE STANDARDS

We took a brief look at interchange standards as we went through the various types of optical store in the last few chapters, but here we shall look at the field as a whole and in rather more detail.

The first thing that must be said is that the optical storage industry has been very slow to develop interchange standards. This has done a lot to discourage potential users. It is true that many of them do not need, at present, to transfer data between systems; but experience shows that even when there is no such need at first, it nearly always arises later. Quite apart from this, a user who buys a non-standard device is 'locked in' to its supplier unless he is prepared to transcribe all his data to a new device. And at a more subjective level, the lack of accepted standards is taken as a sign of an immature industry.

WORM and rewritable disks

It was inevitable that the 'first generation' of optical disk stores would have little compatibility among them; at this stage there were several approaches to drive and media design, and nothing to show that any one of them would dominate the field. As it happens, nearly all of these early devices were 12 inch WORM drives (some with 8 inch versions); those of other sizes have fallen by the wayside. For the first two or three years, nearly all sales were in small quantities for use in pilot systems, so standards were not important. By the time that serious work started on $5\frac{1}{4}$ inch WORM drives, it was clear that standards were needed if optical storage was to be widely accepted. At this point, the companies developing $5\frac{1}{4}$ inch drives divided into two camps. Those in one camp saw the standard as essential, and were prepared to wait for it before bringing out their products. The others realized that this meant a fairly long wait, so they put their products on the market as soon as they could so as to take a share of whatever early business there might be. Some firms in this second camp designed to what they guessed the standard would be like, with the intention of revising their design to meet the standard when it appeared. Others dismissed standards completely, as a brake on progress.

Several independent bodies are concerned with computer standards — in particular ANSI, ECMA, ISO, and JSC. The American National Standards Institute (ANSI) is the standards body for the USA, though for legal reasons the actual writing of standards is done by quasi-independent American National Standards Committees (ANSCs). The European Computer Manufacturers Association (ECMA) is the equivalent body in Europe. The International Standards Organisation (ISO) is, in theory at least, the ultimate arbiter of standards; it can define standards in its own right, but more often (in the computer field anyway) it adopts standards prepared by the other bodies. JSC is the Japanese standards body, although Japanese computer firms often prefer to work through the bodies already named. ECMA, in spite of its name, admits representatives from manufacturers in all countries; it happens that ECMA usually moves faster than ANSI, so many US firms prefer to work through ECMA. It may appear that

ANSI and ECMA are in competition, but in practice there are good relations between them — partly because they have so many members in common. Often there will be informal agreement that only one of them will work on a particular standard. Even when this is not the case, their alternative versions are usually harmonized before submission to ISO. Often ECMA, and sometimes also ANSI, continue to publish their own standards even when the subject has been covered by ISO; but these are invariably compatible with the ISO standard as far as technical content is concerned, although the format may differ. There is also cooperation between ISO and the International Electrotechnical Commission (IEC), through their joint technical committee JCTI.

Of course, whatever may be the formal position, in practice the success of standards depends on 'the market'. If a dominant manufacturer decides to sell a product which does not match the official standards, and takes a large enough share of the market, then his specification becomes the *de facto* standard and other manufacturers tend to fall into line. Obviously some of the anti-standards firms hope that their designs will reach this status, though in the past only IBM has achieved this. (Interface standards are another matter.)

Those firms which believe in the need for a $5\frac{1}{4}$ inch interchange standard decided to pursue it through the independent standards bodies; the alternative would have been a working party formed within the industry, an approach which has been taken for magnetic tape cartridge standards. Unfortunately it has proved very difficult to reach agreement. It was hoped that a standard could be agreed within a year and published not long afterwards, but in fact the arguments have gone on for three years and the standard was still not published at the end of 1988. In fact only a few points remain outstanding, but one major difference has been resolved only by agreeing to two incompatible versions of the standard; it seems unlikely that more than one will survive in the market-place, but it is hard to say which.

This standard for $5\frac{1}{4}$ inch disks will be for WORM disks only, but it has become clear that rewritable drives and media will appear before the standard can be published. There will therefore be a related standard for rewritable media as well. These standards could easily be extended to read-only disks for use on the same drives, but it is not obvious that this is needed in view of the dominance of CD-ROM in the read-only field.

In the meantime, more firms have chosen to put $5\frac{1}{4}$ inch drives on the market which do not follow the standard, so far as it has been agreed. IBM is one of these firms, and two more have now a strong market position. This must raise doubts as to whether the 'official' standard will ever be widely accepted in full, although the prospects are a bit better for the 'unrecorded media' section of it.

If the $5\frac{1}{4}$ inch interchange standard is still far from established, the position is worse for 12 inch disks; there is still no standard of any kind, nor is any effort being made to produce one. Neither does any manufacturer dominate the market, though three early runners — Optimem (now owned by Cipher), LMSI (a Philips/CDC joint venture formerly known as OSI), and Hitachi — are well established. There is little sign of interest in rewritable or read-only disks in this size. 14 inch disks are now being used by only one drive manufacturer, Kodak, and if any other company joins in it will probably make its products compatible with Kodak. The only other disk size of current interest is $3\frac{1}{2}$ inch, mainly for rewritable disk; although there is some activity in the official standards bodies, it may well be that the industry will prefer to follow whichever firm makes most impression on the market.

CD-ROM

The one success story in the field of optical disk standards is CD-ROM, and here the standards have been set in a very different way. Two major companies, Philips and Sony, together developed Compact Audio, and then CD-ROM, which is very closely related to it. They laid down the standards, as the *Red Book* and the *Yellow Book* respectively. These companies control patents which are essential to CD-ROM media and drive manufacturers, and they make it a condition of the patent licence that their standards are followed precisely. In consequence, any CD-ROM disk will run on any CD-ROM drive. This does not necessarily mean that every drive has the same characteristics, as we saw in Chapter 3. The *Red Book* and *Yellow Book* are proprietary to Sony and Philips and were at first released only to their licensees, but a version of the *Yellow Book* is now being prepared by ECMA for issue as an ISO and ECMA standard.

Philips and Sony did not lay down any rules for the file structure to be used on CD-ROM, since at the time the *Yellow Book* was written it was not clear just what customers would want to do with the new medium. As databases began to be issued on CD-ROM, it was realized that the database structure and the access software had to match; and in the absence of any standard for the data, this led to different software being needed to access each database. Obviously the end user would not take kindly to having to learn to use a different software package every time he used a different disk. The problem was tackled promptly by an industry working party, independent of Sony and Philips but with their blessing; it became known as the 'High Sierra' working party after the place where it met (in the USA). The standard produced by the working party is widely known as the High Sierra standard, although it has been adopted by both ECMA and ISO as ECMA 119 and ISO 9660. Recently published CD-ROM disks conform to this standard, so at least a degree of compatibility between disks and software packages is ensured.

Tape and card

There is very little to say about standards for optical tape; only one firm has a product anywhere near the market, and the standards organizations are not involved.

Optical card standards are not yet established either, though it seems to be accepted that the size and shape should be that of the familiar credit card. One media company, Drexler, was early in the field, and for a time it seemed that their specification might become the *de facto* standard as they hoped.

However, several Japanese companies have now come up with alternative media and formats, so the position is wide open. There is no serious activity in the official standards bodies.

In conclusion, then, the present position of interchange standards for optical storage is far from happy, with the one exception of CD-ROM. There is of course a sector of the market where standards are not of direct importance, but customers are still deterred by the failure of the industry to put its house in order. Possibly the formal approach of ANSI, ECMA, and ISO, with its emphasis on consensus, is out of place in this field. The benevolent dictatorship of Philips and Sony is not likely to work for many products; the more pragmatic approach of the industry working party may be the way forward, or we may have to wait for 'the market' to decide. For the sake of the industry, we must all hope that we do not have to wait long.

8
Packaged systems

We have covered the different types of optical storage device in some detail; now it is time to move on to systems. It is beyond the scope of this book to discuss systems in detail, because each is the solution to a specific problem and so there are almost as many system designs as there are users. The next two chapters describe a few examples of systems designed for particular tasks; some of these are unique, others would need little adaptation to suit other users. Because there are tasks which are common to a number of users, many companies have designed packaged systems which include all the hardware and software needed to do these tasks. Some of these are standard systems, sold ready to plug in and go; others are a basis for custom design to meet less common requirements.

Already there are over 200 packaged systems on sale or announced, from almost as many companies. Practically all are based on WORM or read-only optical disk, although many of the WORM systems will be adapted to rewritable disks in the near future. Every one of these systems is different, and it would be impossible to cover them all in this chapter. Instead, the most popular types of packaged system will be identified and some examples described.

A few of the companies which make disk drives or libraries also offer packaged systems. Most of these are Japanese firms; a few are based elsewhere. The rest of the packages come from independent companies, mostly in the USA, although there are also some in Europe and the East. Some of these companies are very small; the prospective user needs to look at the viability of the suppliers as well as the attractions of their products. There is little difference, from the user's point of view, between the supplier of a packaged system which is customized to the user's needs, and a consultant who designs and supplies a tailor-made system.

DATA AND IMAGE STORAGE

Optical storage devices used in the computer field all store data in digital form, as do compact disks even when used to store sound or video sequences. In this they differ from videodisks, which store analogue waveforms that can only represent scanned images (plus a sound channel). The digital information on an optical disk can represent anything — data, still or moving image, sound waveform, or computer program, for example. However for computer purposes the information is nearly always either bit-mapped image, text represented in ASCII or one of the other common codes, or else pure binary data. Some packaged systems are designed to handle only images of documents; others do not recognize images as such, although of course a string of binary data may represent an image or anything else when interpreted by the host. It is worth looking for a moment at the implications of handling data as document images, and as text.

The main point to be grasped is that data stored as character-coded text has meaning to the computer. The structure of the text — letters and figures, words, sentences, paragraphs — can be recognized, and so the computer can process the data. On the other hand, documents stored as bit-mapped images are intended only to be read by the human eye. They are just a string of bits to the computer, which can do nothing more than retrieve the image as a whole and display it on a screen or printer. There are exceptions, of course, in the form of programs which can recognize patterns — in particular, character recognition. These will become important in the future, but at present they are rarely used on stored images; where they are used at all it is normally to convert an image before it is stored.

Storing data in a form which the computer can recognize has two advantages. The first is that powerful methods for access to data can be used; for example those discussed for CD-ROM, which allow a record to be retrieved by the contents or partial contents of any field, or by more complex search criteria. Images on the other hand can only be retrieved by their addresses, or by the use of index data in digital form which has been added to the disk. Usually this has to be keyed in by an operator, although character recognition is occasionally used. Secondly, some or all of the data in a document can be transferred to other programs for further use — for example to a word processor or a spreadsheet.

Another important point is that text can be stored much more efficiently than image. An A4 page of typed text, with around 500 words, can be stored as ASCII characters in about 3 kilobytes. The same page, stored as a bit-mapped image at a reasonable definition, takes about 500 kilobytes, although it is possible to use either hardware or software to compress this to about 50 kilobytes. (Compression takes advantage of the fact that most of the black and white areas on a page of text are much larger than the unit of picture area — the pixel. Thus when the image is scanned, it can be stored not as a sequence of bits representing the state of each pixel, but as a series of numbers each showing the length of a run of black pixels, or of white pixels. Practical methods of compression are not quite as simple as this. Compression can be very effective for text and simple line drawings; it is less so for photographs and complex patterns.)

On the other hand, when data is stored as text it is restricted to symbols known to the computer (e.g. the ASCII character set plus the IBM graphic character set), whereas literally anything can be stored in image form. This includes drawings and photographs, and also animated images and sound waveforms. Also, if the data has not been captured at source, it is very much quicker and easier to pass the document through a scanner than to key the data in character by character. Keying can sometimes be avoided by using character recognition; but this is only effective on typed or printed characters made under careful control, and in these conditions the data can usually be captured at source instead.

It follows that there is a place for both approaches to the storage of data; as text or as document images. Where the data can be captured at source, and is limited to a defined set of characters, storage as text is more economical and allows the stored data to be processed. Where the data is in a less constrained format, or where it cannot be captured at source (as with incoming correspondence), then storage as document images is more practical. Some packaged systems are designed for only one form of storage; many can cope with both. The name of the system is often misleading in this respect; the specification needs to be studied in detail.

FREE-STANDING IMAGE STORAGE SYSTEMS

These were the first packaged optical disk systems; three or four Japanese drive manufacturers brought out products in 1985. The reason why Japan led in this field, even though the West was slightly ahead in the development of disk drives, is to do with the nature of the Japanese Kanji script. This has a much wider range of characters than Western script, and is less amenable to typing; so word processors are relatively little used for everyday correspondence in Japan, and much less data is captured at source. It follows that image storage is of particular interest to Japanese businesses, just as they find fax more useful than telex. As we have noted, image storage is extravagant in storage capacity, so the low cost of media made optical disks look attractive.

A further point is that text stored in image form is very redundant, whether in Kanji or Western script; quite a lot of pixels can be corrupted before the text becomes hard to read. This makes it possible to use optical disks without any error correction, a great saving in development time when error-management codes and hardware were not as well developed as they are now. Of course, any digital data added to index the images needed error correction, but the volume of this was small so relatively simple methods were good enough.

As the data stored by these systems was neither error free nor able to be processed by computer, there was no point in linking them to computers and they were all sold as free-standing systems. A typical system (Fig. 8.1) contained a processor and 12 inch or 8 inch WORM optical disk drive, a scanner, a laser printer, and a high-definition screen and keyboard. Larger systems had more screens and keyboards, and often had multiple scanners and printers as well. When a large amount of data was to be stored there would also be an automated disk library.

Such systems served as automated filing cabinets; they were sold mainly on the speed with which documents could be retrieved and the saving of storage space they made possible. Where there were multiple access

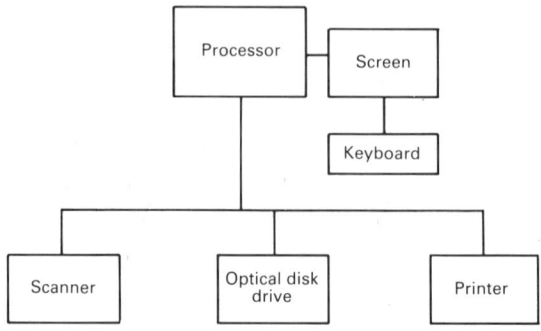

Fig. 8.1 — Free-standing image storage system.

stations, it was also an advantage that several users could see a document at once.

A typical system of this kind, with a single 12 inch disk drive and storing perhaps 20 000 A4 pages, sold for about 10 million yen — around £40 000. With a library mechanism the capacity could be multiplied by perhaps 32. These systems sold in useful numbers in Japan, but there were few takers in the West. They have been superseded by products which use error correction, and can therefore be linked to computers and used for character-coded text as well as image.

GENERAL-PURPOSE SYSTEMS

Error-correction techniques for optical stores have developed rapidly, along with specialized chips which let these techniques be used at a reasonable cost. This makes it practicable to store data in machine-readable form with error rates no worse than those of magnetic disks. Such a system can be linked to a computer, so the optical storage system no longer needs its own full set of peripherals. A simple packaged system of this kind is no more than a disk drive plus software to support it, which runs in the host; others use a dedicated computer (often a PC) and act as servers to a computer or a network, usually linked by a local area network rather than a peripheral interface. Some servers support only workstations rather than a larger computer system, in which case we are back to a free-standing product. The most powerful of these systems include a jukebox.

Of course the data stored in such a system is not restricted to text, and in fact for many purposes much of it is in bit-mapped image form; for example in a system used to store correspondence with the firm's customers, outgoing correspondence may well be stored as text but incoming correspondence will be easier to store as images. Other systems may handle diagrams as well as text. The images can be handled by the host computer, with scanners, high-definition screens and so on attached to it (many standard computer screens have too low definition to be useful for image display). However, transmitting images over the interface between host and server can load it very heavily. If the images are stored only so that they can be read by the human eye, it may be better to attach the image-handling peripherals to the optical storage system rather than to the host (Fig. 8.2).

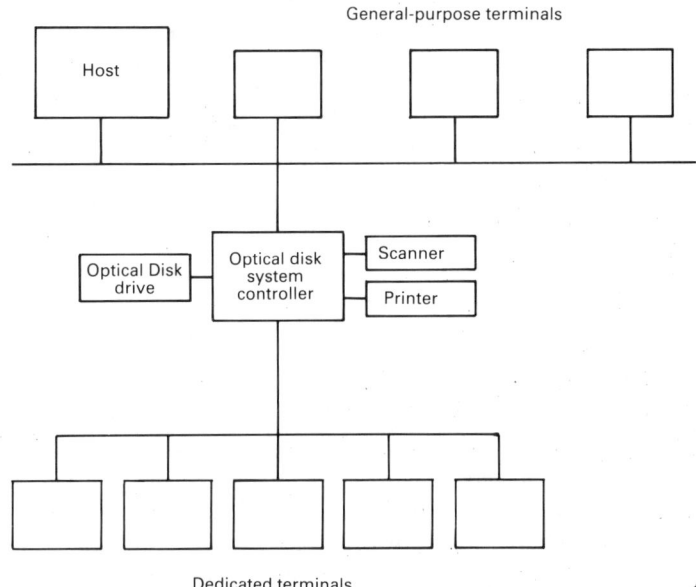

Fig. 8.2 — Optical storage subsystem with dedicated terminals.

Over half the packaged systems now on the market fall into this general-purpose category, and there is a very wide variety of them; at one extreme a $5\frac{1}{4}$ inch WORM drive with interface board and simple software to fit in a PC, and at the other a server using a jukebox, several 12 inch drives, scanners and printers, and a fairly powerful dedicated processor. The approach to software design varies widely as well; indeed many of the firms selling these packages have taken a standard set of hardware and tried to compete with their rivals by writing better software. As yet, optical storage software is less mature than the hardware, so there is plenty of scope for this kind of competition. The simplest approach is to make the system emulate one using either magnetic tape or else magnetic disk, so that the user can simply attach it to his computer without any change to his software. Just what happens if he tries to overwrite a file depends on the particular system. However, this approach does not make full use of the features of optical disk storage, and more advanced software is becoming usual.

At the low end of the range, a system with $5\frac{1}{4}$ inch drive, controller and access software, which holds say 200 megabytes per disk, can be bought for £4000. At the other extreme, powerful systems with 12 inch drives and a jukebox start around £300 000 and can go up to several million pounds.

ENGINEERING DRAWING MANAGEMENT

A few systems are made especially to manage engineering drawings. In fact these are very much like general-purpose systems, since such drawings are normally stored either as bit-mapped images or else as a set of vectors and descriptors. However, the software makes special provision for the indexing and retrieval of these images and for driving special peripherals such as plotters and digitizers. In more advanced systems the software can also manipulate images, or parts of them; however, these are really CAD systems with optical storage as an added feature, rather than optical storage packages. Such systems start around £50 000.

Closely related to these are one or two systems designed for handling maps.

SYSTEMS INCORPORATING MICROGRAPHICS

Microfiche, microfilm and aperture cards have been widely used for storing engineering drawings. Optical storage is clearly a competitor to these; so it is not surprising that many of the companies with a big stake in micrographics — notably Kodak and Canon — are taking an interest in optical disk as well. Optical storage is not yet proved to be as permanent as microfilm, but it allows much more powerful methods of retrieval, and images can be zoomed; most users also find a high-resolution screen better to work with than a microform viewer. If drawings are stored as vectors rather than bit maps, the retrieved data can be returned to the host system for further processing — typically minor revisions. WORM optical disks cannot be reproduced cheaply like microfilm, although where many copies of a large set of drawings are needed it may be possible to press disks as is done for CD-ROM.

Several systems have been introduced which combine microfiche with WORM optical disk. The disk may be used only to store indexes, or the system may store some images on microfiche and some on the disk; or images may be stored initially on disk and output on microfiche when multiple copies are wanted. Most of these systems are tailor-made to suit each individual customer, and are expensive.

FREE-STANDING MEDIA CONVERTERS

Optical disk is a very good medium for archival storage, and so there are special-purpose systems simply to transfer existing data from magnetic media to optical disk. Most of them copy from magnetic tape, in various formats, and some of these can convert the data from a range of input formats to a standard archival format. One such system is described in

Chapter 9. There are also a couple of systems which use floppy disks as the source. Often such a system will be used to convert a large backlog of archives, while new archives are written directly to a separate optical disk drive on-line to the host system

A typical tape to WORM system costs around £30 000.

PACKAGED CD-ROM SYSTEMS

A dozen or so packaged systems on the market are based on CD-ROM rather than WORM drives. This number leaves out those packages which consist simply of drive, interface board and retrieval software, though there are a number of such systems about; they are often sold by the publishers of CD-ROM databases. Of the more specialized systems, several are designed to use map data. Some of these are mobile, fitting in a vehicle and connected to distance and direction sensors so that instructions on route finding can be given to the driver. Applications of CD-ROM systems are discussed in Chapter 10.

OTHER PACKAGED SYSTEMS

Some more specialized systems exist, and no doubt there will be more of these in the future. A couple of them are aimed at CD-ROM producers, converting master tapes to master disks, often with the option of producing a 'proof copy' on WORM disk first for checking. Others are linked with communications systems for storing fax images. One is designed to intercept output formatted for COM (computer output on microfilm) and save it on optical disk instead.

REWRITABLE STORAGE

Now that rewritable disk drives are on sale, packaged systems using them will soon appear; indeed many of the systems designed for WORM disks will handle the rewritable equivalents as they stand, though they may not take full advantage of the ability to rewrite. In fact a packaged system for rewritable disk should be easier to produce than one for WORM, since a rewritable disk emulates a magnetic disk much more closely than WORM can.

9

Applications — data storage, back-up and archiving

In this chapter and the next we shall look in more detail at some of the applications of optical storage. These cover a wide range, and for convenience we shall divide them into two groups. In this chapter we consider the storage of data for re-use within the same computer system; often, though not always, it is re-used in the same software package that recorded it. In the next chapter we move on to the use of optical media to transfer data from one system to another. There is bound to be some overlap, but in general this chapter will be about the uses of WORM and rewritable disks and tape. The next will be mostly about read-only disk and card, though WORM and rewritable media have a place too. In each chapter, a few actual installations will be examined in detail.

DEVICE CHARACTERISTICS

As we studied the various types of optical storage device we looked at their characteristics and at their strengths and weaknesses, and we considered which applications would gain most from the use of such devices. Let us briefly review this with data storage, back-up, and archiving in mind. The obvious alternatives to optical media, for these purposes, are magnetic disk and tape. Cost and performance have to be considered in this context.

Optical storage can achieve a higher density than magnetic storage, and many of the advantages of optical stores stem from this. In particular, an optical disk or tape volume is much more compact than a magnetic volume of the same capacity. The high density also suggests that optical media should cost less for the same amount of data stored. In fact the difference is not large at present, as optical media are not easy to make and the suppliers have to recover a lot of money spent on development; we can expect the price of optical media to fall over the next few years. However, the economy is largely one of scale. When only a small amount of data is wanted on a volume, magnetic media will still be more economical.

The other cost that affects the choice between magnetic and optical storage is that of the device itself. At the low end of the price range, there is little prospect yet of an optical disk drive that is anywhere near as cheap as a floppy disk drive. At the other extreme, where gigabytes are to be stored, the price competition is much closer. This is largely because a whole optical volume can be covered by a single head, whereas a large magnetic disk drive has many heads.

After density, the next important characteristic of optical media and devices is their resistance to damage and contamination. This may not matter when data is stored for re-use within the same system, and the disk or tape is not dismounted. On the other hand, for archival storage it is essential that each volume can be removed and easily handled. The same is usually true for back-up, although some mainframes do a first-level back-up on fixed disk for the sake of performance. Most early magnetic disk drives were dismountable, but more recently the fixed disk has become the norm. Removable magnetic disks are still used, most obviously the floppy disk, but only for low volume capacities; this implies high media cost in relation to the amount of data stored. Magnetic tape volumes can of course be dismounted, and in cartridge form they are easily handled.

The ruggedness of optical disks also makes for easier handling and storage. In particular, optical media can be kept indefinitely in normal office conditions. Also they will survive transport (including the post) with no special precautions. All magnetic media require more care; in particular, magnetic tape needs fairly close environmental control to avoid the risk of loss of data. In the contrasting case where the data must be totally destroyed for security reasons, optical media using plastic substrates can easily be destroyed by fire; those with metal or glass substrates may be more difficult. In either case, since the medium is removable, there is no security risk attached to the drive mechanism.

Data on WORM disks is permanent. This may be an advantage or the reverse, depending on the specific application. Rewritable media will open up applications which were closed to WORM.

Magnetic disks still lead their optical equivalents in performance, both in terms of data rate and of access time. Faster optical disk drives will be developed, but these will cost more; for many applications, the slower cheaper drives will be adequate.

Finally we come to the question of standards. We have seen that optical storage standards are some way from being established and widely accepted. Standards for magnetic disks are also lacking in many areas, but there are strong standards for floppy disks and also for most magnetic tape formats. For internal storage and for back-up this matters very little. When we come to archiving, however, an established standard gives greater confidence that archived data can be retrieved even though the user may have migrated to a new system.

COMPETING TECHNOLOGIES

For the storage of data to be re-used within an application, magnetic disk has been predominant for over twenty years. For this purpose it has completely replaced magnetic tape, except on a very few hobby computers. The earliest 'disks' were in fact drums, because data was recorded on a cylindrical rather than a flat surface, but the principle was the same. However, most of these early drums or disks used a separate head for every track. This made access time short but cost very high, and it was impossible to replace one media volume by another. The type of disk drive with which we are all familiar can have several disks (or platters) and has only one head for each recording surface, which makes it cheaper but slower. These disk drives used to be made with removable disk packs, but as data densities increased this became harder and was eventually given up. Now the only magnetic disk drives with removable media are the ubiquitous floppy disks, and a few cartridge disk drives. In each case the density is relatively low and the media cost, per unit of data, high.

Back-up calls for removable media, although large mainframes sometimes make a first level of back-up on fixed disk in the interests of performance. In very small systems floppy disk can be used, and a few installations use magnetic disk cartridges. With these exceptions, magnetic tape is the universal back-up medium. The main weaknesses of magnetic tape — serial access and poor data retention in the long term — are of little importance for back-up. A tape drive often costs more than the fixed disks it supports, which can cause some discontent. Since tape can be re-used indefinitely it is a very cheap medium for backing up; modern tape cartridges are easily handled and loaded, although open-reel tape is less convenient. In principle, magnetic tape can be used in an automated library mechanism like the jukebox used for optical disk. In practice these libraries are very rarely used.

A new type of magnetic tape system which has recently been announced is based on digital audio tape (DAT). This is derived from videotape technology, using multiple heads set in a rotating drum. It also uses very powerful error correction, not unlike that used in optical storage. A typical device can store about 1 gigabyte (1000 megabytes) in a cartridge about $3 \times 2 \times \frac{1}{2}$ inches and costing only a few pounds. This will make it a strong competitor to optical storage when media cost is important and access time is not. Since the medium is re-usable, it will compete in particular with rewritable optical disks in back-up applications. It is unlikely to have the long-term archival qualities of WORM disks. In addition to DAT there are magnetic tape devices using similar (helical-scan) technology but larger cartridges, based on those used in video recorders; these are less compact but offer even larger capacities, with media cost as low as 0.2 cent per megabyte as compared with 10–20 cents per megabyte for optical disks.

STORING DATA WITHIN AN APPLICATION PROGRAM

Nearly all application programs need to store data for use in future sessions, or for re-use within the same session. Usually the data will be held in the main store of the processor during the session, and saved to non-volatile storage at the end of the session or at various points within it. Sometimes the amount of data is too great for the main memory; then some of it has to be rolled in or rolled out in the course of the session.

Magnetic disk meets this requirement well; it provides rapid access and high data integrity, at an acceptable cost. It has had no competitor in recent years, except in a few specialized applications and in low-priced hobby computers. Clearly WORM optical disk is unlikely to be used for this purpose, except possibly in specialized applications where a permanent audit trail is needed. Rewritable optical disks are more promising. At the moment they do not match magnetic disks in either access time or data rate, and they are more expensive although less bulky for the same data capacity. They do have the advantage that media volumes are exchangeable, and easily handled or stored. This suggests that rewritable optical disks may be attractive in 'open shop' applications, such as universities, where it is desirable that each user has his own disk which he can bring to the machine and take away after use. In some installations the same thing is done for security reasons. In general, however, optical storage is unlikely to be widely used for storing data within applications for the time being. As the technology develops it may come to compete with magnetic disk in performance and cost.

STORING PROGRAMS

This is rather like the last requirement, since programs as well as data are related to particular tasks; the difference is that programs are altered far less frequently than data. In particular they are not altered within a working session (any amendments are a separate exercise). This makes WORM a much more practical proposition. As WORM disks are removable, programs can in fact be supplied already loaded on the disks; but this is trespassing on the territory of the next chapter, and will be looked at in more detail there. WORM (or CD-ROM) will also look attractive in the open-shop situation for individually owned programs, just as rewritable disks are attractive for data. $5\frac{1}{4}$ inch disks should be ample for this purpose and will be preferred because of their compactness and the possibility of standardization. When programs are loaded into main store as a whole there will be competition from magnetic tape. When overlays have to be rolled in and out, optical disk will be more suitable than magnetic tape because of its faster access. However, in the latter case magnetic disk has an advantage if very fast access is needed.

STORING BIT-MAPPED IMAGES

Bit-mapped images are of course just another form of data, but the choice of storage medium is not necessarily the same as for other types of digital data. There are two reasons for this. Firstly, such images are very heavy on storage space. As we saw in a previous chapter, an A4 image at a reasonable resolution can take up half a megabyte — as much as the complete text of this book. Compression can reduce this if the image is of text or a line drawing, but helps very little in the case of denser images such as photographs. Secondly, as such images are invariably retrieved for display on a screen rather than further processing, short access times are not important.

For these reasons, optical disk will often be more cost-effective than magnetic disk where bit-mapped images are stored. Erasable disks can be used if necessary. However, these images have no meaning to the computer and cannot be manipulated by it, so they are less likely to be changed or replaced than most data files. It may therefore be reasonable to use WORM disks. In fact in many applications — such as the storage of medical X-rays or scanner images — the pictures will be retained for some time; the line between archiving and storage within the application program is a thin one.

Optical tape is also a possibility, although its long access time may not be acceptable to the user.

BACK-UP

One result of the trend towards fixed rather than removable magnetic disk drives is that backing up of data has become even more vital. Not only failure of the medium itself, but also any failure of the disk drive mechanism or the electronics that support it, can make the data inaccessible. There are many approaches to back-up. It may be done daily, frequently, or continuously as the data is created; it may be done on a file or a volume basis; whole databases or only changed files may be backed up, and so on. On large mainframes it is sometimes necessary to back up onto duplicate hard disks, in the interests of performance. This does not give protection against a disaster that affects the whole system, so some secondary back-up is needed. On PCs and other small systems, the volume of data may be small enough to be backed up on floppy disk, or occasionally on cartridge disks of some kind. Otherwise magnetic tape is the usual back-up medium.

On large systems, which usually have trained operators, it has been usual to use open-reel tape drives handling $\frac{1}{2}$ inch wide tape on $10\frac{1}{2}$ inch diameter reels. Depending on the coding method used these hold about 30 or 120 megabytes per reel. Average access time is measured in minutes; data rates above one megabyte per second can be achieved, although the fastest drives are expensive and noisy. However, a few years ago IBM introduced a high-performance cartridge tape drive, the 3480. This has similar capacity to the densest open-reel tapes but better performance, and the cartridge is much more compact and easy to handle. This type of drive will progressively replace open-reel tape on large systems. Drives using the same cartridge but different recording standards (which are defined by the 'HI/TC' committee) are coming into use for intermediate systems; they have a similar capacity to the 3480 but lower cost and performance. And at the lower end of the market there are several types of lower-performance cartridge tape drive, usually using $\frac{1}{4}$ inch wide tape and storing from 10 to 120 or more megabytes per volume.

Digital audio type tape cartridges can store about a gigabyte, so they have obvious attractions for large systems. Their performance, however, does not compare with that of the IBM 3480 type cartridge. It is not yet clear whether they will be widely used in the computer field.

Tapes used for back-up are re-used on a cycle of perhaps one or two passes a week. Normally they are only used for writing (apart from any check reading), read access being needed only when there is trouble on the host system. They are usually written serially, so the lack of random access is not a drawback. Magnetic tape is therefore a very suitable medium in most cases. In the few cases where a more sophisticated back-up system is used, random access may be an advantage and so optical disk will be considered. Clearly rewritable disks, when established, will be preferred to WORM on the grounds of media cost. However, at least one system manager has calculated that if he backed up on WORM disk instead of tape, the saving in operating cost (because fewer volumes need be loaded and unloaded) would more than offset the cost of continually buying new WORM disks.

ARCHIVING

In some applications, data may have to be retained for a long time — often tens of years — although access to it is infrequent. Examples of such data are insurance policy and income tax records. When such records are new they may be used often, so they are stored on magnetic disk for immediate access. However, this is expensive, and as the frequency of access falls they are usually 'archived' by copying them to a less expensive medium. This may be kept on-line or off-line, or of course each in turn. Usually archived data is recorded in sequence onto the new medium, but sometimes each volume is partitioned so that different kinds of data can be kept apart. Once archived, data is not normally amended, so only read access is required; indeed, write access is usually barred to cut down the risk of the data being corrupted.

Magnetic tape

Archival records nearly always use magnetic tape, though on small systems floppy disk is a possible alternative. Several forms of tape have been described in the last few paragraphs, and all of these can be used for archiving. DAT-based tape systems have an advantage over the other forms because of their compactness and very high volume capacity. However, there are also other types of magnetic tape drive which have been designed with archival use particularly in mind, although none has proved very popular. One is similar to open-reel tape, but with larger reels and tape one inch wide to give a volume capacity around one gigabyte. Another uses short lengths of tape several inches wide, in special cartridges; these are used with an automated tape library, similar in principle to the automated disk libraries or jukeboxes we have described.

Magnetic tape is not, however, a very satisfactory medium for archiving. The problem lies mainly in the substrate, but partly in the active coating. The substrate is of necessity flexible and very thin. It has to be wound onto its reel under controlled tension, so that each turn stays firmly in place and does not slide over the one below. In the course of time the material gives slightly under the stress, and the tension in the tape is reduced. If this is allowed to go too far, the turns may slip and be damaged. If there are any dust particles on the tape, or any distortions or creases due to poor winding, these can become impressed into the tape during storage. Fluctuations in temperature and humidity speed up these processes, so archive tapes need to be stored in carefully controlled conditions. Also the magnetic pattern stored on one turn of the tape can be affected by that of neighbouring turns; the effect will be familiar to users of audio tapes as 'pre-echo'. With modern tape formulations it is much less of a problem except at high storage temperatures.

To avoid the corruption of archival data stored on magnetic tape, the tape must have not only controlled storage but also regular attention. ECMA has published guidelines for handling and storage of magnetic tape (as document TR/11: there is a corresponding BSI document) which recommend storage and handling conditions; these include a full pass of each tape every six months to restore the correct tension. Normally the tape will be cleaned at the same time to remove any dust particles. The cost of storage and maintenance of tape archives can thus be substantial. It has been claimed that DAT-type tape will be more suitable than other forms for archival storage; presumably this is because of its powerful error correction, but it is still likely to need regular maintenance.

WORM optical disk

WORM optical disk is an obvious alternative to magnetic tape for archival storage. It has several advantages. The recording method is non-reversible, so the risk of loss of data either through accidental mistreatment or through extreme conditions is small. Disks can be stored in normal office conditions — or indeed more extreme conditions, although long periods in a damp atmosphere could cause trouble. No maintenance is required, and as the disks remain in their cartridges they are unlikely to be damaged by handling. Disks are lighter and more compact than tapes of the same capacity, so the cost of storage space is less. In this application magnetic tapes are not re-used, so they lose their cost advantage over optical disk. Indeed, costs are likely to fall once disks are produced in quantity, which will make them cheaper to use than most magnetic tape although DAT tape may remain cheaper. Of course, the cost of the media is not of prime importance in archiving, since it is small in relation to the value of the data carried on it. The vital factor is the continuing integrity of the data. All WORM disk manufacturers guarantee at least ten years' data life, some say thirty, and one has gone on record as saying that 100 years is the probable life. This gives optical disks a clear lead over magnetic media.

For all these reasons, WORM optical disk is an excellent medium for data archiving. The one problem at the moment is that standards for WORM disks are not yet fully established, as we saw in earlier chapters. In contrast, magnetic tape formats are very effectively standardized (though this does not yet apply to DAT-type tapes). Standards are desirable, not so much to aid data interchange but rather to give assurance that mechanisms to read the archived tapes will still be available even if the original maker leaves the business. If that happened it would not mean that the data was lost, of course; but the prudent owner would buy new equipment and disks and transcribe all his archives, and this would cost money.

The standards problem will soon be resolved for $5\frac{1}{4}$ inch disks; however, there will be two or three accepted standards (including of course IBM's) rather than just one. A single standard for 14 inch disks may well come about naturally, as we saw in Chapter 2. On the other hand, there is very little progress towards 12 inch standards. In spite of this, WORM disks in both 12 inch and $5\frac{1}{4}$ inch sizes are being rapidly adopted for archiving by both large and small organizations. There can be little doubt that WORM disk will be the predominant medium for archives in the 1990s.

Rewritable optical disk
It is also possible to use rewritable disks for archival storage, though there seems little point in preferring them to WORM in view of their higher cost and possibly shorter data life. However, the cost difference will be reduced when production is stepped up. If drives handling only rewritable disks were substantially cheaper than those that also handled WORM, users with only a small amount of data to be archived might prefer to use rewritable disks for this.

Optical tape
Finally, WORM optical tape should be mentioned. Most of the features of WORM disks apply to tape also, except of course that access is serial rather than random and so average access times are tens of seconds. The flexible substrate may bring with it some of the long-term storage problems that are experienced with magnetic tape. On the other hand, a given amount of data takes up less space on tape than on disk. The media cost is much less too, if this matters in view of the value of the data stored; a media cost one-tenth of that for disk has been projected. When optical tape drives are available, they may be adopted for archiving by some heavy users who do not need a very long data life. However, the question of long-term data integrity will have to be resolved before WORM tape seriously challenges WORM disk for data archiving. Where long data life and random access are not important, helical-scan recording on magnetic tape offers a media cost rather lower than that of optical tape.

Some of the applications of optical card might be regarded as archival, but it is more convenient to consider them in the next chapter as data transfer applications.

The next part of this chapter describes some actual installations in which optical disk is used for data storage and archiving.

OPTICAL DISK INSTALLATION AT BARCLAYCARD

Our first example is a very straightforward demonstration of the use of WORM optical disk to store text which is captured at source. The system includes a PC and acts as a server, although in this case the host is not a general purpose computer but a dedicated system.

A small optical disk system, including a single $5\frac{1}{4}$ inch WORM drive, is installed at Barclaycard headquarters in Northampton. It forms part of a telex switching system (Fig. 9.1), and is used to archive messages. The

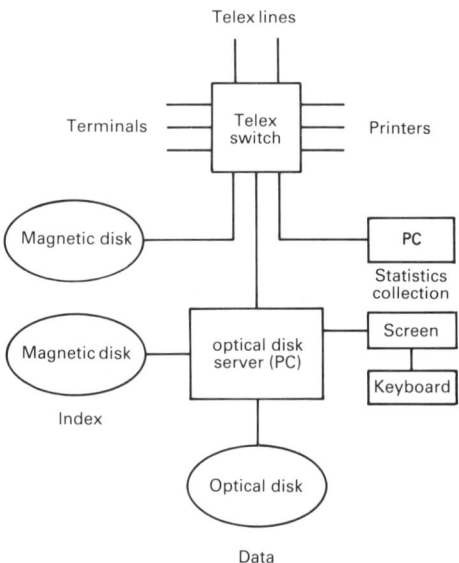

Fig. 9.1 — Telex switch and optical disk installation at Barclaycard.

'Intelligent Archive' disk system, using an ISI drive, was supplied by CACL to Telephone Rentals plc who provided and installed the telex system.

An earlier telex switching system was installed in 1974. A paper copy of each telex message was kept by the telex operators for two months, in case of enquiries, and then destroyed. This became inconvenient as the amount of traffic built up, as an operator had often to read through many messages to find the one needed. In 1987 the telex switch was due to be replaced. Barclaycard specified that the new switch should include means of archiving messages and retrieving them quickly. Optical disk was proposed by Telephone Rentals as the most suitable medium for archiving.

The telex switch handles all telex messages sent and received by Barclaycard headquarters, and most of those to and from branch offices. Many telex users within the company have workstations on their desks and printers nearby. The switch routes telex messages from and to these. The switch also handles other types of message, mostly internal to Barclaycard. Some of these are generated automatically by other terminals or computers rather than keyed in. The telex switch operates on the store-and-forward principle, all messages being stored on a hard magnetic disk. They remain on this disk until deliberately purged to make room for more messages. The disk is large enough to store messages in this way for two or three weeks. Each message, whether incoming or outgoing, is numbered by the switch in a single sequence.

Hardware and software

The optical disk is an ISI model 525 WC which uses 115 megabyte single-sided disks, although double-sided disks of twice the capacity could be used. The drive is supported by a server (Fig. 9.2). This is in fact a dedicated

Fig. 9.2 — Optical storage system at Barclaycard. The disk drive is in a desktop box beyond the personal computer. (Copyright Telephone Rentals.)

personal computer, a Televideo machine compatible with the IBM PC-AT, running under MS-DOS 3.3. It has a 42-megabyte magnetic disk. The optical disk drive itself is controlled by the 'WORM-TOS' operating system provided by ISI. The retrieval software used is 'Corporate Retriever' from Software Solutions, supplied with the disk drive by CACL; some extra software has been written by Telephone Rentals. The optical disk drive is divided into five partitions. The first four are used, one at a time, to store archived messages. The fifth is reserved for system use.

Operation
Each night, all messages passed during the preceding day are archived automatically by the server. They are edited into a form which suits the retrieval software, and copied to the optical disk. The first message partition which is not already full is used. An index covering all messages in the current partition is then generated and stored on the magnetic disk in the server, replacing the index generated the previous night. When a partition of the optical disk is nearly filled (which takes several nights), a final version of the index for that partition is generated and is written into the partition. The rest of the day's messages are then copied to the next message partition of the optical disk, and the index for this replaces the old index on the workstation disk. The system is unattended at night. When the telex operators come on duty they find a message on the workstation screen to confirm that archiving has been completed, or else an error message (for example if the first four partitions are all full). Archiving can also be started manually. It takes about an hour to copy the data, plus a number of hours (depending on the amount of data) to build the index.

A report giving the number of messages copied is printed out automatically in the maintenance department at Barclaycard. For the time being a similar message is automatically sent, as a telex, to the office of Telephone Rentals each night. The telex switch system incorporates a personal computer which collects and reports statistics, including some on optical disk archiving. However, the software for this was not ready at the time of writing.

Any archived message can be retrieved by a telex operator, using the server workstation. A message can be found by its number, if this is known. If not, the operator searches using whatever other information is available. This can be the sender's name, addressee's name or telex number, date, or some combination of these; or it can be text occurring within the message, such as a customer's name or account number. The retrieval software returns a list of messages found by the search. For each message the sender, addressee's name and telex number, date and message number will be shown. If the search was for text within the message, each line containing the search text is also shown. The operator can then call for the full text of one or more of the messages, or browse through all of them.

Once the right message has been found, the operator can send it to any terminal or printer attached to the telex switch. Alternatively it can be transmitted as a new telex message.

Most enquiries are likely to refer to the current disk or the one last filled, but all earlier disks are available. There is no indexing system to tell the operator which disk to load. Usually the approximate date of the message is known; disks are labelled with the period covered, and the operator searches as many disks as necessary to find the message. The operator need not know which partition on the disk contains the message.

The telex traffic through the switch is about 1000 messages a day. However, a further class of messages has now been routed through the switch, in addition to telex. This roughly doubles the traffic to be archived. More than one month's telex messages, with their index, fit onto each disk; with the increased traffic, about one disk a month will probably be needed. The number of messages retrieved is fairly small at present, around five a day on average. As the service becomes known to more users the number will rise. Some users already find it easier to retrieve messages this way than from their own paper files.

There is obviously an overlap between the messages held for a period within the telex switch, and those on optical disk. Messages stored in the switch can be retrieved from any user workstation (with the right password), but only by their message number. Usually the enquirer does not know this number, so has to ask a telex operator to find the message from the optical disk.

Barclaycard have not needed to build any resilience into the system, because of the overlap between messages which have been archived and those which are still held in the telex switch; therefore only a single disk drive and workstation are used. The maintenance contract provides a four-hour response. It is not thought necessary to back up the workstation disk, as the index can be remade from the data on the optical disk.

Experience

Telephone Rentals intend to offer optical disk archiving as a standard option with their telex switch. Barclaycard was one of the first users, so some minor teething troubles were encountered. One of these was with the layout of data on the disk. At first a single partition was used for all messages, but it was found that the index for a full disk occupied about 30 megabytes. This took a long time to produce and to search, and also text searches were liable to return inconveniently long lists of hits. By dividing the message area into four partitions, each index is reduced to about a quarter of the original size.

The telex staff continued to keep paper copies of all messages until the system was proved, but after about six months this was discontinued. The cost of disks, at about £100 each, and of the system itself, is considered to be well justified by the saving in telex staff time and the better service that is now available to telex users. In addition, archived messages are now kept permanently; they used to be held for only two months.

In spite of the minor problems that are always experienced by an early user, management and users at Barclaycard are very satisfied with the system. They have no particular warnings to give to others considering optical disk for this kind of application. They do however make the point that a very close working relationship with the supplier — which they had in this case — is essential to a company taking an early example of any system.

Comments on the Barclaycard installation

This is a good example of the straightforward use of WORM optical disk for archiving. Since the data is already stored as character-coded text the necessary indexes can be generated automatically, and retrieval by searching the text is also possible. Media cost is low because the data is stored as text rather than images. The index is relatively simple, and takes up less space than the data. As the system is not critical to the company's operations, no resilience needs to be provided.

Apart from the expected minor teething troubles, the only problem has been concerned with the management of the index; it was solved by a fairly simple software change. It is interesting to note, however, that creating the index takes a good deal longer than archiving the messages; system designers need to take care over this point when predicting performance.

OPTICAL DISK INSTALLATION AT THE BRITANNIA BUILDING SOCIETY

The next example is at the opposite end of the scale; a large installation, storing data as bit-mapped images and including a jukebox. This is a free-standing installation. It does have a link to another system, but not as master and slave.

One of the largest optical disk installations in the UK is that in the head office of the Britannia Building Society, at Leek in Staffordshire. It is indeed claimed to be, at the time of writing (late 1988), the largest image storage installation outside the USA. Included in it (Fig. 9.3) are 12 inch WORM disk drives mounted in a jukebox; also document scanners, printers, and workstations. It is used to improve access to files dealing with the administration of mortgages (housing loans). It is not used for repayment transactions; these are handled on a conventional mainframe system. Most of the documents are stored in image form, although some text is stored. The system was installed by British Olivetti, who handle European sales for the suppliers Filenet Corporation of the USA. Olivetti and Britannia describe the jukebox as an 'Optical Storage And Retrieval unit', or OSAR.

A paper describing the system was presented at the 1988 Optical Information Systems conference in London by David Mawdsley, Deputy General Manager of the Britannia. The following extract describes the manual system which the Optical Disk system replaces, and the reasons for the change.

> The Britannia Building Society is the ninth largest in the UK, with assets of approximately £4 500 000 000. It has a network of 250 branches covering the whole of the UK and over 1800 employees. The core of the Society's business is the provision of finance for home purchase and improvement to a total of 200 000 borrowers. For each of these borrowers a file of correspondence is maintained throughout the life of the loan (which can be as long as 25 years) and most of these files, some 150 000, are paper based. They occupy 6000 square feet of space at the

Ch. 9] APPLICATIONS — DATA STORAGE, BACK-UP AND ARCHIVING 133

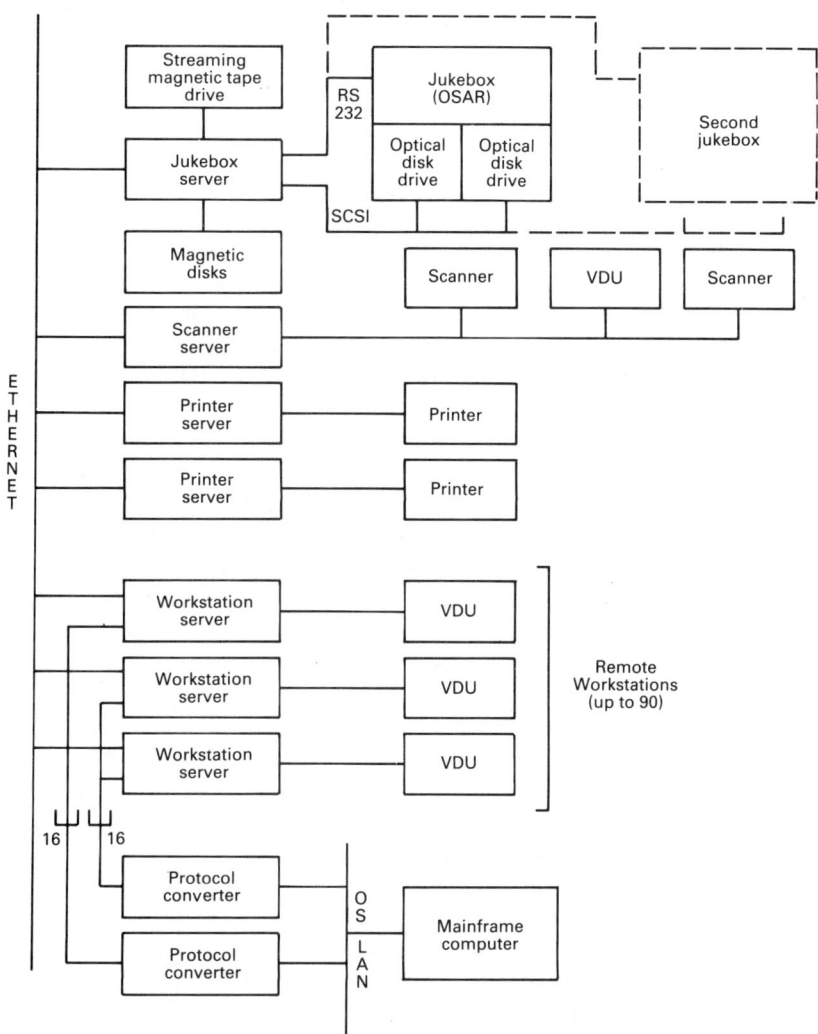

Fig. 9.3 — Optical storage installation at the Britannia Building Society.

head office in Leek, and any activity requiring access to these files is dealt with at the head office by about 130 staff.

Control of the use of this number of files has never been particularly easy, but an upsurge in lending activity in 1985, together with a greater requirement for access to the existing files, made proper control particularly difficult. The reduction in the availability of files to clerical staff when required resulted in a tendency for the 'hoarding' of files by clerks who felt they may need them again in the near future, thus further worsening availability. This resulted in the deterioration of both the level of service to the borrower and of clerical productivity. It became essential that a better way of dealing with the files was found.

The correspondence files are fairly volatile. They average about 60 pages each (although a complex and protracted arrears case may run to several hundred pages) and about ten pages are added to each file in the first few months following initial completion of the mortgage.

The problem
The basic requirement was thus for a system which would handle a large number of correspondence files, to which documents were added from time to time. Each file had to be available to any user on demand irrespective of whether someone else was using it. This had to be done in a way which was cost-effective and acceptable to the users.

Some of the information in future files could be captured at source, but other information — such as incoming correspondence — could not. This would need to be transcribed with a keyboard, or else scanned and stored as images. Britannia decided to store the whole of every file in image form; this made it unnecessary to change the existing paper-based method of generating the documents, and yet avoided the cost of keyboard transcription. The cost of this choice was the need for a very large storage capacity, about 50 kilobytes per document page. Since the files changed only by the addition of further documents rather than the modification of existing ones, WORM optical storage was chosen. A jukebox was included in the system to give rapid access to the very large amount of data.

The correspondence files do not contain total information on each mortgage. There are also files, held on existing mainframe computers at the head office, which record transactions such as repayments and interest charges. These transactions are normally made through branch offices, using terminals which are linked to the head office computer. Transactions with investors are handled in the same way. The head office clerks who handle mortgage correspondence need access to the transaction records, but do not normally make any input to them; the branch staff do not need direct access to the mortgage correspondence files. Britannia therefore chose to put correspondence file management into a system independent of the mainframe, but using workstations which could access both systems at once. This allows a clerk to have both types of information on the screen at once, in separate windows.

Because the two systems have been kept separate, the introduction of optical storage has had little impact on the existing use of the mainframe system. In particular, the heavy traffic involved in transmitting images to the workstations has not affected the mainframe, since separate local area networks are used. This approach has also avoided most compatibility problems. However, the terminals supplied with the optical system are not fully compatible with the mainframe, so a protocol converter is used. Closer integration between the two systems is not planned at present.

The correspondence file system is based on a range of forms which are filled in by hand. Most of these use multi-part self-copying stock. The files also include less formal typed or handwritten papers from within the Society, and correspondence from customers and elsewhere outside the Society. For the time being, all the existing forms and procedures are being used without significant change, except that the document images are read from a screen rather than paper. Changes to enable greater advantage to be taken of the characteristics of the optical storage system will be considered at a later stage.

Implementation
The Society evaluated two potential suppliers in detail. The final choice was based mainly on the suitability of the available software and development tools. The company chosen was British Olivetti. Olivetti use equipment developed by Filenet Corporation of the USA, for whom Olivetti are the UK agents. Standard hardware is used, but the Filenet standard software needed some modification. This was done with Filenet's 'WorkFlo' programming language. The software development could have been done by Building Society staff, but resource problems prevented this and most of the programming was done by Olivetti staff. Future development is likely to be done by Britannia.

Implementation was controlled by a steering committee of staff from Olivetti, from Britannia's data-processing department, and from user departments within the Society. A system administrator was recruited from within Britannia's data-processing department. This post was later split into development and operational functions. The contract specified a development period of about six months to be followed by a six months pilot period, during which eight retrieval terminals were in use. The pilot scheme was completed successfully in early 1988; thereafter user departments were introduced one by one to the system, and the number of terminals is being increased to about 90. These terminals are linked to the system by an Ethernet network. The majority are within the head office building, but some are at another site about a mile away. When all departments are served by the optical system, all new correspondence files will be discarded (after a short holding period) once they have been scanned into the system. This will remove the need for any further increase in storage space for paper files. Older files will remain in paper form, although it is proposed that this backlog will gradually be converted to optical form.

File location and migration
Users often need to refer to more than one document in a file. If they do not know which document contains the information sought, they browse through the file to find it. So that successive documents can be displayed without an unacceptable delay, when a user requests access to a document the whole file is staged to magnetic disk storage. One document at a time is passed on to the workstation as required. To do this efficiently the stored data has to be 'clustered' so that all documents of a file are on the same optical disk. Files grow throughout their life by the addition of further

documents, and the extent to which any particular file will grow cannot be predicted. An allowance is made for this, by limiting the number of files written to any disk. If the allowance proves inadequate and the disk becomes full, all the active files on it are copied to a new disk or disks. Closed files, to which no further documents will be added, are not copied; the old disk is retained, but in shelf storage rather than in the jukebox, as an archival record. When more than half the content of a disk consists of closed files, even if the disk is not full the files remaining active are copied to a new disk. This prevents the jukebox becoming clogged with closed files. Obviously when files are copied to new disks, the disks are shared so that only the appropriate allowance for file expansion is left empty.

If any disk showed signs of a deterioration in image quality, this too would be copied. Britannia believes that this is unlikely to happen.

Users normally request in advance the files they expect to use, just as they did with the paper-based system. Files are requested an hour or so in advance; this helps to smooth the load on the jukebox. However, files can be retrieved immediately when necessary, for example to deal with a telephone enquiry. New documents scanned into the system are held on magnetic disk until a time when the retrieval load is light, such as lunchtime or the end of working hours.

A back-up copy is made of each document scanned into the system. The back-up copies are not clustered, but are simply recorded in sequence. Software is available to allow documents to be retrieved from the back-up disks if necessary. These copies too are transferred from magnetic to optical disk when retrieval traffic is light. Since the back-up copy is normally in the jukebox (until a disk is full, when it can be shelved) it gives protection only against media problems and not against catastrophe. In this respect it is no worse than the paper filing system.

Document generation
As we have already seen, the approach taken by Britannia is to retain — for the time being at least — the existing paper-based procedures for producing the documents which form the correspondence file. Some documents, such as correspondence from customers, are in free form. The more standard items use preprinted forms, usually as multi-part self-copying sets, which are filled in by hand rather than typed. This does lead to some difficulties in the scanning, particularly when a bottom copy uses coloured paper, or when an entry box is emphasized by a dot screen which is nearly the same colour as the ink or carbon. One or two minor changes to the procedure have been made; for example the assignment of a higher copy from the set to the scanner, instead of to the customer's solicitor.

Although most documents in each correspondence file are stored as images, the system can handle documents as text when this is available. In particular, a header document for each file, containing basic information such as file number and the customer's name and address, is keyboarded and stored as text.

Document input

It is not considered essential to enter documents into the optical storage system immediately they are generated. A backlog of two or three days is allowed, and this smooths out the minor peaks and troughs of data entry workflow.

The scanning of documents of mixed type has been more difficult than was expected. The problem has been reduced by batching documents according to those characteristics which affect the scanner — particularly colour and thickness of paper. This makes it necessary to take each file apart and sort the documents. Staples and clips are removed, and documents too small to be fed reliably through the scanner — such as notes on the backs of envelopes — are first photocopied onto A4 size sheets. The same is done with documents such as book pages which cannot be separated.

The scanners have automatic batch feed. The scanner operators attend to document feeding, and where necessary adjust the scanner threshold to suit the documents in the batch. An optimum setting has now been reached which suits most document types. The operators have terminals which allow them to monitor the scanning, but they do not at this stage check each individual document.

Verification and indexing is carried out at a separate workstation (the operators take turns at the various tasks). The operator views each document in turn, checking for the common faults that affect readability. Where an image is unacceptable it is flagged, and the operator identifies and offsets the original document in the pile which comprises a batch. This operator also indexes each image according to information which appears on it. The index information is entered with the keyboard, and is stored by the system for use in document clustering and retrieval.

The batch is then returned to the scanner operator. He re-scans the rejected documents, but this time he is responsible for verifying the image; therefore a third cycle is never necessary. The re-scanned image replaces the old one so the key information does not have to be re-entered.

Until all departments have access to the optical storage system it is necessary to reassemble the original file, so that a complete paper file is available to those departments which still need it. When this requirement ceases, documents will be held in their batches for a few days and then destroyed.

Document indexing

Most documents are stored in a non-machine-readable form, so retrieval depends on the keys entered at the scanning and verification stage. For the sake of system efficiency the number of keys has been kept to a minimum. All documents are keyed with the document type, the account number, the number of the department which generated or received it, and the date. Some types of document may have additional keys. The date used is the date at which the document is scanned, and this is entered automatically. All the other keys are entered by the verification operator, using information which appears on the document image itself. This has not required any change in the society's procedures, except that clerks must ensure that the account and department numbers are added to incoming documents if they are not shown already.

Documents can be retrieved on any of these keys or combinations of them, together with simple calculated criteria (such as 'all documents dated between X and Y'). In addition, if a user does not know precisely where in a file to find information, he can browse through the file from a selected starting point, one document at a time. However, because each document is transmitted to the terminal only when requested, browsing is slower than some users would wish.

File and document indexes are held on magnetic disk. The optical disks do not contain a current index of their own contents, and the index cannot readily be reconstructed from them. The index is backed up from the magnetic disk to magnetic tape daily.

Hardware
The system (Fig. 9.4) is based on a Filenet OSAR 64 automated disk library

Fig. 9.4 — Jukebox (right) and scanner (centre) at the Britannia Building Society. (Copyright British Olivetti.)

(jukebox) with a capacity of 64 12 inch WORM optical disks. This is fitted with two Hitachi disk drives. Each disk is double-sided and has a capacity of 2.6 gigabytes (1.3 per side), or about 50 000 page images: this gives a total jukebox capacity of about 3 million page images. (The ratio of pages to megabytes would not necessarily be the same in other systems.) It is likely that a third drive will be added, to improve performance and resilience, and also a second jukebox. This will have a single drive, and will be used for scanning a backlog of files which were in use before the introduction of the optical system but are still active.

Associated with the jukebox is a server which incorporates a processor and 2000 megabytes of magnetic disk storage. The second jukebox will have to share this server. A streaming magnetic tape drive is provided for security back-up of the magnetic disks.

Data is input to the system by batch-feed scanners. Two, handling documents up to A4 only, are in regular use. A scanner for larger documents has proved unnecessary, but at least one more scanner will be used with the second jukebox to capture the backlog of paper files. Documents are scanned at 200 dots per inch; they can be printed out at this resolution, but the resolution of the workstation screens is lower. Scanning at this density allows standard scanners and printers to be used. Images are compressed before storage. This compression, which is based on the method used in Group 3 facsimile transmission, achieves an average compression ratio of about 10:1. It thus reduces the storage requirement for a typical page image from 500 kilobytes to about 50 kilobytes.

Each user workstation has a 20 inch diagonal landscape screen and 5 megabytes of RAM storage, but no disk. The program is downloaded to the terminal from the OSAR at the start of each working day. The screen definition is 115 dots per inch, and internal and mainframe data is displayed at this resolution; it has been found to provide satisfactory image quality. These workstations are described in more detail in a later section.

Laser printers (made by Ricoh and Hitachi) are provided for producing hard copy, at a resolution of 200 dots per inch.

The system controller is able to monitor and control the system through four simple terminals, and can carry out some functions not available to other users such as deleting documents and files.

Some resilience is provided by using several optical disk drives and scanners, and by dividing the total magnetic disk capacity between a number of drives. However, there is no provision against jukebox failure. In theory, disks from the jukebox's storage cells can be manually loaded into the drives, but this has proved difficult in practice. The nature of Britannia's business is such that even a fairly long system failure would not be a disaster. After the first couple of hours there would be a loss of effective working time as clerks ran out of files to work on. There is a resident site engineer, and the only OSAR failure so far has been dealt with quickly.

Most of the hardware, apart from the optical disk drives, is manufactured by Filenet, although the scanners and printers are of other makes.

Software

Filenet offer a standard software package with their system. They also offer a programming language (WorkFlo), with which this package can be modified or replaced. Britannia took advantage of this to tailor the user interface to meet their requirements. About nine man-months of programming effort (in fact provided by Olivetti staff) were required. However the interface is at present a common one for all departments; Britannia plans to develop versions which are tailored to the needs of individual departments, and now has staff to do this.

Software for all the workstations is held on the magnetic disks of the central system. It is downloaded to each terminal over the Ethernet network. Originally each item of software was downloaded as required. This led to unacceptable delays, partly because WorkFlo is not a particularly sophisticated language, so now the software is downloaded at start-up each morning and held in the RAM memory of each terminal. To accommodate this it was necessary to increase the amount of RAM in the terminals.

Fully validated software was available from the supplier, but this lacked certain features needed by Britannia; in particular the ability to cluster files so that all documents in a file appeared on the same disk. The software installed was therefore based on an advance version of the next issue — in effect Britannia acted as a beta test site for this issue. This led to poor system reliability and performance at first, and some delay to the pilot programme. However, reliability now exceeds the specification and workstation availability is about 99%.

Workstation design and operation
The workstations (Fig. 9.5) have high-definition screens, and represent a major part of the cost of the system. The present workstations are connected individually to the Ethernet, and thence to the jukebox server, each workstation having its own server which stands under the desk. Clustered workstations, four per server, will be available in future, and these may be fitted with magnetic disk. This will solve the problem of software downloading that has just been discussed.

Each workstation is also connected to Britannia's ICL mainframe computer. As the Filenet workstation servers do not recognize ICL communication methods, protocol converters are provided; each of these supports up to sixteen workstations, with a separate RS232 link to each. The protocol converters are connected to the mainframe's 'OSLAN' local area network.

The software supports multiple windows on the terminal; the large screen, in landscape format, allows these to be used to full effect. The use of the windows is flexible. Typically one half of the screen will be taken up by a life-size display of a stored document, while other windows will show data from the mainframe and a menu. It is possible to cut and paste between windows and thus transfer data in text form between one and the other, even when the windows show data from different systems. In fact this is the only channel for such transfers, since there is no direct link between the two systems. The header document for each file on the OSAR is stored in text form, as already described, so the user can identify the file to the mainframe by transferring this header. Obviously data in image form cannot be transferred in this way.

Ch. 9]   APPLICATIONS — DATA STORAGE, BACK-UP AND ARCHIVING   141

Fig. 9.5 — Terminal screens at the Britannia Building Society. (Copyright British Olivetti.)

The new system allows several users to have access to any file at the same time, unlike the old paper-based system. To help users keep in touch with the interest of other departments, whenever a document is displayed the details of the previous two users of the file — department code and date — are shown on the screen. This facility has been found useful and will be extended to list the last three users.

The system allows users to annotate documents. The notes, entered with the keyboard, are in fact stored separately on the magnetic disk and overlaid on the document whenever it is displayed. This facility has been little used, perhaps because it is not easy to use.

The user has to log in to each system at the start of the working day. Once this is done the terminal remains connected to both systems, and both can be accessed at the same time. Some minor problems arise because the facilities of the Filenet terminals differ in some respects from the terminals belonging to the ICL mainframe system. The first problem, incompatibility of communications protocol, is solved by the protocol converters which act as gateways between the Ethernet network used by the optical storage system and the OSLAN network of the ICL system. Another problem is that the Filenet workstations do not have a personal identification device, which results in a security weakness. For the time being, the users of optical system workstations are allowed only read access to mainframe files and write access is barred. As a general solution this is clearly inadequate. There are differences of keyboard layout, but these do not affect many staff because few have access to both types of terminal.

Training
A three-day training course was at first provided for those clerks who were to use the optical storage system. This is now being reconsidered. It was perhaps too much to learn at once, as many clerks are found to be using only the simplest facilities rather than some more advanced features which could improve their productivity. Refresher courses, to emphasize such features after users have had some experience with the system, are being considered. In general clerks do not fully appreciate the differences between the optical system and the mainframe computer; they fail to understand why it takes longer to retrieve images from the optical system than data from the mainframe.

Experience
The pilot phase of the project was successfully completed at the beginning of 1988, a couple of months behind schedule. Full-scale implementation is taking place in stages, adding user departments to the system one by one. Not all of the applications considered when the system was proposed have yet been implemented, but there is no reason to think that this cannot successfully be done.

Performance requirements were specified in detail in the contract; the specification has now been met, although it took some time to achieve this. The time to retrieve the first document of a set to a terminal (assuming it has already been pre-fetched to the magnetic disk) is about 8 seconds. Each subsequent document in the set takes about 4 seconds.

The system has proved acceptable to the users, whereas an earlier pilot scheme based on microfilm was not. There are several reasons for this. One is that the new system is built round procedures which were already familiar. Another is the use of a single terminal to give access to both the optical store and the mainframe. A third is the high definition of the screen. Including end users in the steering committee has also helped. In the early days, reliability and performance weaknesses caused some disappointment; however, these are now considered to be good enough, although some users dislike the delays in image retrieval when browsing. This last point is a problem of specification rather than implementation, since performance does meet the specification.

Hardware reliability has been very good. In particular the jukebox, the most vulnerable part of the system, has had only one failure — though it has not yet been intensively used. However, when this failure occurred, the staff did not succeed in loading disks into the drives by hand. Although there have been difficulties in scanning, these are due to the marginal suitability of some of the documents rather than to failings of the scanners themselves. Software reliability was at first disappointing, for reasons that we have already discussed; it is now satisfactory.

The initial plan predicted that the cost of the system would be recovered over four years through higher productivity. At the time of writing it has not been demonstrated that this will be achieved. The fact that the system is not yet used by all departments, and lack of user experience, partly account from this. Improvements in some areas may be achieved by relatively minor procedural changes — for example, redesign of some forms to remove the need to batch documents before scanning. Substantial space savings, both in the central file storage and at work positions, should arise from the elimination of paper files when all departments have gone over to the optical system. Management information on the use of files will be more readily available (though software for this has yet to be written); if decentralization of access to these files should be required in the future, the system will support it. Recent legislation allows building societies to introduce new services, and the system may also play a part in these.

There has been no adverse comment from the Society's auditors on the optical storage system, nor on the intention to destroy paper files once they have been copied to optical disk. Britannia recognizes that the legal acceptability of data stored on optical disk will not be established until a test case is tried, but is confident that no problem will arise.

Some advice and warnings
A number of points of interest emerge from this case study. Most of the following are the author's observations, but some points are taken from David Mawdsley's OIS conference paper.

The scanning resolution needs to be established at a very early stage. It has a drastic impact not only on the capacity and throughput of the storage device, but also on the performance of the channels which carry images from the optical system to the user terminals. The storage required is not necessarily proportional to the square of the resolution, because of the effects of image compression.

The method of loading software into user terminals needs careful consideration. In this case the initial scheme failed, and the alternative needed extra memory in the workstation. Hard disk storage in clustered workstation servers may be a better approach.

In a system of this size, the design of the network supporting the user workstations may be more critical than that of the optical storage and retrieval subsystem itself. In this implementation it does appear that performance is limited at least as much by network bandwidth as by the optical storage components.

Paper-handling requirements should be given a good deal of attention. A limited test may not reveal all the problems.

The system is designed to work in an office environment. However, the heat output of the jukebox is substantial, and some air conditioning may have to be installed. This would no doubt be taken for granted in a US office.

Finally, too much trust should not be put in theoretical predictions. It is important that guarantees of system performance and reliability, as perceived by the user, are written into the contract.

The Society has not found it necessary to take special precautions against jukebox failure, nor is it worried about the unproven legal acceptability of optical records. Other types of user may need to take a different view.

Comments on the Britannia installation

The Britannia optical storage system is a pioneering installation, and one of the largest in Europe. The Society followed a cautious course in its introduction, specifying system performance requirements and a pilot scheme before full implementation. It also chose an introduction path which retained the paper system in full as a fall-back. After some teething troubles the system has proved a technical success and seems likely to be cost-effective, although the pay-back period may be longer than had been predicted. The way in which the system has been kept at arm's length from the mainframe computer system, and yet common access to both given to users, is of particular interest. The fact that performance may be governed by factors outside the optical system itself — particularly by the bandwidth of channels over which images are transmitted — is demonstrated. The importance of the scanning resolution should also be noted. Image storage makes heavy demands on storage capacity, and the choice of resolution has a drastic effect. Higher resolution increases not only the cost of storage, but also the power of the system needed to handle it. In this system there is an imbalance between the definition at which data is scanned and stored and the definition of the terminal screens. The extra cost of storing images at the higher resolution is partly offset by the ability to use standard scanners and printers.

OPTICAL DISK INSTALLATION AT THE PUBLIC RECORD OFFICE

Our third example is another simple system, storing text rather than image, but in this case it is a free-standing system for transferring archived records from magnetic tape to optical disk. This demonstrates the value of WORM media for very long-term preservation of data.

The UK government, unlike that of the USA, has been slow to try out optical storage. However, two pilot systems are being used to copy data from magnetic tape to optical disk. One is at the Property Services Agency at Hastings, the other at the Public Record Office at Kew. The Kew system will be described.

The task of the Public Record Office is to preserve records passed to it by other government departments, and to make these available to the public for historical research. Each department decides which of its records are to be preserved, with the assistance of Inspecting Officers from the PRO. Various rules decide when records are released to researchers; normally this is not before they are 30 years old.

The records are usually on paper. However, a lot of data is now stored on computer tape, and some departments would like to pass magnetic tapes to the PRO for preservation. Besides saving storage space, this would allow researchers to use computers to help them find the items they wanted more easily. They could also copy extracts into their own reports without the need for re-keying. Unfortunately, computer tape is not a good medium for archiving. It has to be stored at a controlled temperature and humidity. It also needs regular attention, which usually means rewinding every six to twelve months and a more extensive check every two years. This is expensive, and as the PRO does not know how many tapes it would be sent, the total cost cannot be predicted. This has made the PRO reluctant to accept tape for preservation.

The problem was discussed with CCTA, the government agency which has the task of giving advice to departments on the use of computers. This was at the time when optical storage was beginning to be talked about, although not yet on the market, and CCTA suggested that it should be considered. By 1986, optical disk systems were on sale. The PRO, with advice from CCTA, drew up a statement of requirements for a pilot system to copy records from magnetic tape to WORM optical disk. This was sent out to those firms which were thought to be interested. From several bids, the PRO selected Data General to develop and supply the pilot system. The contract was signed in September 1986 and Data General delivered the system in March 1987. It was the first system of this kind that Data General had made, and some further work was needed before the PRO began the full evaluation in November 1987.

Hardware
The system (Fig. 9.6) consists of a processor with 120 megabyte hard disk, tape drive, optical disk drive, two terminals and a matrix printer. The optical disk drive is the Optimem 1000 model, which stores 1 gigabyte on each side of a 12 inch WORM disk. The disks are made by 3M. The tape drive is a vacuum column type made by Kennedy, which handles $\frac{1}{2}$ inch wide tape in NRZ, PE, or GCR format at 75 inches per second. This tape drive is of the vertical type, fitted into a tall cabinet with the optical disk drive mounted beneath it. The processor is in a small under-desk cabinet and the other items stand on desks. The whole pilot system is installed in a small room. It is designed to run in a normal office environment, though air conditioning might be needed. The tape drive is noisy and would probably not be accepted in an office; a tension arm or streaming tape drive would be more suitable for office use.

There is no link to any other computer. Indeed the PRO has no large-scale computer system, although it has a small computer to handle readers' search requests; and a few personal computers are used.

Software
The software was developed specifically for this project; the PRO has however granted DG a licence to use it in systems for other customers. The smallest unit of data it handles is a file. In fact most government departments make a rule of recording only one file on a reel of tape; so, for the PRO's purposes, the unit is a whole tape. The software allows files to be copied from tape to magnetic disk, from magnetic disk to optical disk, and from

146   APPLICATIONS — DATA STORAGE, BACK-UP AND ARCHIVING   [Ch. 9

Fig. 9.6 — Tape to optical disk system. (Copyright Data General.)

optical disk to tape. It also allows a byte-by-byte comparison to be made between files in any two of these forms. Data is recorded on optical disk as an image of the tape, with no change of format. It can be copied from disk back to tape in the same format, so that the copy tape is identical to the original. However, the system can also convert data to ASCII or EBCDIC format as it copies from disk to tape; this is so that data can be given to researchers in the form which suits them best.

The system creates an index entry for each file written to the optical disk. This is added to the directory on that disk. Index entries take up about 2% of the data space. They form a simple cumulative index, no inverted indexes are used. A complete index of all optical disks known to the system is kept on the magnetic disk.

The user drives the system through a set of simple menus. Each choice from a menu selects one operation, such as copying from one medium to another, or checking one file against another. The menus also let the user look at the index and do various housekeeping jobs. The user is prompted to type in entries such as file and disk numbers; the system checks that these are valid, and lets the user confirm or cancel the operation. Various 'help' screens can be called up. There are no macros which would let one menu choice start a sequence of steps, such as copy tape to disk and then check the disk file against the tape; nor can file and disk numbers be carried forward from one step to the next without retyping. If the PRO needed these features, they could easily be provided.

When a new disk is first used, the system writes a short test file at the beginning of it. This test file is then checked automatically each time the disk is mounted on the drive. Each month, as part of its evaluation, the PRO checks about one in ten of the files recorded on optical disk, including both early and recent files. Some of these are copied back to tape, and sent back to the department that wrote the file, which checks that the tape can be read. If and when the system is put into full use, each tape will be copied onto two separate disks which will be stored in different places.

Experience

This is only a pilot project, so the PRO is not yet accepting tapes for preservation. However, it has borrowed tapes which are typical of those it may accept in the future. At present it can only handle tapes written on ICL 1900 and 2900 computers, excluding those written in GCR mode. In fact most tapes written by government departments are within these limits, and it will not be difficult to adapt the system to others. A wide variety of tapes is being sampled so that any problems can be sorted out. The PRO is trying to assess the type, condition, and quantity of the tapes that may be passed to them.

A rough estimate is that there is a backlog of about 2000 tapes to be archived, and a flow of about 200 per year. If the tapes were full, about thirty could be fitted onto one side of an optical disk; but most of them are only part full, and an average of 60 go on a disk side. Allowing for two copies from each tape, about seven disk sides would be filled each year and the backlog would fill seventy sides. This is well within the capability of this system. For the time being there are no plans for powerful methods of retrieving the data; it should be sufficient to load disks in the drive by hand, and copy to tape those files which interest a researcher.

The National Physical Laboratory is looking at sample disks to see if any problems are likely to occur after long storage; for example, whether the plastic might tend to deform if the disk cartridges were stored on edge.

The PRO has had no serious problems with the system, although it was the first of its kind so there were minor teething troubles. One of these prevented the whole capacity of the disk being used. This turned out to be the result of a program error which was soon put right. DG and the PRO worked very closely together at the start of the program, and the PRO is pleased with the results. When the pilot scheme is completed, at the end of 1988, the PRO will write a report. This will recommend whether this system, or some other, should be put into regular use, what extensions may be needed, and what it would cost to staff and run.

Comments on the PRO installation

This is a very straightforward use of WORM optical disk for archiving. Once again it was the first system of its kind from this supplier, and the value of a close relation between the supplier and the user is seen. In this case there seems to have been little difficulty in meeting the (fairly modest) specification, apart from a minor design error which prevented all the disk capacity being used. Only the simplest of retrieval methods is proposed. This is reasonable for the PRO, since these records will not be made available to the public for many years yet, but other users of systems like this may need something more powerful.

The choice of a vacuum column tape drive is a little surprising. Something simpler would have been fast enough for the limited amount of data being dealt with, and this would have made the system quieter, cooler and cheaper.

OPTICAL DISK INSTALLATION AT SHAREWARE MARKETING

Finally a very brief description of a system which is interesting because it stores software, rather than text or images.

Shareware Marketing, of Tonbridge, is a small company which specializes in the retail supply of public domain software and shareware for personal computers. Public domain (or PD) software consists of programs which are available to the public without charge, and can be distributed and used with no restrictions. Shareware is software which can also be distributed without restriction, but the user is trusted to pay a fee to the originator. This is in effect a 'try before you buy' arrangement, since the user is not expected to pay unless he finds that the program is of use to him. User groups and small companies such as Shareware Marketing distribute this software, usually on floppy disks, at a price which covers the cost of the media and overheads but not any fee which is due for the use of the software.

Shareware Marketing selects the best of these programs and groups them into sets for sale. Each set fits onto one, or sometimes a few, floppy disks. There are several hundred such sets; new sets are published each quarter as new programs are received. Amendments to existing programs are rare, although some do appear.

The usual approach has been to keep a set of master disks and to copy these to floppy disks for sale to customers. Commercial equipment is used for copying. The copier can record several disks at a time, so the more popular disks are recorded in batches and held for stock. Others are copied on demand. This obviously means that a lot of master disks are stored and handled.

Instead of keeping the master sets on individual floppy disks, Shareware Marketing now keep most of them on one large disk. The sets add up to hundreds of megabytes, and although there are frequent additions there are few amendments. Shareware Marketing have therefore chosen to use WORM optical disk. The mechanism they use is the Maxtor RXT 800s; this is a $5\frac{1}{4}$ inch WORM drive which stores 400 megabytes per side, using dye–polymer media. The disks are used in CLV (constant linear velocity) mode. This maximizes capacity rather than access time, which is appropriate for this application where several hundred kilobytes are read at each access.

Neither media nor recording formats conform to the forthcoming international standard, or to the formats used by IBM. However Maxtor have established a strong position in the optical disk drive market, so users can feel reasonably sure of continuity of supply.

The drive is in the 5¼ inch full-height format, and it is mounted with a power-supply unit in a desktop box. Its interface is SCSI, and it is supported by an SCSI interface adaptor board located in the host personal computer. This in turn drives a commercial disk duplicator made by Autofax which can write up to four floppy disks at a time, in various sizes and formats. Program sets are always selected by number, so there is no need for multiple indexes or powerful retrieval software.

There are a few program sets whose authors issue frequent revisions; these are still held on magnetic disk rather than on the optical disk.

Shareware Marketing have found the system works well. Their one complaint is that the software provided with the drive does not show which side of the disk holds any particular file, so usually both sides have to be tried. Because both drive and media are compact and rugged, the whole system can be taken to trade shows, and disks can be duplicated on demand. In this case, of course, only one of the output stations of the duplicator is used at a time.

It is interesting to compare Shareware Marketing's use of WORM disk with that of an American user group which, as we saw in Chapter 4, has published its entire library of PD and shareware programs on CD-ROM. In principle Shareware Marketing could have used this disk as their source for sale disks. However, they are interested in only a small proportion of the programs which are published; they have also added value by careful selection and by grouping the programs into sets, and in some cases adding indexes or comments. For this reason it is much more convenient for them to have full control of the contents of their master disk.

As for the end users, few will have CD-ROM drives; those who do could get a lot of software very cheaply that way, but keeping up with new issues will be more expensive in proportion to the amount of new material. There is also the problem of picking the useful programs from a choice of several thousand without expert guidance.

DISCUSSION OF EXAMPLES

The examples make it clear that optical disk can meet a range of data storage needs. These are pioneering installations, in the sense that each is the first of its kind made by the supplier; both supplier and user were learning as they went along. Inevitably there were minor mistakes and delays. However, close liaison between supplier and user has paid off in each case, and all the users are satisfied.

Only WORM disks have been considered in these examples. This is unavoidable, since rewritable disks are only just reaching the market and tape and card are not there yet. There will be more to learn with these new media, and a new generation of pioneers.

As optical storage comes into wider use, many needs will be met by standard systems and fewer will need such a close relationship between the user and the supplier. However, there are lessons in these examples which will be of interest to all prospective users. Some of these relate specifically to optical storage, others are more general.

Character-coded text or bit-mapped image?
Perhaps the most important lesson is that the choice between storing text and storing document images is absolutely crucial. A page of text needs typically 20 times as many bytes when stored as a bit-mapped image as it would if character coded. Not only does this add to media cost, it may need a more powerful system to support it and a faster interface to transfer the data to workstations or a host computer; without this, retrieval of documents for display on a terminal screen may be unacceptably slow. Against this, image storage can be used when the data cannot be captured at source. The Britannia Building Society chose the image approach even though much of the source data could have been captured; this removed the need to change the way documents were used. It thus made acceptance easy, and provided a safeguard against problems with the new system. In any case, some of the documents could not be stored in any other way. On the other hand, storing everything as images has led to a large and expensive system.

The choice also affects document retrieval. Images must be indexed as a separate process, usually by keying in references or keywords. This may be necessary for character-coded text as well, but often text can be retrieved by internal keys such as addresses and dates (as in the Barclaycard case), or by searching the text for character strings. Text can also be further processed, and passed on to other applications. A page of text can be displayed on a screen, or printed out, faster than a bit-mapped image. However, in many cases at least part of the data can be stored only as images; either because it is pictorial in nature, or because character recognition would be too expensive or unreliable, as with handwritten text. In this case it may be better to store everything in image form than to mix the two methods. It is worth noting that even if character recognition is not reliable enough to capture text in full, it may be able to pick out a more limited repertoire of words and so allow bit-mapped documents to be indexed automatically.

Resolution
If image storage is chosen, the next decision to be made is the resolution at which images will be scanned, stored, displayed and printed. Roughly speaking, the number of bytes needed is proportional to the square of the resolution. This is not exactly true because images are usually compressed, and compression is a bit more effective at higher resolution. The lowest resolution that is acceptable depends on the application, and also on the form of output; usually printed images need a higher resolution than images on a screen. For internal purposes, 200 bits per inch is usually good enough, but staff not used to computers may expect a higher standard. Publishing to

letterpress standard calls for a much higher level, sometimes as high as 1000 or 2000 bits per inch.

Obviously images must be scanned and stored at the highest resolution that will be needed. If some of the output devices use a lower level, conversion is needed and this can be quite complex, especially if the ratio is not a simple one (like 2 to 1) or the image is stored in compressed form.

Standard resolution levels for scanners and printers tend to come from the makers of fax transmission devices; 100, 200, and 300 bits per inch are common and 400 bits per inch is becoming accepted. On the other hand, video screens have different traditions and it may be difficult to get an exact match.

Indexing and retrieval
The next consideration is that of indexing and access methods. In some cases the simplest methods will do, as in the Shareware Marketing case where program sets are always accessed by a unique reference number. In other cases a record may be reached by several different paths; this calls for either a more complex index system or else retrieval by scanning the data for text strings. Optical storage is no different from magnetic storage in this respect, but the capacity of each volume is generally higher so better indexing may be needed to manage the data. In any case the method chosen will affect the design of the system and its performance.

Performance
This brings us to the point that system performance can be difficult to predict. Again, this is not unique to optical storage, but optical devices often hold more data than their magnetic equivalents. Also they are more likely to store images. Until there is much more experience of optical storage, the prospective user will need either a demonstration of a system doing a job very similar to his own, or else a pilot scheme. He should also make sure that the level of system performance is specified in the contract, and that it is fully checked before the system is accepted.

In image systems, scanner performance can be a problem, as we saw in the Britannia study. Practical tests need to be made with every relevant kind of document, including those that have not been carefully handled. And again the requirement should be part of the contract.

Reliability
Related to performance is reliability. Optical disk drives are possibly less delicate than magnetic disks, and hardware reliability is likely to be as good or better. However, some of the supporting software is not yet so mature, and care should be taken in its choice. In particular its compatibility with the operating system should be checked; some, such as MS-DOS, need special measures to handle large amounts of data that can be stored on optical disk.

Jukeboxes are mechanically complex, and inevitably they will break down more often than simpler devices; a typical figure for mean time between breakdowns is 10 000 hours. System designers have to think hard about resilience. If a failure would have serious results, they may need to duplicate the jukebox and all the disks in it. In spite of claims, it seems unlikely that the work of a jukebox can be done by hand if the picker mechanism fails. It would be more practicable to remove all the disks and use them in a separate drive, although care would be needed in keeping track of the disks.

Standards
Standards have already been discussed at length. All we need repeat here is that interchange standards not only help with the exchange of data between systems; they also ensure that drives will be available when they are needed.

Data life and acceptability
We have also discussed data life. Ten years is now the figure guaranteed by most manufacturers, and some offer thirty. Disks with glass substrates may have the edge in this respect, although it is very hard to prove either way. In any case, a much longer life will be normal; one company has predicted 100 years. Deterioration is gradual, and can be detected well before any data is lost, so disks can be copied in good time.

One loose end is the legal acceptability of data stored on optical disk. In the USA, this has been established in one or two states though not generally. In the UK it can only be proved by a test case; there has been none yet. However, there now seems to be confidence that this method of storage will be accepted, and organizations like the Britannia are happy to proceed. If legal acceptability is vital to an application, the user will for the time being need to use caution.

Implementation
Finally we can turn from system design to implementation. The few points we shall mention are general, rather than specific to optical storage; they arise mainly from the novelty of the new technology.

The first question is whether optical storage is the right answer to the user's problems. In this chapter we have compared optical with magnetic storage; but before he makes this comparison the user needs to decide if computer methods are really going to be more cost effective than paper or microfiche. There can be no general answer to this question. In a straightforward case he can make the comparison himself, bearing in mind that it can be difficult to predict system performance exactly. In a marginal case, or if a lot of money is at stake, he may want the help of a consultant. Remember, though, that the consultant's estimates of performance will not be precise either.

Next the prospective user must choose whether to design his own system, have it designed by a consultant, or buy a complete system from one supplier. In the latter case he may be able to use a standard packaged system, or he may have one custom-designed; custom design will obviously cost more. A consultant may simply help the user choose a supplier, or he may design the whole system using a mix of suppliers and possibly adding his own software. The user needs to be aware of any commercial links the consultant has with suppliers, since these may limit or influence his choice.

As with all new developments, it is wise to move in easy steps and to keep a fall-back position open. The Britannia study is a good example of this. No significant change was made to business methods. This ensured that, on the one hand, the users readily accepted the system; and on the other that the old methods could have been resumed if the new system had not been satisfactory. Also worth noting are the involvement of the end users in the planning, the close relationship between customer and supplier, and the inclusion of system performance levels in the contract. A more radical approach would have brought a faster pay-off, but at a risk which would have been too great in a system of this size and novelty.

In each of the installations described, except that at Shareware Marketing where standard hardware and software were used, there was very close liaison between supplier and customer. This meant that the system was designed with a full understanding of the user's needs, both from management's point of view and from that of the staff actually working with the system. It also meant that potential problems were picked up in good time, and that users had reasonable expectations as to what the system would do for them.

Finally, although the level of performance was carefully defined in each case, the time-scale was flexible. In a novel installation, performance is hard to predict; a rigid time-scale may force the customer to accept a system which is not really up to his requirements, whereas with more time the specified level could have been reached. In each of these cases, plenty of time was allowed; in fact there were no major over-runs, and all the customers were happy with their systems.

CONCLUSION

We can sum up this chapter on applications in data storage, back-up and archiving in a few paragraphs.

In the field of archival storage, WORM disks have many advantages over magnetic tape, which until now has been the usual medium. Most new installations, and many that already exist, will benefit by using WORM for this purpose. Where there are many volumes, or rapid access is important, there is a case for using a jukebox. In cases where data need only be kept for a few years, and fast access is not important, helical-scan magnetic tape is a possible alternative to WORM disk, with lower media cost. WORM optical tape may also be suitable when the amount of data is very large, although long data life has yet to be proved; media cost is a little higher than helical-scan magnetic tape. Optical card can be regarded as archival, on a very small scale, but this is not its prime application. Rewritable optical disk can be used for archiving, but data life is not quite as long as for WORM; in most cases WORM will be more suitable.

For back-up, rewritable disks can be used as an alternative to magnetic tape although here the pros and cons are more evenly balanced. Optical disks are more rugged and give random access; cartridge magnetic tape drives are less expensive and often smaller. Once optical media prices settle down, they will probably be competitive with tape except in those cases where DAT-based tape is acceptable.

For internal storage, rewritable optical disk is not yet a strong competitor to magnetic disk because of its lower performance and higher price. This may change in the next few years. In the meantime, optical storage is useful in those cases where removable media are needed.

10

Applications — data exchange, distribution and publishing

In the last chapter we looked at those applications of optical storage where data is re-used within the same computer system. We now turn to the use of optical media to transfer data from one system to another. This includes the publishing of data for use on many separate systems, whose owners may or may not be within the same organization as the publisher.

Read-only media are very suitable for publishing, and CD-ROM is dominant in this field. When data is being transferred within an organization, the number of identical copies is often small — sometimes only one. In this case WORM or rewritable media are more suitable.

DEVICE CHARACTERISTICS

We went over the characteristics of optical storage devices in the last chapter. Most apply also to read-only storage, in particular the high data density and the ruggedness of the media. However, there is one more characteristic that is important here. This is the cost of making many copies of the same data, and distributing them widely. WORM and rewritable media must be written individually, so the cost of copying is in direct proportion to the number of copies. Read-only media, however, are copied mechanically (or sometimes photographically) from a master. The master is expensive but copies from it are cheap, and this is what makes read-only media so suitable for publishing.

In fact, hybrids are possible. WORM and rewritable disks have sector headers, and sometimes a clock signal, impressed on them during manufacture; permanent data could be added in the same way, so that part of the disk carried common data and part was available for data written by the user. This has not been done in practice, probably because it combines the high mastering cost of read-only disks with the high cost per disk of the other types. However, the idea may come up again in the context of the forthcoming 'CD-PROM'. Another proposal which has not been followed up is the use of a WORM disk as a master for mechanical copying. This is possible where the recording technique changes the surface relief; the bubble-formation technique is an example. But disks using this technique are built as a pair of substrates back to back, with the sensitive layers inside for protection. Copying would require the disk to be taken apart; this is a very delicate operation.

Production
Once the pre-master tape has been prepared, CD-ROM disks are made in just the same way as Compact Audio disks, and often on the same production line. These lines are designed for high volumes and thus low unit costs. CD-ROM disks share these benefits, but they are tested to a higher standard than audio disks, and so the reject rate is higher. Nevertheless, CD-ROM disks (as distinct from the data they carry) are very cheap if the quantities are large enough to spread the mastering cost widely.

Other forms of read-only disk do not have this advantage; they need dedicated plant, and cannot ride on the back of a high-volume consumer product. For this reason they are considerably more expensive than CD-ROM, and will be used only where they offer something extra. The only formats likely to be used (other than videodisk, which is now of marginal interest to the computer industry) are those which run on drives which also handle WORM or rewritable disks. If the user already has such a drive, these disks save him the cost of an additional drive for CD-ROM. However, this helps only if he does not want to use both media at the same time, and CD-ROM drives are relatively cheap. The other advantage of those read-only disks which are not tied to the CD-ROM standard is that performance can be higher. In spite of this, these formats are scarcely used at present. Where performance is important, it is more usual to distribute the data on CD-ROM and then copy it to a magnetic fixed disk for rapid access.

Handling
All optical disks are rugged; read-only disks are even more so because they do not have a sensitive layer. They do need a reflective coating, but as this is inert there is a wide choice of materials, and it is easy to make a tough and long-lasting coating. In fact CD-ROM disks, because of this ruggedness and their especially powerful error correction, do not need cartridges and are not affected by normal handling. There is in fact a move towards supplying the disks in caddies, but this is for convenience of loading rather than protection.

Capacity and performance
CD-ROM disks have a rather higher data density than other optical disks, with room for about 600 megabytes on a 120 mm (4¾ inch) disk; all CD-ROM disks are single-sided. Other read-only disks are compatible with their writable equivalents, and so have the same data density and capacity as these.

CD-ROM drives are relatively slow. Normally the data rate is 153 kilobytes per second; in principle the disk could be spun faster to improve the data rate, but this has not yet been done. Current drives have an average access time of about half a second with a maximum of one second. Some

Ch. 10] APPLICATIONS — DATA EXCHANGE, DISTRIBUTION AND PUBLISHING 157

drives are faster; but CD-ROM disks are used in CLV (constant linear velocity) mode, which prevents very fast access because the rate of rotation has to be adjusted for each access. Other read-only disks do not have this limitation, so might be preferred where performance is important. However, data can be copied from a CD-ROM drive to a magnetic fixed disk for access; this gives even better performance than other types of read-only optical disk, at much the same cost.

Access methods
Retrieval methods for data on CD-ROM were discussed in Chapter 4. It was shown that the low cost per byte of this medium makes it practical to use complex data structures and indexes, and thus very powerful access methods. There has been a problem of compatibility in the absence of data layout standards, but the 'High Sierra' standard has gone a long way to solving it. Other read-only disks have room for complex indexes too, but do not benefit from universal standards.

Data integrity
Error rates for CD-ROM are better than those for other optical disks or for magnetic media, because of the very powerful error correction. Paradoxically, good error rates are less important in a medium used for publishing, since if the error is detected the disk can be cheaply replaced. However, the *undetected* error rate is still important, and this is presumably improved in the same proportion; in fact it is so low that it is almost impossible to measure it. Error rates for other read-only disks are similar to those of the matching writable disks. As we saw earlier, there is no active layer and the reflective layer can be made very tough. There is thus no reason why a read-only disk, if properly made, should not last indefinitely — certainly for several tens of years. Such long life is rarely needed; the data is usually obsolete in a few years, if not months.

APPLICATIONS AND COMPETING TECHNOLOGIES

Clearly the major application of CD-ROM is the publication of information for sale. The sellers are mainly specialist CD-ROM publishers, or else organizations which also publish data in print or as on-line computer databases. A second, closely related, application is the distribution of data within an organization or from the organization to its agents or tied clients; and a third is the distribution of software. We shall look at specific applications later in this chapter, but now we shall consider how CD-ROM compares with the older alternatives.

CD-ROM or paper?
The broadest of these alternatives is, of course, ink on paper. Here there is a very wide range of applications. At the one extreme, no-one predicts that readers of fiction will ever prefer the computer screen to the printed book; at the other, CD-ROM is already popular with professional information users,

because software can give them so much help with their searches. The choice depends on a number of factors; the quantity of information to which the user may want access at any time, the complexity of its structure, how often it is revised, whether the latest news is essential to the user, where and how the user accesses the information, and so on.

We have seen that it costs a few thousand pounds to prepare the master for a CD-ROM disk that can hold up to 600 megabytes of data; thereafter the cost per copy is very low. Printed paper has a similar price structure, except that the production cost per volume depends on the amount of data it contains; a CD-ROM costs the same to make whether it contains one megabyte of data or 600. In fact the mastering cost and the cost per disk of CD-ROM are not very different from the equivalent costs for a book of say 200 pages, which would contain about half a megabyte of data. It follows that the cost of mastering and making a CD-ROM which uses anything more than a trivial proportion of its capacity is less than that of the equivalent in print. In fact the cost of making the disk is usually trivial when compared to the value of the information carried on it.

However, when the user has bought a printed book he needs no further equipment to make use of it. CD-ROM is a very different story. If the user already has a computer system he may need to buy only a CD-ROM drive, which will cost him a few hundred pounds. Otherwise he needs to buy a complete 'delivery system', usually a personal computer with a CD-ROM drive attached, and this will cost him well over a thousand pounds. (When CD-I players are on the market they will be much cheaper than this; it remains to be seen whether they will handle CD-ROM in a way that is useful to the professional.) Clearly the user needs to buy a lot of data before CD-ROM is justified on cost grounds alone — probably the equivalent of a hundred or more books. But a hundred books take up a lot of space. More important, finding a particular item of data in a library of a hundred books is often a difficult and time-consuming task. CD-ROM, on the other hand, is organized to make it much quicker and easier to retrieve data, and it is on this ground rather than cost that most CD-ROM installations are justified.

Some users will want not only to read the data but also to process it in some way. They may copy text from it, via a word processor, to a book or report of their own; this presents no problem if the CD-ROM stores the text as characters rather than as images. They may similarly want to copy images from the disk. If the data is numerical, they may want to make calculations based on it. In all these cases CD-ROM has an advantage over print; it avoids not only the cost but also the possibility of error involved in re-keying the data.

The absence of wear on a CD-ROM disk, however much it is used, is also an advantage when compared to reference books.

CD-ROM has a further advantage where data is regularly revised, since it costs little to replace the original disk by a new one. In contrast, the cost of printing means that reference books may be updated by supplements rather than complete reprints, and this makes access more difficult and liable to error. The time taken to produce and distribute an update is also likely to be less for CD-ROM than print, although in each case special measures can be taken to get a turnaround of only a few days.

However, there are some disadvantages in using CD-ROM. Perhaps the most obvious is that the data has to be read from a screen rather than a page; this is not welcomed by many potential users, although of course computer users will already be used to it. Allied to this is lack of portability; you can take a book almost anywhere, whereas you have to go to wherever the computer may be. Of course portable computers can have CD-ROM drives, but this will not be a common arrangement. Again, this is not a problem for the professional data user with a PC or terminal on his desk, but it can be a deterrent to the casual user.

Some other difficulties exist with current CD-ROMs and delivery systems, but these may be overcome in the future. One is that the time to replace a screenful of data by the next can be very noticeable. This is a hindrance when reading straight through a text; even more so when browsing to see whether an item is really of interest. The other current problem is that CD-ROM is not yet able to handle integrated text and images as well as print can do it; the most acceptable solution to the user may be a double display so that the two can appear side by side, but such displays are expensive. Also, a standard PC display cannot show images with anything like the high definition of the printed page. Again, technical solutions exist but are too expensive for most users.

In conclusion, therefore, CD-ROM is likely to be preferred to paper where many megabytes of data must be available for more-or-less random reference; particularly by professionals who have delivery systems at their desks or very close by, and by those who need to extract data for further use. It is less likely to be used for small quantities of data; where the data is read systematically so that only a small part (say a book) is used at a time; where the data is needed away from the desk; or, except perhaps for CD-I, by non-professionals. The combination of text and image data on CD-ROM is not yet fully developed.

CD-ROM or microform?
The next publishing method with which CD-ROM competes is microform (i.e. microfilm and microfiche). Here we must make a distinction between text and images. For text, CD-ROM has considerable advantages. It is cheaper and more compact; retrieval of a particular item is very much easier and faster; it is (or can be) machine readable and so suitable for further processing; and (for applications where it matters) it is more accurate. Against this a CD-ROM delivery system is more expensive than a simple microform reader, though a microform system which automatically finds and displays the required image costs more. Images on video screens are usually more acceptable to users than microform readers, although this may not be true of the cheapest PC displays. As before, the fact that there is no wear on a CD-ROM disk will be of value in some applications.

Most of these arguments also apply in the case of images, but here the higher definition possible with microform — especially when printed out on paper — may shift the balance in its favour.

Microform depends on photographic processes which have been known for over a century, and on this basis it is sometimes claimed that the life of data on microform is 100 years. CD-ROM has been known for only a fraction of this time. Nevertheless there is no evidence that CD-ROM has a shorter life. Whether compatible readers for either CD-ROM or microform will be available in 100 years is another question; there will be few cases where the potential data life will determine the choice.

Note that these arguments apply to microform as a publishing medium, which presumes that a fair number of copies will be made. Microform as an internal storage or distribution medium, where only one or very few copies may be needed, is another matter.

CD-ROM or magnetic media?
Moving on to magnetic media, publishing on magnetic tape or disk is of course aimed entirely at computer users. Software is almost always published on these media, although it may also be obtainable from an on-line database; in the case of the PC user the latter can be a 'bulletin board'. Any form of data may be sold on floppy disk, or on tape or hard disk; however, this is not an important method of publishing data other than software. It is of course widely used for data transfer within an organization, or between related organizations.

CD-ROM offers an alternative medium for publishing software. Its attractions are the very high data integrity that can be guaranteed (with the right choice of drive, as discussed earlier), and the compactness and resistance to damage of the disk. In the latter respects it is of course matched by floppy disk, though not in general by tape or hard disk. The economics of its use, as a medium, depend on the amount of data or software and the number of copies required; magnetic disks or tapes have to be copied individually, while CD-ROMs are stamped in quantity. However, the cost of the medium and of putting the data on it is usually small compared to the value of the data, so a choice will not be made on media cost grounds. Not many software packages exceed a few megabytes, so most will fit on a single volume of tape or a small number of floppy disks; the high volume capacity of the CD-ROM is not of particular value.

More important to the user is the cost of the equipment he needs to use the data. Practically every user has a tape or floppy disk drive, since he needs it for back-up and often for off-line storage or archiving and for data interchange; it costs him nothing to use it also for access to published data. On the other hand, no system yet comes with a CD-ROM drive included in the price (apart from those sold specifically as CD-ROM delivery systems) so this is an extra cost. All these considerations suggest that CD-ROM will be slow to replace magnetic media for the publication of software.

Magnetic media are rarely used for publishing data other than software, and it seems that CD-ROM will easily become dominant in this field. However, tape or floppy disks will still be more suitable for those users who do not already have a CD-ROM drive and who do not expect to buy a large quantity of data. In principle, access software designed for CD-ROM can easily be adapted to magnetic media; it remains to be seen whether there will be enough demand to make that adaptation worth while.

CD-ROM or on-line databases?
The final method of publication that competes with CD-ROM is the on-line computer database. This is a very different matter from print or microfiche. The data is already in digital form, and powerful access software is available; indeed, much CD-ROM access software is only slightly adapted from software designed for on-line access. The choice therefore depends on two main factors; cost and currency. Taking the latter factor first, an on-line database can be updated as often as the owner chooses; daily updates are common, and for critical information — such as stock market prices — the database can be updated continuously as revised figures come to hand. The production time for a new or revised CD-ROM, as we have seen, is typically around a month. Three days can be achieved on demand, or even 24 hours at a pinch; but of course the time for delivery, by post or otherwise, has to be added. It is therefore unusual to update CD-ROM databases more often than monthly, although there are a few cases of weekly updates.

It follows that CD-ROM, used on its own, is not suitable where it is important that the information is right up to date. It is, however, possible to use a hybrid approach if only a small proportion of the data changes each month (or within whatever period is selected for the disk update). The CD-ROM is used for normal access, but where there is later data available on-line this can be accessed. Obviously the user must be able to tell when recent data exists. One possibility is for a key list of revised entries to be transmitted daily (at a time when communication is cheap) to the user and stored on magnetic disk; another is for the user to make a brief on-line access, simply to check the date and time of the entry, whenever he makes access to the CD-ROM. In either case, the access software will need to be more sophisticated than that for a single type of database. Which method is more economical will depend on the circumstances.

This brings us to the question of cost, the other major difference between CD-ROM and on-line databases. CD-ROM disks are usually sold outright, either as a single purchase or by a subscription which covers the initial disk and all updates for (usually) one year. The user can then make as much or as little use of the disk as he wants, within the terms of the agreement; these will usually prevent him passing the data on to a third party, and may or may not allow him to extract data for further use. Access software does exist which allows the publisher to charge according to the amount of use, or to limit the number of accesses made to the disk: it seems unlikely that this will come into general use.

In contrast, the cost to the user of access to an on-line database always increases as he uses it more, although there may also be a fixed subscription charge. In a few cases (such as bulletin boards) he may only have to pay the cost of the telephone call — though this can be substantial if a lot of data is transferred, since remote transfers are slow. More often there is a charge proportional to the time he is connected to the host computer; sometimes also a separate charge for the time he is connected to the database itself, or for the amount of data transferred. The cost obviously varies very much with the circumstances, but can be quite high — in some cases as much as $200 per megabyte of data seen by the user. This compares with a few dollars per megabyte for data bought on a CD-ROM. The catch is, of course, that the CD-ROM user has to buy all the data on the disk, not just what he needs.

Which approach suits a particular user will depend on the actual charges, and on the extent to which he accesses the database and the nature of each access. If he uses the database infrequently, extracts only a small amount of data each time, and can go directly to the data he wants, then the on-line database will be attractive; if he uses it a lot, and if he cannot define his needs precisely so that he needs to refine his searches in the light of the results, or if he simply wants to browse through a section of the database to see if it is of interest, he will prefer CD-ROM. CD-ROM is also attractive to the trainee and the occasional user because the psychological pressure of 'time is money' is removed. Clearly the efficiency of the access software is much more important for an on-line database then for CD-ROM; unfortunately the user is unlikely to be able to make a choice in the former case, since the access software will be integral with the on-line database.

Of course a choice between CD-ROM and on-line will not always be available, but the owners of many on-line databases have published CD-ROM versions. This will probably become common practice except where the essence of the database is its currency; for example if it lists share prices or news items. When both versions exist, the owners naturally try to pitch the price of the CD-ROM to maximize their total profit — which involves a lot of intelligent guesswork. As on-line databases are expensive to use, the prices of the corresponding CD-ROMs are high; subscription rates of $1000 to $4000 per year are typical. (Prices for disks based on printed databases are usually lower.) Very roughly, the breakpoint between CD-ROM and an on-line database could be in the region of one access per week.

Distributing data on a smaller scale
That concludes our comparison of CD-ROM with other methods of publishing data. We noted earlier that CD-ROM is useful also for the controlled distribution of data within an organization, or to its registered agents or clients. Many of the points we have considered in connection with publishing apply to this kind of application too. One difference is that the originator controls the equipment used by the recipients, or at least knows what it is, so standards are less important; this gives more scope for data structures and retrieval software designed to suit the particular needs of the user, and perhaps integrated with his other systems. The originator may choose to prepare his own data and master tape, but is more likely to use one of the specialist CD-ROM publishers or a consultancy. Cost considerations will be quite different from those involved in publishing. The originator will not usually need to account for the value of the data, so the cost of the medium

may have more influence on his choice; internal communications will be cheaper than the use of a public network; and the number of users is more easily predicted. However, the number of copies will often be smaller; it may be so small that it is more economical to use WORM disks copied individually. A number of companies in the computer field are now issuing their product manuals on CD-ROM.

Other read-only disks
We have up to this point been looking at CD-ROM and its competitors. We must now consider the other read-only optical storage media.

We shall spend little time on videodisk, since we have seen that as a computer storage medium it has been largely displaced by CD-ROM. When videodisk is associated with computers as 'interactive videodisk' the link is a loose one, with the computer used simply to control the selection and presentation of video sequences by a self-contained player. Videodisk is used almost entirely for images (although these can be images of pages of text), and particularly for animated sequences; so it competes with videotape rather than with computer media. It does have the advantage over videotape that images and sequences can be selected at random rather than serially, and this makes it useful in training and education. An interesting example is the 'Domesday' project run by the BBC in conjunction with schools in the UK. Data, pictures and maps relating to a wide spread of communities in Britain were collected and presented on two videodisks, and special players were produced for school use.

Other forms of read-only optical disk are at present confined to those which are compatible with WORM or rewritable disks, and there are very few even of these. They have the same competitors as CD-ROM, but because there is no single standard for these drives they are much less attractive for general publishing. They may be chosen where all the customers for a particular kind of data have similar equipment, as could happen in some vertical markets, and for internal broadcasting of data within an organization.

Optical card
Optical card differs from disk in being even more compact and easy to handle, and in having a much lower data capacity; typically a card holds a few megabytes whereas a disk holds several hundred. Card has not yet been tried as a publishing medium, although it does have the property of being cheap in large quantities because it can be reproduced photographically from a master. Software publishing has been suggested as a use for these cards, but the drawback here is that each user would need to have a card reader which would be of no other use to him, and readers are still not cheap; on balance, therefore, floppy disks or other magnetic media are not likely to be displaced by optical card for software publishing. Much the same applies to the publishing of data, although some applications have been suggested.

A more promising field is the transfer of personal data from one system to another. There is a lot of interest in the use of these cards for medical records. The idea is that each customer of a medical insurance scheme (particularly in the USA, where these schemes are widely used) should have his medical history recorded on an optical card, which he would carry at all times. When he visited a doctor or a hospital, the card would be put in a reader and all the usual access methods would be available. Further data could also be added to the card. This application is attractive because there is no existing way to do the job; a complete record on paper would be too bulky for most pockets, and would not allow computer access or automated access methods. The alternative is for the record to be held centrally and accessed by a communication link, but this is likely to be slower, more complex, and more expensive. Several experiments with cards are in progress, but no scheme is yet in full operation.

WORM and rewritable media
Finally, we must remember that WORM and rewritable media can also be used for data interchange, distribution and publishing. Indeed the first of these three usually involves only a single copy, so read-only media are ruled out. The choice of medium depends on much the same factors as those discussed in Chapter 9. However, standards, or at least agreed formats, at every level become of prime importance.

For publishing or distribution to a relatively small number of users, it may be cheaper to make individual copies on WORM or erasable disks. The break-even point will probably be around 25 to 50 copies but depends on the amount of data, since this determines the time taken to make each copy. When the data is selected to suit each customer (as is often the case with software), read-only disks are obviously not suitable; also when a fast turnaround is important, the mastering processes required for CD-ROM may take too long.

INFORMATION SOURCES
Most CD-ROM users will be interested in access to information published by others, rather than in recording and distributing their own data. Here we shall survey the kind of information that is published on CD-ROM. No attempt will be made to list actual publications; that would be beyond the scope of this book, and in any case change is very rapid. Some sources of current information are included in Appendix 1, 'Further reading'.

Types of information
Apart from demonstration disks, the first information published on CD-ROM (or, in a few cases, on videodisk) consisted of databases which were already available on-line. These included company information, financial statistics, bibliographic data, and scientific and medical data. Such databases were easy to put on CD-ROM; not only were they already in digital form, they also had access software which needed little modification for use on a CD-ROM delivery system. Access to an on-line database is normally charged by connect time (and telephone charges also depend on time); the

same database on CD-ROM is usually an outright purchase. The supplier will aim to price the CD-ROM version so that heavy users, or those who need to browse, will benefit by choosing CD-ROM while occasional users will find the on-line service cheaper. Of course the on-line database can be updated almost instantaneously, whereas that on disk cannot; the choice will depend partly on how much this matters for a particular database and a particular user. Many CD-ROM databases are updated regularly; usually each month, quarter or year. Often this involves issuing a replacement disk, but if the database is cumulative the original disk will be retained and a supplementary disk issued. We saw in a previous chapter that the High Sierra standard provides for this arrangement.

The other common source for CD-ROM data is information which is already available in print; this includes directories, encyclopaedias and reference works in general. Nowadays these have often been generated on word processors or typeset by machine, and so are available in digital form. However they were not designed for sophisticated access methods, and quite a lot of work is needed in arranging and indexing to prepare the information for CD-ROM publication. When the publication is illustrated the amount of work is much increased; in fact very few illustrated works have yet been published on CD-ROM.

However, the case is rather different when the original consists almost entirely of illustrations, as for example in an atlas of road maps or a diagrammatic car parts catalogue. Such data can best be stored as bit-mapped images. These are created simply by mechanically scanning the original pictures (on paper or microfilm), which is a relatively inexpensive process; in fact for this reason, some CD-ROMs store even text information as scanned images rather than as coded characters. It takes a lot of bits to store such an image, the number depending on the definition required and on whether the digitized image can be compressed; in general line drawings and text can be compressed effectively but photographs cannot. Typically an image occupies 50 to 500 kilobytes. The number of images that can be held on a disk is therefore very much less than the number of screenfuls of character-coded text, and the problem of indexing is simpler.

All the CD-ROM data we have discussed has originally appeared in other forms. However publication on disk can be most effective when the data is specially chosen to suit the characteristics of CD-ROM. At the time of writing this approach is still in its infancy.

Publishers

Various kinds of organization have published data on CD-ROM. Some of these are conventional publishers who are used to publishing directories or reference works on paper; some are government agencies or research establishments; some are organizations which control on-line databases. However, a number of specialists in CD-ROM publishing have emerged, either independently or as branches of existing organizations, and many information providers are choosing to have their data published by these rather than doing everything themselves. Even these specialist disk publishers rarely have their own disk pressing plants, or even their own disk mastering facilities; they deliver the data on master tapes to disk manufacturing companies. Most of these make Compact Audio disks as their main business, but there are exceptions.

Pricing

The nature of CD-ROM makes it natural to sell the disk outright, with the right to free access to its contents within defined limits (which will often prevent the purchaser passing data on to a third party). Where regular updates are available it is usual to sell the disks on a regular subscription basis; for a yearly sum the user receives the current disk and then a replacement every month or quarter. If the database is a cumulative one there may be a one-off charge for the current disk and then supplementary disks are covered by subscription. Whilst there were problems of compatibility it was common for the subscription to include a free-standing delivery system, but as standardization improves this is becoming less usual. Some existing CD-ROM databases are designed for non-standard delivery systems so must remain bundled.

In a few cases, CD-ROM and on-line databases are combined. The user can access the bulk of the data from CD-ROM and use the on-line service for additions or alterations since the issue of his disk. This obviously calls for more sophisticated access software as well as more complex methods of charging.

A few information suppliers would prefer to charge CD-ROM users in proportion to the amount of use they make of the disk, much as they charge for on-line services. Access software is available which makes this possible, but it seems unlikely that the approach will be acceptable to many users.

We shall continue this chapter by describing a couple of actual applications of read-only optical storage. The examples are both concerned with catalogue data on CD-ROM, since as yet few other applications have passed the development stage. The exception is the use in libraries of bibliographic data on CD-ROM, but most librarians are overworked and the author was unable to find one who could spare the time to demonstrate his system.

THE WHITAKER BOOKBANK SERVICE

CD-ROM is well suited to the publication of catalogues, and the Whitaker *Bookbank* is a good example of a catalogue which is entirely in text form. J. Whitaker and Sons Ltd publish reference books (including *Whitaker's Almanack*), and *Whitaker's Books in Print*, formerly *British Books in Print*, has been published for over a century. A microfiche version, updated every month, was introduced ten years ago, and a CD-ROM version under the name of *Bookbank* began at the end of 1987. *Bookbank* is issued monthly, and each disk is a complete replacement for its predecessor.

The databank

The list of *Books in Print* includes nearly half a million titles, and in a typical month about 5000 new titles and up to 100 000 amendments are listed. There seems every prospect that these figures will increase as desktop publishing makes it easier to introduce new titles, and 'on demand' printing helps to keep books in print. The CD-ROM also includes details of about 12 000 publishers, and information on forthcoming titles and those recently out of print. Whitakers charge £980 a year for the service, including the access software but not hardware. This is about twice the price of the microfiche version; the extra cost is justified by ease of use, more powerful search facilities, and the ability to link the system to other computer applications.

Books in Print lists, for each book, the title, author, publisher, date, price, and availability (in print, forthcoming, out of print); there is also a classification code added by Whitakers. The CD-ROM includes all this data, and there is also an inverted index so that a record can be retrieved by any word within any of its fields. Even with this index, the database occupies only about half of the disk.

Access

The arrangement of data on the disk conforms to the 'High Sierra' standard. It is also compatible with the US equivalent, Bowker's *Books in Print Plus*, so that both CD-ROM databases will run on the same system. The access software is provided on the CD-ROM, apart from an installation program on floppy disk which only has to be run once when *Bookbank* is added to a computer system. This access software was developed by BRS Europe and is a customised version of their 'BRS Search'. It is menu-driven, and gives the user a choice of three modes of access to the main list — novice, intermediate and expert. In the novice mode the user is presented with a screen with fields for the title, author, publisher, ISBN and so forth, and he keys in a partial or complete entry to any one or more of these. The intermediate mode is similar but more concise, and the user can set up more complex search criteria. Amongst these are stems and wildcards (i.e. incompletely defined words), and words which must *not* appear. The expert mode is command driven. It is quicker to use once the commands have been learnt, and so is best for frequent users. It also allows the user to store sets of search criteria for future use. Whitakers are considering whether a thesaurus could be added to the search software. This would allow *Bookbank* to find titles containing words which were synonyms of those used as search criteria.

Once the search criteria have been keyed in, the time taken for the search depends largely on the number of criteria and the number of hits (i.e. records which meet one or more of the search criteria). It is typically a fraction of a minute, but the user soon learns to avoid criteria which will score too many hits. The screen then shows how many hits satisfy each criterion separately, and also how many satisfy all of them at once. If the user is satisfied with the result — which usually means that there are some combined hits, but not too many — he can display the records found; otherwise he either eases or tightens the criteria and searches again.

Several display formats are provided, and the user can also design his own. One of the standard formats shows each record in full, one record per screen in a spacious layout. Another shows ten records per screen but only shows a selection of the fields and truncates some of them. An intermediate version shows three records per screen, complete but packed in a form which is less easy for the novice to read than the full screen version. In each case the user can page through all the records. He can also print all or selected records, and can transfer them to a disk file or into other applications which he has on his computer; stock control or order-placing systems, for example.

At present the software only supports single users. However, Whitakers intend to introduce software which will allow *Bookbank* to be accessed by a number of computers connected by a network.

Hardware

Bookbank runs on IBM-compatible personal computers under MS-DOS, and uses any CD-ROM drives for which the Microsoft extensions to MS-DOS are available. At the introduction of *Bookbank* this included drives from the three best-known suppliers, but others will be added.

Applications

There are two main ways in which *Bookbank* can be used by booksellers. The first is to provide a service to counter staff and customers. Any title can be retrieved by name, author, ISBN (International Standard Book Number), or a word or combination of words which appear in one or more of the fields. Details of the book or books that satisfy the search criteria are read from the screen or printed out for the customer to take away. If the bookshop uses a computer for stock records or for producing orders to suppliers, data can be transferred to these applications from *Bookbank*.

Bookbank can also be used 'behind the scenes' to help the bookseller manage his stock records (and in a similar way by librarians). This can be described best by looking at an actual case, that of Bookland & Company. Bookland is a retail bookseller with a head office in Chester and a dozen branches in neighbouring towns. The head office uses several Tandon personal computers, linked by a local area network, and a Hitachi CD-ROM drive is installed in one of these. Most of the branches have their own computers. These are equipped with modems, and data is exchanged at night between each branch computer and those at the head office. The most important application of these computers is stock control, and a complete record of each shop's stock is kept both at that shop and at the head office. A list of transactions is sent from each shop to head office each night to keep the two in step.

When the computer stock-control system is introduced at a branch, the first task is to enter details into the computer of every book held by that branch. This used to involve keying in the title, author, publisher, price and ISBN for each book; a typical branch would stock perhaps 20 000 titles, so it was a long and tedious job. With *Bookbank* the task is greatly reduced; the staff have only to enter the ISBN for each book. This need not even be keyed in, since most books now carry the ISBN in bar-code form on the cover. Bookland use a portable device (a Psion Organiser) to go through the stock, reading the ISBN from each volume with a light pen. The Organiser is then connected to the shop computer and the data transferred to it (Fig. 10.1).

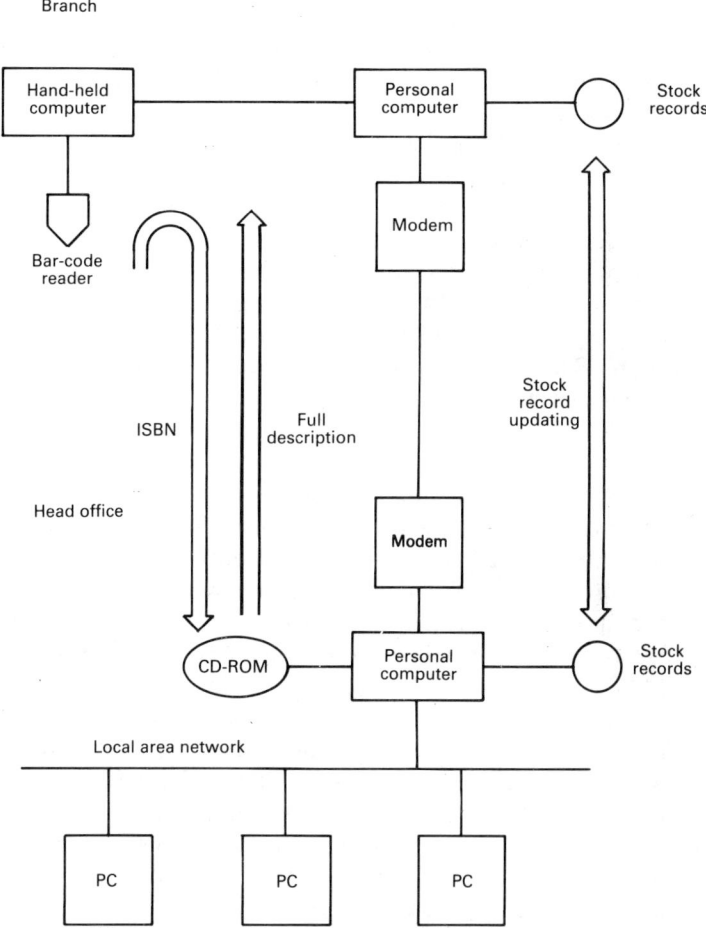

Fig. 10.1 — Stock record management at Bookland.

From there it is passed to the head-office computer, where the stock-control system looks up each ISBN on the *Bookbank* disk and completes the stock record with it. Finally the completed stock list is transmitted back to the branch. No data is keyed anywhere in the process, except the ISBNs of the few books which are not bar-coded. Bookland estimate that this saved so much effort that the first year's cost of *Bookbank* was covered when one branch had been treated in this way. In addition, of course, keying errors were avoided. The process is not very fast — about two seconds for each record retrieved from the CD-ROM — but Bookland run this as an overnight task so the time taken is not a problem.

Stock changes and orders also use *Bookbank*. When a book not already known to the stock-record system is introduced, only the ISBN need be entered, and *Bookbank* is used to fill in the details. The stock-control system at Bookland is linked to 'Teleordering', a central ordering system used by many book publishers and wholesalers. Book orders from Bookland's branches are collected at their head office and some are transmitted overnight to the Teleordering system, while others go by mail to individual publishers.

Bookland still use the microfiche lists in their retail shops. Each shop has several sales positions and several microfiche readers, but fewer subscriptions to the updating service. The most critical sales points have a new microfiche set each month, and the old sets are used for a second and perhaps even a third month in less critical positions. Bookland intend to introduce CD-ROM here too, but this will not be economical until multi-user software is available so that one disk and drive can serve several sales points. This software will be available from Whitaker, though Bookland is also working on its own version.

Data preparation and publication

The process of producing each month's *Bookbank* disk (Fig. 10.2) begins with the entering of the month's additions and changes (based on information sent by publishers) in machine-readable form. This is done at the Whitaker headquarters in London, and the data is first assembled in Whitaker's own format and then converted to the MARC exchange format. MARC, which originated at the US Library of Congress, is the nearest to an international standard for data about books that exists at the moment, although designed primarily for library use. Standards committees are working on common formats for data to be used within the whole book trade, and MARC is likely to play an important part.

The next step is carried out in London by BRS. They merge the new data with that carried over from the previous month, create the inverted index, and lay out the data to conform with the High Sierra standard and their own search software. Data and index are then written onto tape in a format that suits the disk manufacturers. This tape is sent to a suitable manufacturer — at present the former Polygram plant, now part of PDO (Philips Du Pont Optical), at Hanover; here the disks are mastered and pressed before being sent to Whitakers for checking and distribution.

The *Bookbank* system is so arranged that access to a disk can be prevented once its month's validity — plus a safety margin of a few weeks —

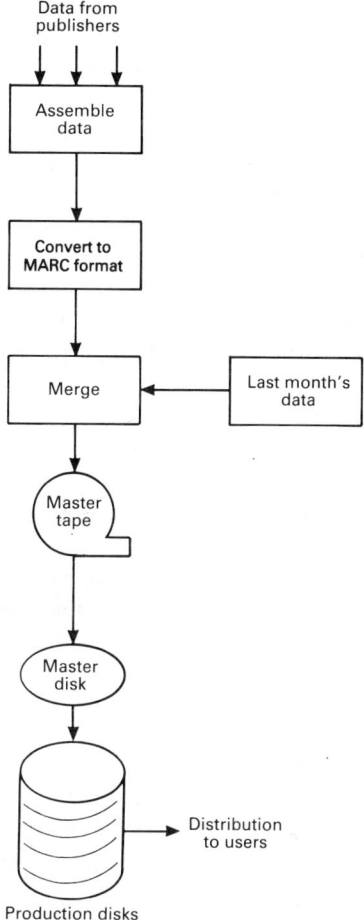

Fig. 10.2 — Preparation of the Whitaker *Bookbank* disk.

has expired. This ensures that obsolete information is not used, and also prevents users passing on old disks to others who would otherwise take out their own subscriptions.

Experience
The *Bookbank* system has been well received by those booksellers whose turnover is high enough to bear the cost of it, although some of the larger shops need the multi-access version to make it worth while. As with most of the applications we have discussed, its close resemblance to an existing (microfiche) system makes it readily acceptable. However, as the case of Bookland shows, it is at its most useful when doing things that microfiche cannot do.

Bookland are entirely happy with the system, apart from the lack — for the time being — of multiple access. The relatively slow response of CD-ROM is not a problem to them at present; but booksellers using *Bookbank* at the counter may find it slow if they are careless in their choice of search criteria. This will be more apparent where there is multiple access to the CD-ROM disk.

A minor weakness of the search software is that when the user adds an extra criterion to reduce a long hit list, the whole index rather than the existing hit list is searched for the new criterion. If the latter is fairly general, as it often is, this can take quite a long time. For example, searching the title field for 'Chester' produced about 300 hits, in a reasonable time; specifying that the title should also include 'plays' took a long time because 'plays' produced several thousand hits, even though there were only half a dozen which satisfied both criteria.

Incidentally, an interesting variant on the book catalogue idea is being developed by Nimbus Records. This is a catalogue on optical disk for recorded music shops. The number of music titles is only about 100 (a limit set by the number of 'tracks' in the CD format), so indexing is simple. However, the special feature is the use of digitized sound to record an extract from each title, to help the customer to identify the particular piece he wants. A colour image of the record cover can also be displayed. The system can include a touch-sensitive screen for ease of use, and can be linked to an electronic till.

THE BELL AND HOWELL ELECTRONIC PARTS CATALOGUE

The use of CD-ROM to publish data in image form is well demonstrated by the Bell and Howell Electronics Parts Catalogue. This is intended for use by motor parts dealers, or the spare parts stores of car repairers. It takes the place of illustrated parts catalogues on paper or microfiche. The arrangement is that a vehicle manufacturer makes its parts catalogue, and all updates, available to Bell and Howell, who convert them to CD-ROM disks. B & H sell the disks and workstations, either directly to parts dealers or else to the vehicle manufacturer. So far this has been done for two of the three big US car firms — Chrysler and General Motors — and for the US importers of Honda and Mercedes Benz cars. The system is not yet sold in Europe, but two continental manufacturers are likely to adopt it.

The disk-based system is designed to be used in very much the same way as the paper catalogue it replaces. This makes it easy to introduce. Manufacturers do not all arrange their catalogues in the same way, so B & H supply different versions of their system. The one described below is that sold to Chrysler dealers under the title PAIS (for Parts Access Information System); other versions differ only in detail.

Hardware
The hardware which supports the catalogue is based on Bell and Howell's IDB 2000 image retrieval system; IDB stands for Image Data Base. It

consists of one or more workstations and a server unit (Fig. 10.3). The workstations have large screens in portrait format; touch-screen input is an optional extra. All workstations have standard PC-type keyboards, but some keys have special labels. The server contains a few circuit boards, and slots ($5\frac{1}{4}$ inch footprint) for up to eight peripherals. A typical server uses three of these slots for a CD-ROM drive, a hard magnetic disk, and a cartridge tape drive. One or more printers can be attached. The server is built into a box which will fit under a desk, and is linked to the workstations by an Ethernet network. One server will support up to fifty workstations. Large systems can have extra magnetic disk storage in the server, and the contents of the CD-ROM are copied to this to reduce response times. Normally there are at least two workstations; many dealers buy only two, although some have up to thirty.

Database design and use

A large part of each catalogue is made up of diagrams, each of which shows some sub-unit of a particular model of the vehicle; for example a clutch assembly. The unit is drawn in 'exploded' form so that each part can be identified, and the parts on the diagram are numbered in sequence (Fig. 10.4). A typical diagram shows twenty or thirty parts. The screen is large enough to display a full page diagram at a size 25% larger than that in the printed catalogue. Screen definition is 120 pixels per inch. However, two bits per pixel are used, giving a four-level 'grey scale'; in other words each pixel can be white (which is the background colour), black or light or dark grey. The image quality is as acceptable to the user as that given by 300 pixels per inch in black and white only.

The diagrams are selected by means of a set of menus; these invite the user to choose vehicle type (car, truck or imported vehicle), model, year and subassembly. If the touch screen is fitted, the user need only touch the screen at the place where his choice appears (Fig. 10.5); or he can enter the item number from the keyboard. In the same way, he selects the part he wants from the diagram by touching its image, or keying its number. He can select any number of parts. He then presses a key, and the diagram is replaced on the screen by the catalogue text for each of the parts he selected. There may be more than one entry for a part; for example if there are options, or if a part was changed in the course of the year. Each entry shows the part number and description, and how many are used in the subassembly; also the way the part is supplied (singly, in packets of so many, or in a service kit with other parts), and other technical information. It also shows the list price, and prices at various discount levels. The discounted prices can be left out if preferred, for example when the screen can be seen by customers.

If a part has been superseded by some other, information about this is shown with the catalogue entry, as are any notes provided by the manufacturer. The dealer can also add his own notes against any entry — for example a warning if he finds one part is often confused with another.

When the user has identified the parts he wants, he marks them and they are put onto a list. He can then go on to other subassemblies, and add parts

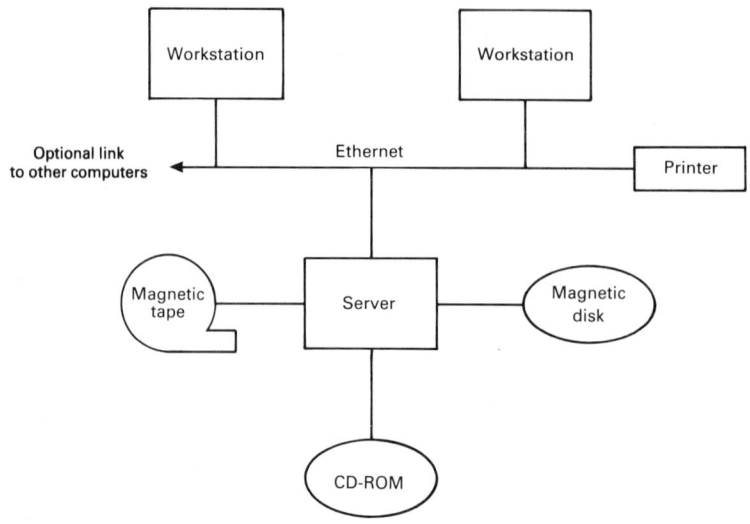

Fig. 10.3 — Bell and Howell motor parts catalogue.

from these to his list. When he has finished, he can print out the list so that the parts can be picked from the storage bins. He can call up the total cost at any of the discount rates.

The IDB 2000 system is free-standing, but if the dealer has a computer he can link to this, using an RS232 connection. The workstation screen is split into two windows, and one of these is used to emulate a computer terminal. Text can be moved from one window to the other; so for example an order list can be transferred to the computer so that it can be compared with stock records.

The CD-ROM disk is replaced by a new one at intervals, usually every three months. However, the system can handle updates in between disk changes; these are sent out on tape or, if the dealer is equipped for it, downloaded over a communications link. The updates are stored on the magnetic disk in the server and automatically replace the older data from the CD-ROM. The user sees only the latest information and need not be aware that it is an update. Notes can be added by a dealer, as already mentioned, and these are held on magnetic disk in the same way.

The optional touch screen makes the system very easy to use, and most dealers buy it for that reason. However, regular users often find it quicker to use the keyboard. This can be taken a stage further; command lines can be used to avoid the sequence of menus in selecting a diagram. Other functions are also provided, such as calling for information on a part by its name or number, and finding which models use a specific part. Appendices to the catalogue are stored as images; for example a list of addresses of parts depots. Brief 'Help' notes can be called up at any time.

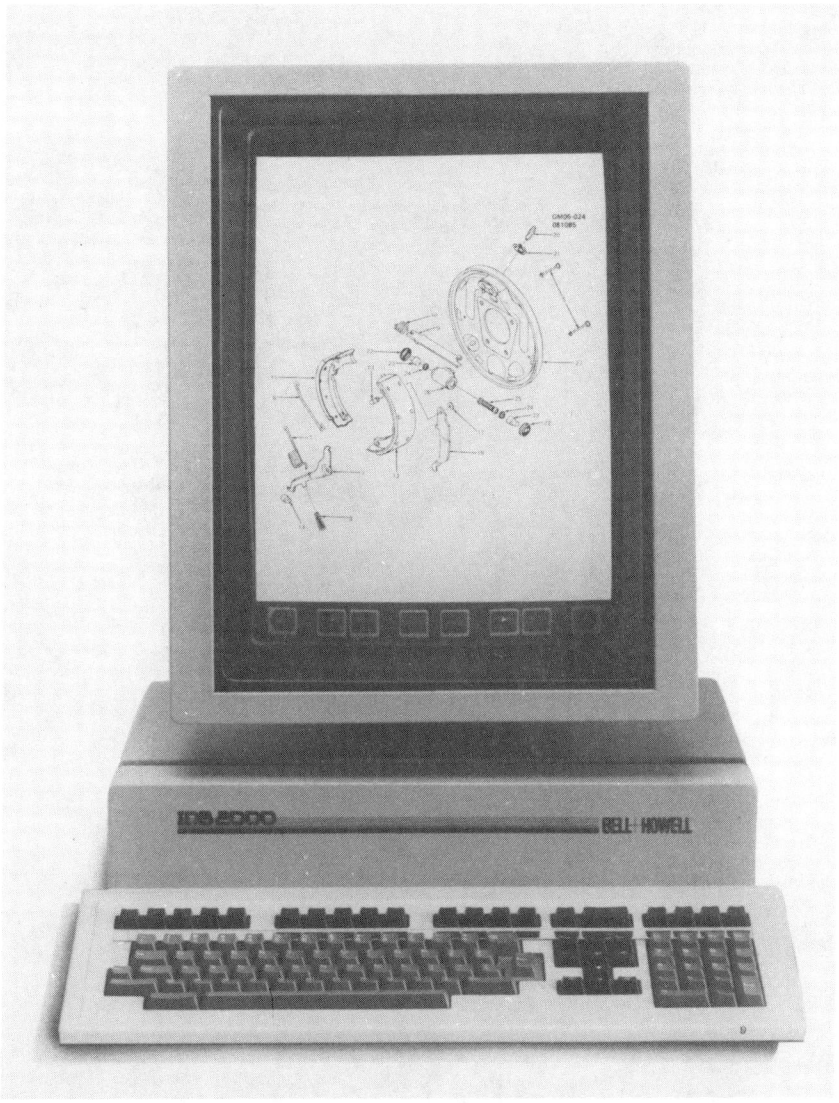

Fig. 10.4 — Page of motor parts catalogue as displayed on workstation screen. (Copyright Bell and Howell.)

Database preparation and publishing

Bell and Howell do all the scanning, editing and indexing needed to convert the catalogue from paper to CD-ROM format, and make a master tape. They pass this to any suitable disk manufacturer for mastering and pressing, and the disks are sent back to B & H for distribution. The initial preparation of the catalogue for issue on disk may take six months; after that an update can be issued within a fortnight. The Chrysler catalogue, which covers seven

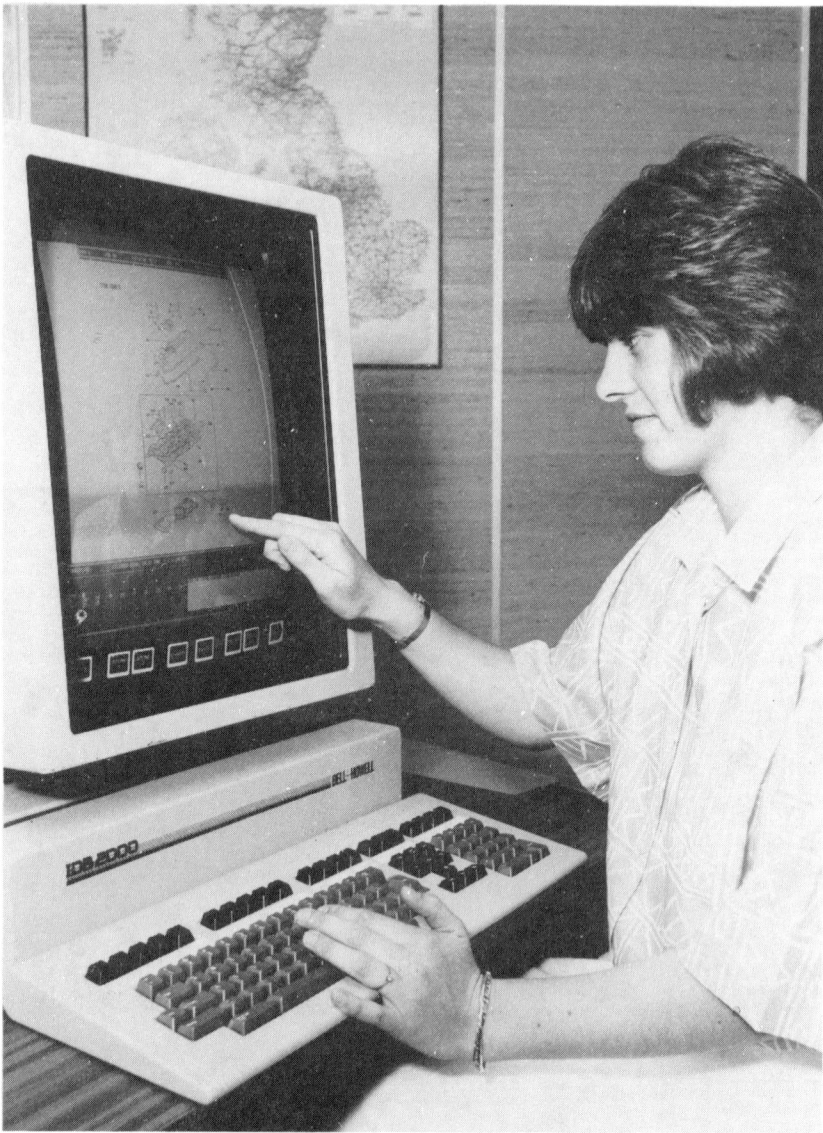

Fig. 10.5 — Touch screen terminal. (Copyright Bell and Howell.)

years' models, fits on one CD-ROM; the General Motors catalogue takes two, as there are more models, so the server sold to GM dealers has two CD-ROM drives. Diagrams are actually scanned at 300 dots per inch and eight bits per pixel; the image is then converted to 120 dots per inch and two bits per pixel, enhanced, and compressed using a method similar to Group 4 fax. A typical image, when compressed, takes up 30 kilobytes, though a more complex one may need up to 60 kilobytes. These figures apply only to line drawings; the parts catalogue does not use photographs.

Hardware

The workstation is of Bell and Howell's own design, and is built round a Motorola 68000 processor. The operating system and the retrieval software are Bell and Howell's own. The touch screen works by sensing the position of a finger with infrared beams. The screen is not coated, and a sealed version of the keyboard is available, so the workstation can be used in workshop surroundings, and some dealers give workshop staff direct access. The server is normally placed in an office.

Future versions of the system may include one to run on a PC rather than a dedicated workstation. This would be slower than the version described.

Experience

Reaction from dealers in the USA is said to be enthusiastic, and about 500 systems were sold in the first 18 months. Two major benefits are savings in space and time. The paper catalogues, in several volumes, take up several feet of shelf space. Each reference may involve looking up several pages, and only one person can use a volume at a time. Just as important is the reduction of errors in the supply or ordering of parts, as part numbers no longer need to be remembered or copied. It is claimed that new recruits can use the system effectively within days, whereas the paper system took as many months. Users also find that the screen images, being larger than those in the printed catalogue, are easier to read. (Microfiche is not used by the motor trade in the USA.)

Bell and Howell will extend the use of their CD-ROM system to other kinds of data, such as service manuals. For European motor manufacturers these may be combined with the parts catalogue in a single product. This would include photographs as well as diagrams. Image compression is far less effective for photographs than for line drawings, so fewer images would fit on a disk. The possibility of using CD-ROM to store airline servicing data is also being considered; this data is mainly text with few diagrams and photographs.

Comment

This application shows the benefits made possible by the high data density of CD-ROM, and by the ease of access to the data when it has been suitably prepared. Care has been taken to make the system acceptable to customers, even to the extent of providing an access method (the touch screen) which may be by-passed by many users. Notice that although the catalogue diagrams can be directly scanned, this does not complete their input; it is also necessary to define 'touch points' for touch-screen response, and links to the text. The use of grey-scale image coding and compression gives good image quality at a fairly low cost in storage (30 kilobytes per page), but this only works well for line drawings; photographs need much more storage space for each image.

DISCUSSION OF EXAMPLES

The examples show two very different approaches to the publishing of catalogues on CD-ROM. In the first example, the catalogue stores text only, and standard (though slightly customized) access software is used to give very flexible access to the data stored. The disk and access software are designed to run on any drive and any PC that conform to the standards which have now been established; the publishers do not aim to sell hardware to support the disk. The disk is sold by subscription, and each issue is a complete replacement for its predecessor; there is no provision for updating information in between issues.

The Bell and Howell system, in contrast, stores all the data as page images, even when it is available as text (with minor exceptions). The access system is designed for this specific application, and emulates the existing paper-based methods with as little change as is possible. The disk is intended for use with a specific hardware system, which is proprietary; and Bell and Howell's interest is in selling this hardware, rather than in selling the information carried by the disk. The disk is replaced less frequently, but there is provision for combining the disk data with updates and other information entered at the site.

There are some features in common. In both cases the catalogue follows closely a version which has appeared in another medium, paper or microfiche. In both cases there is provision for linking the system with existing computers and transferring data to them from the disk. And in both cases, but particularly the second, a good deal of thought has been given to how the customer will actually use the system.

In the last chapter there was a strong emphasis on the importance of close contact between the system supplier and the user. In the case of publishing the situation is rather different; most of the design problems have to be resolved between the publisher, the supplier of the access software, and the company which actually makes the disks. The user buys standard hardware (though from a single source in the motor parts case) and expects it to 'plug and play'. In fact the hardware design presents no unusual problems; most of the effort goes into designing the access software, and arranging and indexing the data on the disk, to produce a product which requires little skill to use. These are very specialized tasks, and in neither case has the data publisher tried to do them in house.

Although the examples both refer to catalogues, many other applications might have been illustrated. Bibliographic data is very much like catalogues, but often the aim is not only to identify an item but to present an abstract of its contents. Sometimes this is transferred into another system, such as a word processor. Financial data may be examined in the same way, or it may be transferred into a spreadsheet or some other program as a basis for further work; indeed, one publisher issues CD-ROM disks which use a spreadsheet as their access software. Maps and charts may be displayed in a ship or vehicle and used for navigation. The one common feature is that the data structure and the access software make it easy for the user to find his way through a vast amount of data, and to have it presented in the way that suits him best.

CONCLUSION

CD-ROM has established itself as a publishing medium, and is well ahead of all other forms of optical storage in this respect. Some data is published in this way because it needs to be in machine-readable form, so that it can be further processed or copied for use elsewhere. However, most CD-ROM disks carry data which will be presented on a display for human attention. The advantage of optical storage over conventional publishing methods in this case depends on the access software, which helps the user to find what he wants quickly and easily from amongst a very large amount of data. The same approach — indeed, often much the same software — is used in on-line databases. The choice between these and CD-ROM depends on the nature of the data, and in particular on the frequency with which it is updated. It also depends on the way in which the customer wants to use it; a professional information worker can make very effective use of an on-line database, but a less experienced user may find it expensive and rather unnerving.

Even so, these are early days for optical publishing, and many possibilities remain to be explored. In particular, the integration of text with images has not yet been mastered. This is demonstrated by the Bell and Howell system, which stores the text in image form, in spite of the limitations of this approach; and by the few illustrated reference books which have appeared on CD-ROM, which require the reader to switch between text and picture rather than presenting the two in context. We may expect a good deal of progress over the next two or three years. We can expect the CD-I (or CD-ROM XA) and DVI formats, which combine static or animated images and possibly sound with data, to be introduced as well; but these are intended primarily as products for the home and it has yet to be seen whether they have much to offer the professional.

Meanwhile the rate of publication is increasing fast. In mid-1988 there were about 200 databases available on CD-ROM, but this number could well double over the next year. The published disks can be classified according to the data they carry, as follows:

Bibliographic	44%
Commercial and financial	18%
Administrative and legal	13%
Scientific, technical and medical	11%
General reference (e.g. dictionaries)	5%
Education	4%
Non-alphanumeric	5%

However, it is not likely that these proportions will persist. In particular, librarians and information scientists have been quick to take up CD-ROM as an alternative to microfiche or on-line databases, and the field is now quite well served. In other areas CD-ROM is only just getting a foothold, and more rapid development is likely.

Under 'non-alphanumeric' are several disks carrying maps of various kinds, two carrying sound samples, one carrying only pictures (although a few of the disks in other classes carry pictures as well as text), and a single one carrying software — this is published by one of the PC user groups and carries its whole library of public domain (and user supported) programs.

In summary, CD-ROM now seems to be poised for take-off; hardware, software, standards and databases all exist and have been proved. Interaction between an increasing range of CD-ROM databases and a growing number of users will see read-only disks firmly established as a publishing medium over the next two or three years.

Other forms of read-only optical storage are far less advanced. Videodisks are used for training and education, including the 'Domesday' project, but nowadays rarely for storage of computer data. Read-only optical disks to other formats are scarcely used. Optical cards are showing more promise, especially in the medical record field — which of course is a data transfer application rather than publishing. However, although a number of trials have been carried out, there has not yet been a full implementation of a system based on optical card.

11

What next?

In this final chapter we shall review the way that optical storage is developing at present, and try to foresee how things may go in the future. First, however, to put this in context, we shall take a quick look at the history of optical storage.

A LITTLE HISTORY

In a sense, optical storage began when photoelectric readers were first used, in place of mechanical devices, to read punched tape and Hollerith cards. Since the data was still mechanically recorded, this did not lead to higher data density; nor, so early in the development of microelectronics, did it do much to improve reliability. Once photoelectric readers had this foothold, however, effort was put into their development, and this led eventually to the excellent devices which are a vital part of modern optical stores.

Punched tape and card were significant in another way; they made the computer user familiar with write-once storage media. This was not a matter of choice, and when rewritable alternatives — magnetic tape and disk — came along, they were adopted with enthusiasm. Even so, many programmers clung to punched cards long after their machines were fitted with magnetic peripherals.

Magnetic storage was a big enough step forward to keep the user happy for several years. However, some computer engineers recognized that there was a limit to the storage density that was practical with magnetic media. Optical media offered a way round this limit, and several computer companies and research laboratories began to take an interest in it. The ultimate aim was always erasable storage, but write-once or read-only media were seen to be useful development tools. One or two researchers foresaw that they might also be the basis of a commercial product.

Photographic media
The obvious step was to start with photographic media, since these were well developed and understood, and high-resolution materials were already available. The problem then was to develop access mechanisms which would allow digital data to be written onto photographic film at high density, and retrieved at high speed.

A simple device using photographic film was developed in the research laboratories at ICL. In this, a light beam could be moved in two dimensions over a rectangular piece of photographic film. To write data, the beam was scanned over the film; it was left on where a '1' was to be written, and turned off to write a '0'. The film was then developed to make the latent pattern of data permanent and visible. The film — or a photographic copy of it — was replaced in the same device or a similar one, but this time the beam was permanently on and a photodetector sensed the light passing through the film. This was a truly random-access device; it functioned as a read-only rather than a WORM store, because of the processing stage between writing and reading.

This store never went beyond the laboratory, but a lot was learnt from it; not least the fact that a long beam path, such as was needed to scan the static media in two dimensions, calls for an extremely rigid structure.

IBM used photographic media in a much more elaborate device, which did go into production but without much commercial success. This was the 'Photochip' store. The data was recorded on small glass plates; a number of these were loaded into a mechanism which could pick any one of them and load it into a reading station, in the same manner as the jukeboxes which we described in an earlier chapter.

Holographic techniques

Another device which never reached production was 'Mnemos', proposed in the late 70s. This was a cross between microfiche and computer data storage, storing photographic images on a rotating disk. Each image on the disk was rectangular and corresponded to a single source image, but instead of conventional optics the device used holography. Holography is an optical technique based on the interference between light beams. It is not easy to describe in simple terms (though an attempt is made in Appendix 2), but its chief feature is that light from every point in the source contributes to every point in the image. The image bears no visible resemblance to the source, but nevertheless the source can be reproduced from a recorded image (or 'hologram'); even if a part of the image is obliterated, the whole of the source can be reconstructed although with reduced contrast. This is a very useful property when dealing with imperfect media, and allowed Mnemos to use images much smaller than those used on microfiche; several thousand images were stored on a 12 inch disk. A powerful laser light source was necessary becuse the images were so small, and this and the very high definition required of the film were probably the main reasons for the failure of the scheme.

Another proposal based on holography was put forward by a firm in the USA called Holofile. It was based on a prototype developed by one of the big American research laboratories, with government funding. The medium was again photographic, and was a flat film of the same size as a standard microfiche. A two-dimensional array of light sources, or rather shutters, was used (called a page composer); this had 100×100 elements, and the pattern displayed by it was recorded as a single hologram. 20 000 such holograms were to be recorded on the 4 inch by 6 inch film, giving it a capacity of 200 megabits (or about 25 megabytes). The proposal was not followed up; probably the page composer turned out to be too expensive or unreliable, and again a high-powered laser would have been needed.

Ablative media

A more successful product, and one which broke away from photographic media, was called Unicon. This took advantage of the power of the laser to introduce what we now call the ablative technique. The medium took the form of a very short wide polyester tape coated with a thin metal film, which was wrapped round a drum for use. As the tape passed under the reading station, the laser beam was turned on or off to record a single track of data, with holes burnt by the laser representing one signal level and untouched film the other. The laser was moved a short way across the tape before the next track was recorded. There were various models; a typical one stored 800 megabytes with a data rate of 1 megabyte per second and average access time 8 seconds. The Unicon was an expensive device, but its speed and high data capacity made it attractive for some purposes; one was the recording of seismic data by oil companies. It had a modest commercial success.

Meanwhile the search for rewritable media went on, and very many materials were tried without much to show for the effort. IBM even experimented with materials which had to be used at extremely low temperatures; in one device a disk coated with such a material spun inside a cryogenic enclosure, and was accessed by a light beam passing through a window from an optical system at room temperature.

Photochromic media — and holography again

A rather more practical medium was developed in the UK by the Plessey Company. This material worked on the photochromic principle (a variant of that used in some sun-glasses). When light of a specific wavelength fell on a thin film of the medium, it became opaque; light of another wavelength turned it clear again. The gas-filled lasers which were just becoming available at this time made suitable light sources, and the medium took the form of tape; the sensitive film was deposited on a clear substrate (in fact cine film base). The device could also use tapes carrying photographic emulsion, though of course this turned it into a read-only store.

The Plessey development was another that used holographic rather than classical optics; holography not only reduced the effect of media defects, it also made the location of the tape relative to the optical head less critical. In this device the array of light sources representing data bits was linear rather than two dimensional (Fig. 11.1). Successive holograms along the tape could be overlapped without interfering with each other. However, the low sensitivity of the photochromic material and the high cost of lasers of the right wavelengths made it unlikely that a commercial product would result, so Plessey abandoned the device.

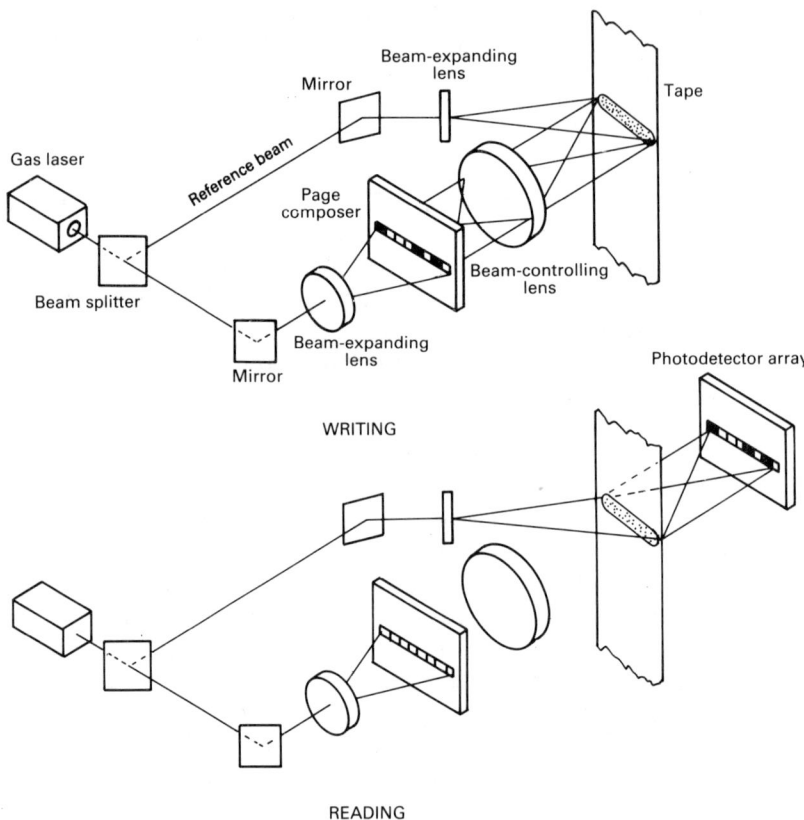

Fig. 11.1 — Plessey holographic tape store (simplified).

Consolidation

By this time the mainstream of development was centred on conventional optics, and media in disk form. Disk mechanisms could give adequate performance in terms of both data rate and access time, with purely mechanical means of access; electronic scanning of the medium, and multiple light sources (or page composers), had proved too expensive and unreliable. Several developers had also realized that there was a commercial case for WORM media, without losing sight of the long-term aim of a rewritable disk.

Developments in the computer field were not isolated. In the entertainment field the videodisk, though not a commercial success, was a remarkable technical development. The spin-off, in the form of reliable lasers, optical detectors, and servo tracking and focus systems, made practicable the first successful optical stores for computers. Not surprisingly these used the same disk size, 12 inch, as the videodisk, although both media and mechanisms diverged from the videodisk design.

Compact Audio disk followed a little later, and unlike videodisk it has been a winner. CD-ROM has ridden on its shoulders, adopting not only design principles but even media production plant set up for the audio product. The fusion of sound, graphics and data in CD-I and DVI is a natural progression. Compact Audio, unlike videodisk, used semiconductor rather than gas lasers from the start; these have become universal in optical storage for computers.

Dealing with imperfect media
A major hurdle faced by optical store developers was the difficulty of making media free from defects. This had less to do with the nature of the materials themselves (substrates as well as coatings) than with the very high data density. On optical media, a small defect may obliterate several adjacent data elements; on magnetic media, where signal elements are much larger — at least in one dimension — the effect is far less. Holography looked like a solution, since in a holographic recording there is no one-to-one relation between data bits and points on the medium; quite a large defect can be tolerated without any loss of data, but only a fall in the signal-to-noise ratio. However, as we have seen, all the work that went into holographic methods has failed to produce a commercial product.

Some Japanese manufacturers recognized that bit-mapped images could take advantage of the high degree of redundancy contained in written text; the human eye and brain make up a very powerful error-correction system. Thus the level of defects found on optical disks was acceptable in this particular application. Optical document storage systems based on bit-mapped images without error correction were introduced in Japan, though they did not attract many customers in the West.

Error correction
The eventual solution to the problem of disk defects was the development of powerful error-correction codes. Error correction had of course been in use for a long time (and error detection even longer) in communication systems, on magnetic tape devices and also in some semiconductor stores. However, relatively simple codes sufficed for magnetic storage, since the lower data density meant that most defects affected only a few storage elements. In addition, data was normally rewritten if found to be in error. It was widely believed that more extensive error correction would require a great deal of redundancy in the data. The low cost per bit of optical storage made higher redundancy acceptable, but in fact error-correction methods have been developed which are surprisingly economical in this respect. They do involve complex algorithms, and so need powerful processing to implement them. The rapidly falling cost of processing power, which results from the increasing degree of integration of microcircuits, has made this acceptable. In fact it is now easy to provide, at a reasonable cost, error rates as good as most customers require. This is demonstrated by the fact that (as we have seen) many CD-ROM drive manufacturers do not feel it necessary to support the 1 in 10^{16} error rate which can be achieved with CD-ROM. It is

interesting that powerful error-correction systems are now being adopted for magnetic tape, for example in the IBM 3480 cartridge and in the computer version of digital audio tape.

In this brief look at the history of optical storage we have only touched on a few examples of early development work. There was of course very much more, particularly in the USA, where a great deal of government money was spent; not to mention the millions of dollars spent on a 14 inch disk development programme which passed through several companies before it was finally abandoned.

WHERE WE ARE NOW
This brings us up to the present, where WORM optical disk is an established product; so is CD-ROM, and there is a limited market for other read-only disks.

The market has taken a cautious view of optical storage, more so in Europe than in North America and Japan. Although WORM devices have been on the market since 1985, it was only in 1987 and 1988 that they began to be used here for much more than pilot schemes. This was partly due to the natural caution of users, who know from experience that pioneering can be painful and joining the second wave can bring much more benefit. However, two other factors have had an effect. Firstly, optical storage was oversold when it was in its development stage. It was 'a year away' for several years before it actually appeared. This caused a credibility gap, which is only now being filled by the demonstration of successful projects like that at the Britannia. Secondly, many users are holding back until the issue of standards is resolved. They may not be interested in data interchange, but they are very much concerned with continuity of supply and competition between suppliers.

12 inch WORM
12 inch WORM disks have attracted some important users, though not many of them yet; in contrast to the USA, the government in the UK has not been in the forefront. A large proportion of the early users are storing text as document images rather than in character-coded form. This is often because they have a backlog of data which was not captured at source, or because they want to retain existing procedures for creating documents. The balance is likely to move towards character coding. In most cases the application is, for obvious reasons, partly or entirely archival. 12 inch disks seem to appeal most to large companies, maybe because of the scale of the investment involved. It has been predicted that at least half the 12 inch drives will be used in jukeboxes, although this is not yet the case because so many installations have been pilot or small-scale schemes.

$5\frac{1}{4}$ inch WORM
The $5\frac{1}{4}$ inch WORM disk, on the other hand, is a mainstream product which suits a much wider range of users. In spite of its later start it has made very rapid headway in the market; no doubt many users are prepared to

experiment who would be less willing to meet the cost of a 12 inch system. Also users can see that there is some progress towards standards, at least to the extent that standard unrecorded media can be used in many drives. There is plenty of competition in this disk size; there is also the prospect that disks recorded in current drives may be playable in future multi-function drives which will take rewritable disks as well.

CD-ROM

CD-ROM has been slow to find customers outside the USA too, but for a different reason. There is less of a credibility gap, because Compact Audio is well known and successful. Instead there is the 'chicken and egg' problem. Data publishers are reluctant to invest in CD-ROM versions until there is a large population of users who can handle CD-ROM; and users are reluctant to invest in CD-ROM drives until they can see a good choice of databases to run on them. Although the number of published disks is now increasing fast, quite a few of them are of little use outside the USA. Of course some users go into CD-ROM for the sake of a single database which is of particular interest to them, but these seem to be in the minority at present. The typical user is the librarian or information scientist with a range of interests to satisfy.

CD-ROM has also suffered from a standards problem, but to a far less extent than WORM because CD-ROM is well standardized at the physical level. Now that the 'High Sierra' format has been defined, standards are no longer a deterrent; but disks to other standards will exist for some time yet. An effective means of integrating images and text has yet to be developed; this may be found in the CDI format (or its derivative CD-ROM XA).

Other read-only disks

Other read-only formats are not important, although a number of disks based on videodisk formats have been published. These have the advantage (in the 12 inch size) of a rather higher volume capacity than CD-ROM; but access time is much longer, disk cost per megabyte is no lower, and mechanisms are far more bulky and expensive. Most databases (with their indexes) are in any case within the 600 megabyte capacity limit of a single CD-ROM disk; where they are not, it is cheaper and often more convenient to use two CD-ROM drives rather than one of the other type. For these reasons, it is unlikely that videodisk-based devices have much future as computer peripherals. On the other hand, for non-data purposes the 'interactive videodisk' — a player with its own screen, but under loose control from a computer — does have its place in training and advertising applications.

Read-only stores using other disk formats have been proposed, but little has been seen of them. There is likely to be a small, rather specialized, market for such disks aimed at users who already have WORM drives, or in applications where the higher performance is thought to justify the higher cost.

A number of other optical storage products — rewritable disks, cards, and tape — are in advanced stage of development; indeed rewritable disks should be widely available by the time this book is read. The next section will consider the prospects for these new products.

WHAT ABOUT THE FUTURE?

It is always rash to try to predict the future, especially in a book which may be read several years after it is written. It is doubly dangerous in a field where change is as rapid as it is in optical storage. Even so, it would be unfair to readers not to include some intelligent guesses about what may come about in the next few years, based on research and development that is already taking place.

As a start, there are some products which are so near the market that their technical success is a safe bet, although their reception by the market is less easy to forecast. The most important of these is rewritable optical disk.

Rewritable disk development

Rewritable disk drives, using magneto-optic techniques, have been announced by several companies although at the time of writing only a few have been delivered. They will certainly find a place in the market, particularly for the storage of data and programs which have to be immediately available but are not often accessed. In spite of some sweeping claims in the press, it is unlikely that rewritable products will destroy the market for either WORM optical storage or magnetic disk, though they will obviously have some impact. They will have a bigger impact on the market for magnetic tape devices where these are used for back-up, just as WORM drives are already replacing magnetic tape for archiving.

Drives designed for magneto-optic disks can be made to handle WORM disks as well without great difficulty. (The converse is not the case.) They can easily handle read-only disks in compatible formats too, although we have seen that these are not particularly attractive. Such 'multi-function' drives, handling at least two types of media, are likely to be popular on smaller systems where the ability to mix disks is thought to be useful. Larger systems may prefer to have separate drives, each optimized for its own type of disk.

At present, the $5\frac{1}{4}$ inch disk is the most popular for rewritable storage, as it is for WORM. A lot of effort is being put into $3\frac{1}{2}$ inch rewritable disk drives, and rather less into $3\frac{1}{2}$ inch WORM. Only two products were announced in 1988, but as more appear they will obviously be popular in personal computers and other small systems whose peripheral slots use the $3\frac{1}{2}$ inch footprint. It has even been suggested that they will compete with floppy disk, but it seems unlikely that either drive or media price will approach that of the floppy disk for several years — if ever.

All the rewritable disks announced so far use magneto-optic recording; it has proved easier to produce this type of disk with an adequate lifetime than other types. There is still room for argument as to what is adequate, and while the number of rewrite cycles is finite, users will have to take care; especially with test programs, which can repeatedly and rapidly access a single address on the disk. However, the figures now being specified are good enough for most purposes, so long as the system is able to recognize the signs of over-use and warn the user to transfer his data to a new disk. These caveats do show that a rewritable optical disk cannot be regarded as simply a plug-in replacement for a magnetic disk.

In the course of two or three years it is likely that two more recording technologies, phase change and dye–polymer, will be introduced for rewritable disks. These have been in development for some time, but the manufacture of media which allow a large number of rewrite cycles has been harder than expected. It is perhaps significant that both these types of media are used in WORM storage. Once the media problem is solved, phase-change and dye–polymer rewritable stores should be cheaper than the magneto-optic kind, because they do not need additional magnetic components. Indeed they are so similar to existing WORM drives that conversion may be possible.

A semiconductor laser has recently been developed which emits blue light, at half the wavelength of that from the red lasers in common use. In principle this makes possible a fourfold increase in density, and hence in disk capacity. As yet only low-powered devices have been made; if blue lasers of adequate power and reliability can be made at a reasonable price, they are likely to replace the red lasers.

The future for WORM
WORM drives for 12 inch disks are unlikely to be made in multifunction versions; indeed there has been singularly little interest in making rewritable media in this size. Large WORM disks are likely to continue to be adopted as the best medium for archival storage. However, there will be strong competition for 12 inch disks from the 14 inch WORM disks that are just reaching the market. These have three or four times the capacity of the 12 inch disk, a ratio which is likely to persist as both varieties of disk are upgraded. It also seems likely that they will have the advantage of a single standard; the one maker now in the market has established such a lead over potential competitors that they may well find it wise to adopt the same standard. There are not likely to be many competitors, and prices will remain much higher than those for $5\frac{1}{4}$ inch products.

The blue laser mentioned in the last section would be equally usable with WORM media.

Read-only disks
It seems safe to predict that CD-ROM will be the dominant read-only format for some years, with image and sound being integrated with text by the CDI (CD-ROM XA) extensions to its format, and animated images by DVI. The higher-capacity version being developed by Nimbus is likely to make more headway in the entertainment market than the computer field, but it will probably win a modest following. The use of videodisk formats for

computer data is not likely to be continued. Disks compatible with WORM or multi-function drives may be used, but they are likely to take only a small place in the market.

Card and tape
The future of other forms of optical media is uncertain; the disk format has intrinsic advantages with which it is not easy to compete. Optical card is convenient where a small amount of data has to be stored in pocketable form, but has little attraction for other purposes. Optical tape claims very high volume capacity, but in a less convenient form than disk, and tape-based media have not proved ideal for archiving in the past. The same applies, to some degree, to flexible optical disks. On the whole it seems a safe bet that rigid disks will continue to dominate optical storage.

The impact of DAT
There have been claims in the press that digital audio tape will not only displace Compact Audio disks, but will also in its computer form take over the optical storage market. This seems — in both cases — an unlikely prediction. DAT is far from ideal as a publishing medium, since unlike Compact Audio and CD-ROM each volume has to be copied separately. Admittedly the audio cassette has been a success, but this does not imply that a rewritable medium has any advantage in itself, at least for publishing data rather than music. We have already seen that the cost of the medium is usually trivial in comparison to that of the data it carries; also that the random access feature of CD-ROM is of great importance — in fact faster rather than slower access is desirable. For archiving, there is no evidence that tape can offer the data lifetime and ease of storage that is a feature of WORM disk. DAT may be a cheaper medium than rewritable optical disk for back-up, but it is a good deal slower. Probably DAT will find itself a place in the computer market; it is hard to see that it will be a dominant one.

Back to holography?
One possible joker in the pack is holography. We have seen that previous attempts at holographic storage came to nothing. This was partly because the technology proved hard to implement, and partly because its main advantage — immunity to media defects and damage — can now be matched by modern error correcting codes. However, fresh work on holographic components is reported from Japan and this could lead to novel products — probably still based on the disk format.

And after that?
These predictions should take us into the early nineties, perhaps even the mid-nineties. Beyond this it is hard to go; there is time for new technologies which are as yet unknown to be developed into real products. However it is reasonable to guess that WORM optical disk will continue to be the preferred medium for archival storage; also that rewritable disks will eventually develop to the point where they pose a serious challenge to

magnetic disks. They will have displaced magnetic tape for most purposes before this point, and will also have made major inroads into the micrographics market. In the publishing field, CD-ROM is still likely to be important, with its format extended to cover an effective combination of text, image, and probably animated images and sound as well. However it will need to be supplemented by a more advanced format which will offer higher performance; no doubt it will also offer higher capacity and perhaps smaller physical size, something which the precise standards of CD-ROM make it unable to support.

So we have to conclude this book on a note of uncertainty. In a second edition this chapter would no doubt be much changed — maybe removed altogether. But without any doubt, optical storage in one form or another will be playing an increasingly important part in the computers of the next decade, and beyond. If this book has made any contribution to the better understanding and application of optical storage, it has served its purpose. Goodbye, and good computing!

Appendix 1
Further reading

There is a distinct lack of books which cover the whole subject of optical storage, although there are plenty of high-priced reports; most of these are concerned with the market prospects. However, electronic publishing (including CD-ROM) has an extensive literature, mostly American, and much of it is listed in the *CD-ROM Directory* discussed below. Many papers in technical journals discuss details of the technology, and articles in business journals discuss the progress of optical storage and the pros and cons of using it. The technical literature is almost entirely in English, since European and Japanese engineers find it convenient to publish in this language.

BOOKS

Optical Storage Technology 1988 — a State of the Art Review
W. Saffady: Meckler (USA), 1988

A fairly concise account (about 100 pages of text) in two sections covering read-only and read/write optical disks, with some mention of tape and card and of turnkey systems. It thus covers much of the same ground as the book you are reading, though in a very different style. There are many references to papers describing technology, commercial products and applications; the book tends to list these rather than discuss them in detail. The references are linked to a bibliography of about 35 pages and thus form a useful guide to the literature. There is also a list of vendors' names and addresses (only 4 in the UK). The book is revised annually; the first (1986) edition was called *Optical Disks for Data and Document Storage*.

Principles of Optical Disk Systems
G. Bouwhuis, J. Braat, A. Huijser, J. Pasman, G. van Rosmalen, K. Schouhamer Immink: Adam Hilger (Bristol), 1985

The authors are members of the team at Philips Research Laboratories whose work led up to the development of the LMS range of WORM disk drives and also to CD-ROM. The book is thus very authoritative. It discusses the physics and engineering of optical recording, and the use of error-correcting codes, in detail. Some chapters are highly mathematical. Anyone concerned with designing, rather than using, optical storage devices cannot afford to be without the book.

Videodisc and Optical Memory Systems
J. Isailovic: Prentice-Hall (USA), 1985

This is mainly a detailed technical account of videodisk hardware and the underlying physics. A short chapter on optical data storage is almost an afterthought, but does include some useful material on the physics of the recording process. Worth reading if you want to know more about videodisks.

The Brady Guide to CD-ROM
L. Buddine and E. Young: Prentice-Hall (USA), 1987

A comprehensive guide (nearly 500 pages) to the technology and applications of CD-ROM, including detailed descriptions of a number of commercial retrieval software suites, a small selection of CD-ROM databases, and the processes involved in publishing on CD-ROM. It also summarizes the contents of the *Red Book* and *Yellow Book*, which are the detailed specifications of CD-audio and CD-ROM but are not yet generally available. Very useful to any prospective CD-ROM user who wants to do more than buy a ready-made system.

The CD-ROM Directory 1989
K. Churchill (ed.): TFPL Publishing (London), 1988

This will presumably be published yearly. It gives brief tabulated details of over 400 databases published on CD-ROM, together with information on publishers, books, journals and conferences and a very brief summary of the technology and prospects of CD-ROM. A useful reference book for prospective CD-ROM users. A similar directory is published by Meckler, although this has a more American outlook and the first edition was not well edited.

ECMA Standard 119: Volume and File Structure of CD-ROM for Information Interchange — 2nd Edition December 1987

This defines the 'High Sierra' format. It is technically identical with ISO standard 9660 (but ECMA standards come free!). Not easy reading. It will shortly be joined by a standard defining the low-level structure, equivalent to the *Yellow Book* mentioned in Chapter 4.

Optics
W. T. Welford: Oxford University Press, 1981

A typical textbook; gives a more rigorous explanation of holography than that in Appendix 2 of the book you are reading.

Optical Information Systems 1987/88: Buyers Guide and Consultant Directory
N. Desmarais: Meckler (USA), 1988

Optical Storage Technology: a Bibliography
W. Saffady: Meckler (USA), 1988

The last two items are in principle available from Meckler's office in the UK, but since I have been unable to get copies I cannot comment on their contents.

JOURNALS

There are a number of these, mostly published in the USA. The most useful are:

Optical Memory News

This is published in the USA as an offshoot of the consulting activities of Edward Rothchild, a leading expert in the field. It is published monthly, and although an American publication it gives full coverage to events elsewhere. Its interest has diminished since Rothchild Consultants set up a (more expensive) information service in parallel, but it is still much the most useful journal for those interested in current and forthcoming commercial developments.

Optical Data Systems

Published monthly in the UK by Microinfo, this is a slighter publication than *Optical Memory News* and the news is sometimes less fresh. Although much of the contents refer to developments in the USA, it gives good coverage of British and European products, and is worth reading for this reason, or as a cheaper and more accessible alternative to OMN.

CONFERENCES AND EXHIBITIONS

The main UK conference on optical storage is *Optical Storage International*, which is held in London annually — usually in June. The proceedings are published in book form by Meckler. It is a two-day event with parallel sessions; it covers technical and commercial developments and a good deal of time is given to applications. The standard of speakers is very variable but the best are excellent. A series of purely commercial presentations was included in 1988, but these were so poorly attended that they may not be continued.

A small but fairly comprehensive trade exhibition is associated with this conference; it is open to those not attending the conference.

Rothchild Consultants hold a *Technical Opportunity Conference* and exhibition in London yearly, usually in April.

Many other conferences are held in the USA, and a few in Japan and Europe.

New products are usually announced at Comdex or one of the other trade shows in the USA, or at Hanover Fair in Europe, but many of them can be seen at the annual *Which Computer* show in Birmingham (January or February). CD-ROM drives and small WORM drives can also be seen at the various personal computer shows.

OTHER SOURCES

The names of manufacturers, distributors, value-added retailers, consultants and trade associations are not listed in this book because such a list would soon be out of date. They can be found in reference books such as the *Computer Users' Year Book* or obtained from bodies such as the Department of Trade and Industry's Business and Technical Advisory Service, the National Computing Centre, the Association of Professional Computer Consultants, the Association of Independent Computer Specialists or (for small systems) the nearest Microsystems Centre. Trade shows, and their catalogues, are also a useful source of information; but not all the major companies choose to exhibit. Directories published in the USA tend to have very few entries for companies elsewhere.

Appendix 2
Holography

The optical storage devices which are on the market at present all use conventional optics, and data is written and read serially along a track which is only a micron or so wide. There are other approaches, of which the most interesting is the use of holographic images. Much of the early development work in optical storage was based on holography, and some development work continues.

Holography is not easy to explain without using mathematics, and what follows is very much simplified; but for our purposes we need not go into detail. We can start from the fact that when light beams from two separate sources fall on the same area of a surface, they do not simply add to produce a brighter patch; they actually interfere with each other to produce a pattern. We do not notice this in ordinary life, because all the usual light sources are relatively large and give out light which is made up of a mixture of wavelengths, and random in phase; the interference patterns are so complex, and so blurred, that they are not distinguishable. However, we do occasionally see interference effects, for example the coloured streaks we see when we look at a compact disk, or coloured bands on an oily puddle. We can also see interference patterns in another medium if we throw two stones into a pond; where the two sets of circular ripples meet, a static pattern is formed.

Sharp, simple interference patterns occur if we use monochromatic light from two point sources which are locked to each other in phase; for example, two pinholes illuminated by the same lamp. If we add more sources, the pattern becomes more complex. It can be shown that the pattern holds all the information we need to work out the number and position of the sources which caused it, if we know about just one of the sources. The science of holography came into being when it was realized that the physical process can itself be reversed; given an interference pattern and a light source identical to just one of those used to create the pattern (described as the reference source), it is possible to re-create an image of all the light sources which produced the pattern. An interference pattern with this property is called a *hologram*.

As we add more sources we find that the calculation of their position from the interference pattern gets much harder, but it is just as easy to re-create them physically as it was before. A logical step, therefore, is to use a row or matrix of sources which can each be on or off, together with a constant reference source (Fig. A2.1), and in fact some optical stores have

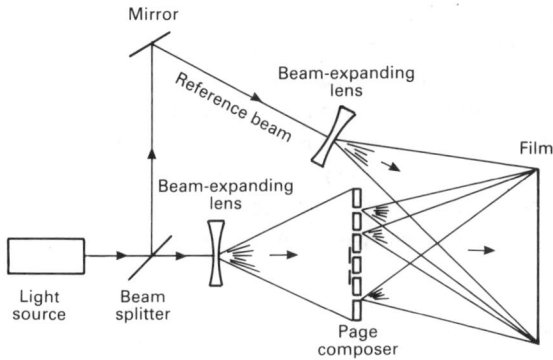

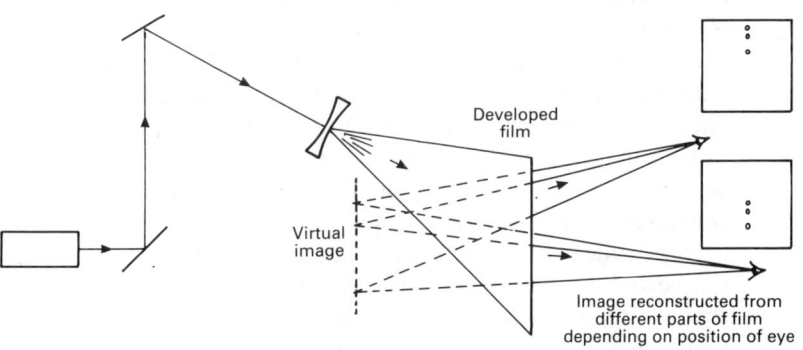

Fig. A2.1 — Principle of holography.

used this principle (Chapter 11). If we make the matrix large enough, and allow each source (except the reference) to vary in brightness, we can use the matrix to present an image similar to the halftone photographs used in newspapers; and if we record the hologram — for example on photographic film — we can reproduce the original picture using only the reference source, even though the hologram on the film has no obvious resemblance to the original picture. In fact there is no need to divide the picture into discrete sources; a continuous image illuminated by a beam which is phase-locked to the reference beam produces a hologram just as well.

Notice that there is no lens between the source matrix and the recording surface. Light from every part of the source matrix falls on each point of the recording surface; this is in contrast to a conventional optical system where each point on the surface corresponds to a particular point in the matrix. This gives holographic recording some very interesting properties. One is that each point on the recording surface has a complete, but different, view of the source; as a result, if the source is a three-dimensional object rather than a plane, the image re-created from the hologram will also be three-dimensional (Fig. A2.2). This is one of the best-known features of holography, as many such holograms have been shown to the public. Taking this a stage further, different parts of the recording film can be exposed to the source at different times, between which the source may be changed in some way. Some of the holograms which have been introduced on credit cards use this effect to produce an image which moves when viewed from different angles.

Holographic recording has another property which is more useful in optical storage. As each part of the recording has been affected by every point in the source matrix, we can re-create the image of a plane source from any part of the recording plane; we need not use the whole of it. Indeed we could not do so, since in principle the interference pattern extends to infinity in each direction; our choice of a part of it for the recording is arbitrary. If less of the surface is used, the re-created image will be less bright and have less contrast — in technical terms the signal-to-noise ratio will be reduced. However, most systems will tolerate quite a large variation; typically, an image reproduced from only half the recording area will be quite acceptable. The result is that small defects in the recording medium, which we have seen are hard to avoid, will have very little effect on the re-created image. This compares with conventional optics where such a defect would certainly corrupt some of the data elements. Put another way, holographic recordings have error correction inherent in them. This was the feature of holography that was of most interest to early workers in optical storage; it matters less now that we have better error-correcting codes, and low-priced chips to implement them.

There is very much more to holography than this, of course. In particular we have skirted round the question of what is a suitable light source. It turns out that for most purposes we need what is called a 'coherent' light source — one which behaves rather like an infinitely small pin-hole — which emits monochromatic light. For practical use it must be a reasonably powerful

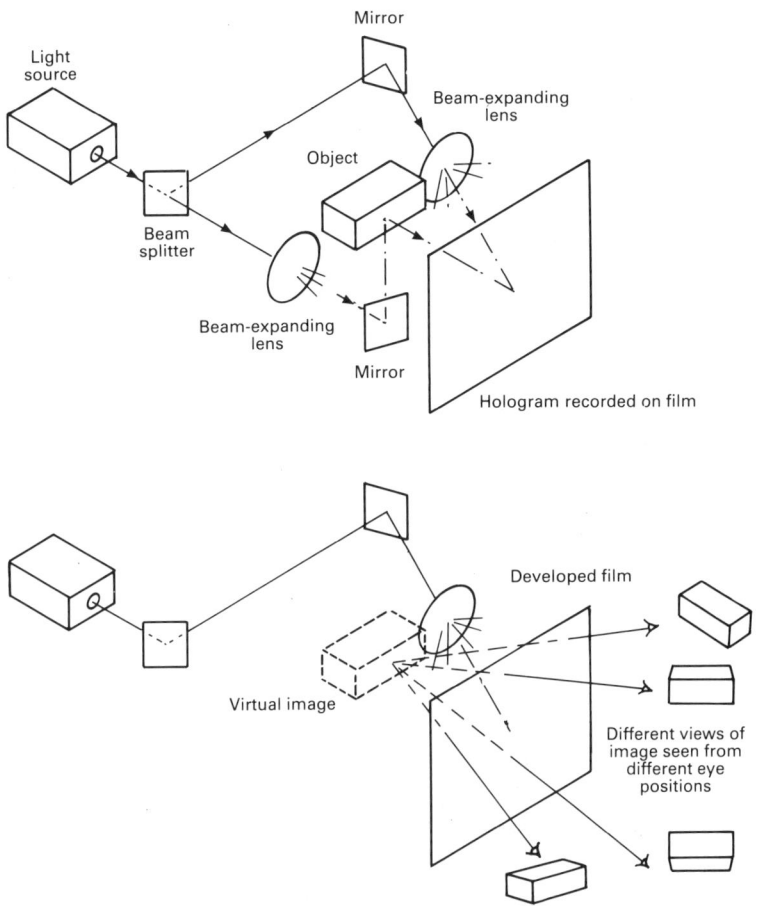

Fig. A2.2 — Holographic recording of a three-dimensional object.

light source, which an infinitely small pinhole obviously is not. Fortunately such a source is now available; the laser.

In Chapter 4 a new type of optical head is described, in which a diffraction grating is used as a beam splitter. This has been described as a 'holographic head' (and the grating as a 'holographic diffractor'), though this is a rather misleading use of the term. Apart from the grating, conventional optics are used and the light is focused to a spot rather than a holographic image at the recording layer of the disk.

Lasers were first introduced into optical storage because they were needed for holographic recordings. Once in use, they turned out to be convenient for other reasons as well, and they have continued to be used even though holography has dropped out of favour.

For a more rigorous discussion of holography, see any modern textbook on optics; one example is listed in Appendix 1.

Appendix 3
Some typical data sheets

In the earlier chapters of this book we looked at data sheets for devices of various types. These were not based on specific products, but were concocted to illustrate the points to be discussed.

In this appendix are actual data sheets for products of several types. Each is representative of its class; it is not necessarily either the best or the latest device on the market.

The data sheets cover:

    12 inch WORM disk drive (Optimem)
    5¼ inch WORM disk drive (LMSI)
    5¼ inch rewritable disk drive (Maxtor)
    CD-ROM drive (Hitachi)
    Jukebox (OSI)

OPTIMEM 1000

OPTICAL DISK DRIVE		
KEY FEATURES: • 2 GBYTES CAPACITY	• REMOVABLE 12-INCH DISK MEDIA	
MICROPROCESSOR-CONTROLLED ELECTRONICS	• BUILT-IN DIAGNOSTICS	
• COMPACT SIZE • LOW POWER REQUIREMENTS	• LOW COST ARCHIVING	
• ADVANCED SCSI INTERFACE (OPTIONAL)	• MODULAR DESIGN	

OPTIMEM 1000
OPTICAL DISK DRIVE

Description

The Optimem 1000 is the first in a family of optical drives using write-once laser technology to read and write digital data. With a storage capacity of 2-billion bytes (two gigabytes) on a removable 12-inch disk, the Optimem product is an ideal low-cost mass storage device for advanced, image-oriented office systems, transaction processing, data archiving and other high-capacity data-storage applications. In addition, since the Optimem drive uses write-once technology and removable media, it is well suited as a backup device for Winchester drives or in financial applications like audit trails.

System integration is simplified through the industry standard SCSI (Small Computer System Interface), which accommodates up to eight drives per controller. The card cage provides two slots for a SCSI and error detection (EDAC) card. A system can be designed in a master/slave configuration with the master drive incorporating the SCSI controller and up to seven slave drives. The Optimem drive can be used alone or in conjunction with floppy and Winchester drives.

The Optimem 1000 occupies only seven inches of panel space in a standard 19-inch rack, and is 24 inches deep. It requires less than 230 watts to operate, including controller, greatly reducing power and cooling requirements. Microprocessor-controlled electronics and modular design simplify field maintenance and repair.

Information is recorded and played back on a removable 12-inch disk which is protected during operator handling, transport and storage by a hard shell cartridge. The cartridge also accommodates labeling information and incorporates write protect and operator interlock features. The Optimem media is pregrooved for servo-tracking and preformatted with sector address information.

SPECIFICATIONS

PERFORMANCE SPECIFICATIONS

CAPACITY (Formatted)
- Per Disk — 2.05 Gbytes
- Per Track — 25 kbytes
- Per Sector — 1,024 bytes
- Sectors Per Track — 25

TRANSFER RATE
- Burst — 625 Kbytes
- Sustained — 483 Kbytes

LATENCY (avg) — 27 msec

SEEK TIME (includes settling)
- Track-to-Track — 3 msec
- Average — 150 msec
- Maximum — 250 msec
- Motor Start/Stop — 8 sec (max.)

FUNCTIONAL SPECIFICATIONS

ROTATIONAL SPEED — 1,122 rpm
RECORDING DENSITY (inside track) — 15,300 bpi
TRACK DENSITY — 14,500 tpi
TRACKS PER SIDE — 40,000
MEDIA — Optimem 1001 or 1002 Cartridge (removable)
INTERFACE — SCSI (optional)

PHYSICAL SPECIFICATIONS

ENVIRONMENTAL LIMITS
- Ambient Temperature: 50° F to 109° F (10° C to 43° C)
- Relative Humidity: 10% to 90%
- Maximum Wet Bulb: 80° F (26.7° C)

DC VOLTAGE REQUIREMENTS (N.A. with optional power supply)
- +15 V DC ± 5% @ 4 A peak
- −15 V DC ± 5% @ 4 A peak
- +5 V DC ± 5% @ 14 A peak

AC VOLTAGE REQUIREMENTS
- Master (with power supply)
  - 90–132 VAC @ 1.3A 50/60 Hz
  - 180–260 VAC @ 0.65A 50/60 Hz
- Slave (with power supply)
  - 90–132 VAC @ 0.9A 50/60 Hz
  - 180–260 VAC @ 0.45A 50/60 Hz

MECHANICAL DIMENSIONS
- Height: 6.81 in. (173.0 mm)
- Width: 17.6 in. (447.0 mm)
- Depth: 24 in. (609.6mm)
- Weight: 55 lbs. (25kg)

HEAT DISSIPATION
- Master (with power supply) 528 BTU/hr typical
- Slave (with power supply) 358 BTU/hr typical

RELIABILITY SPECIFICATIONS

MTBF: 10,000 POH typical (incl. power supply and controller)
PM: Not required
MTTR: 30 minutes
DESIGN LIFE: 5 years
ERROR RATES
- Non-Recoverable Errors: 1 per 10^{12} bits read
- Non-Detected Errors: 1 per 10^{16} bits read

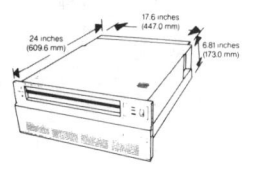

Specifications are subject to change without notice.

Corporate Headquarters
297 N. Bernardo Ave.
Mountain View, Ca 94043
Phone (415) 961-1800
Fax (415) 961-8913

WEST
18400 Von Karman Ave.
Suite 340
Irvine, Ca 92715
Phone (714) 261-5087

MIDWEST
15851 Dallas Parkway
Suite 1020
Dallas, Tx 75248
Phone (214) 960-8405

EAST
1850 Centennial Park Drive
Suite 300
Reston, Va 22091
Phone (703) 648-1568

167 Flanders Street
Rochester, NY 14619
Phone (716) 436-0150

EUROPE
Optimem
Cipher House
Ashville Way
Wokingham, Berkshire
England RG11 2PL
Phone (44) 0734 775757
Telex 846535

Optimem

LASER MAGNETIC STORAGE INTERNATIONAL COMPANY

LaserDrive® 510
High Performance 5¼-Inch Optical Disk Drive

Designed for Original Equipment Manufacturers (OEM)

Description

The LD 510 is a random access write-once optical disk drive that has been designed for permanent memory applications that require high performance and high capacity in a 5¼-inch full-height form factor. Its unique design features a stationary optical path for faster seek times, and advanced self-calibrating circuitry for higher reliability. The LD 510 utilizes a removable ANSI/ISO standard data cartridge to provide 654 megabytes of formatted user capacity per disk.

A PHILIPS AND CONTROL DATA JOINT VENTURE

Applications

Because of its industry-leading transfer rate and fully embedded SCSI controller, the LD 510 opens new applications to optical storage technology. It is ideally suited for applications that require fast access to on-line data and image archives. Its compact design, large capacity and high throughput capability also facilitate its use for data acquisition systems or tape replacement.

The LD 510 is also a cost-effective way to distribute databases or software. Its fast access and planned jukebox compatibility make it an ideal choice for central databases in multiuser environments. The use of convenient removable cartridges also qualifies the LD 510 to be used for applications where data security and data transportability are important.

Hardware Features

- 600 KByte/Sec sustained user throughput (nominal)
- 2160 RPM spindle rotation speed
- Less than 75msec average access (1/3 max seek + 1/2 latency + focus time)
- 654 MBytes user capacity per disk
- Embedded SCSI Controller/full height 5¼-inch Form Factor
- 15000 POH MTBF (90% confidence)
- 64 KByte cache buffer
- Industry standard interface, data cartridge & data format
- Does not require preventive maintenance

Technology

The LD 510 utilizes optical technologies and components that have been developed by Philips, a world leader in optical recording technology. These products are manufactured by LMS in Colorado. In operation, the LD 510 uses a Philips Laser-diode to burn (ablate) pits in a tellurium-based sensitive layer. To read data, laser light is reflected at varying intensities caused by the presence or absence of a pit. This reflected light is converted into electrical signals by a photodetector.

Design

With the LD 510, LMS has advanced the state-of-the-art in WORM technology. It represents the first true second generation optical disk drive by virtue of its unsurpassed performance, planned compatibility with erasable optical technology and conformance with industry standards.

Reliability/Serviceability

- The LD 510 meets the industry demand for higher reliability.
- The LD 510 requires no field adjustments or preventive maintenance.
- There are *no* potentiometers to cause reliability problems.
- A long-life direct drive brushless motor and minimal number of parts increase reliability.

Interface

The LD 510 contains a fully embedded SCSI Controller that performs the following functions:

- Data Buffering (64 KBytes)
- Drive Interface and Controller (SCSI)
- Media defect management
- Error detection & correction
- Self diagnostics

Software Features

- Disk formatting not required
- SCSI (CCS) command set
- Supports arbitration, disconnect/reconnect
- Four-zone auto-reallocate capabilities optimizes defect mapping performance

Recording Format

- 512 byte logical block length
- Preformatted spiral data track
- 4/15 modulation scheme provides uniform 20% duty cycle and allows the use of differential detection
- Sampled servo approach decouples tracking, focus, timing and data signals to facilitate cross-technology compatability

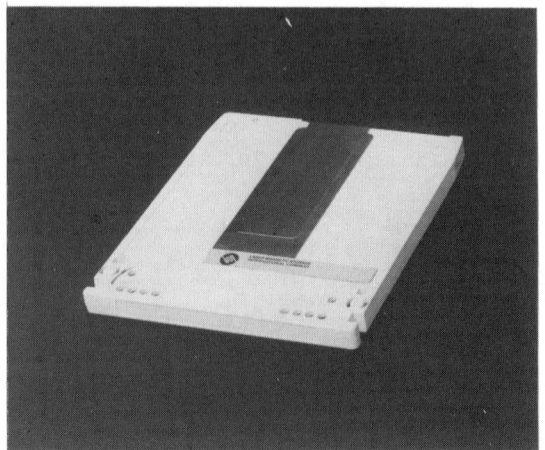

Disk Cartridge

The LD 510 provides the largest data capacity (654 user megabytes) available in an ISO/ANSI standard cartridge. The cartridge protects the disk from contamination and handling and uses a sliding window to provide controlled access to the media. Cartridge features also include grippers for automated insertion, media identifiers, and a write protect switch.

Error Correcting Capabilities

The LD 510 utilizes an advanced error detection and correction code to handle random byte and multiple burst errors. All user data is written to the disk with ECC check symbols that are used to find and correct errors during read operations.

SPECIFICATIONS
LaserDrive 510 — High Performance 5¼-Inch Optical Disk Drive

Functional
Interface	— SCSI/CCS
Burst Transfer Rate	— 1.25 MBytes/sec
Max Sustained User Throughput	— 600 KBytes/sec (nominal)
Average Access Time	— 75 m/sec
Spindle Speed	— 2160 RPM
Average Seek Time	— Less than 60 m/sec

Reliability
Drive
- MTBF — (90% confidence) — 15000 Power on Hours (preliminary)
- 1 Year Hardware Warranty
- No Preventive Maintenance
- No Potentiometers

Media
- 5 Year Unwritten/10 Year Written Disk Warranty

Data

Raw Error Rate	1 Byte in 10^4 Bytes
Error Rate (with ECC)	1 Byte in 10^{12} Bytes
Recoverable Read Error Rate	5 Errors in 10^4 Bytes

Interface
SCSI — ANSI Standard X3.131 — Common Command Set

Environmental / Physical / Electrical
Operating Temperature	— 10-46°C/50-114.8°F (preliminary)
Non Operating Temperature	— −10-50°C/14-122°F (preliminary)
FCC Certification	— Class B
Voltage	— +5 +12
Power Consumption	— 14W Max
Dimensions	— 8"L x 3.25H x 5.7W (20.32cm x 8.25cm x 14.6cm)
Weight	— 6 Lbs/2.72 kg

LaserDrive Removable Cartridge

Capacity
327 MBytes/Side

Disk Characteristics
Cartridge	ISO/ANSI Standard
Disk Construction	Preformatted Polycarbonate Sandwich
Sensitive Layer	Te Alloy
Specifications	512 Bytes / Sector, 32 Sectors / Track, 19,928 Tracks
Data Life	10 years

Specification subject to change without notice

LASER MAGNETIC STORAGE INTERNATIONAL COMPANY
OVERSEAS BRANCH OFFICE
P.O. BOX 218, BUILDING HWA-1
5600 MD EINDHOVEN
THE NETHERLANDS
Tel. +31 40-758753
Telex 35000 PHTC NL/NLMEVSQ
Fax. 31-40-758742

Distributed by:

LASER MAGNETIC STORAGE INTERNATIONAL COMPANY
CORPORATE HEADQUARTERS
4425 ARROWSWEST DRIVE
COLORADO SPRINGS, CO 80907
Tel. (719) 593-4269 (4270)
Telex 910-920-4908
Fax. 719-599-8713

THE MAXTOR TAHITI™ FAMILY

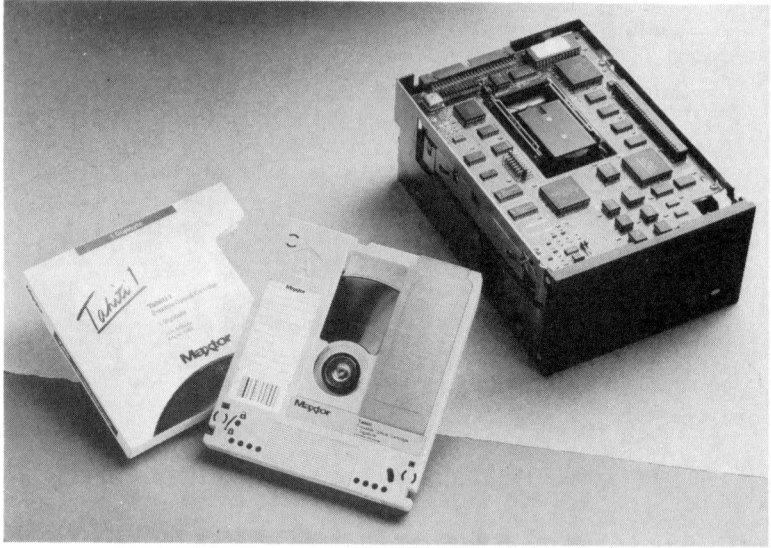

5¼-inch Optical Disk Drive, with 1-gigabyte or 650-megabyte
Removable Erasable Media

The Tahiti 1™ optical disk drive features a 5¼-inch form factor, using removable/erasable 1-gigabyte or 650-megabyte formatted double-sided media with an embedded SCSI controller. Tahiti 1 has an average seek time of 30 ms and provides a high-capacity, high-performance mass storage solution.

Maxtor

THE MAXTOR TAHITI™ FAMILY

KEY FEATURES — OPTICAL DISK DRIVE
- Uses front loading, removable, double-sided erasable media offering 1 gigabyte or 650 megabytes of formatted user storage capacity.
- Highest capacity, 5¼-inch SCSI optical disk drive on the market.
- Physical dimensions and mounting holes identical to 5¼-inch Winchester and floppy disk drive industry standards.
- Motor driven cartridge system for orderly spin down/eject.
- Zoned Constant Angular Velocity (ZCAV) recording method offers superior data capacity, with fast access.
- Extensive LSI circuitry offers maximum function and reliability for minimum cost.

- Stored data is randomly accessed by the drive.
- Media removal/Lock controllable by software.
- Power supply requirements compatible with industry standard 5¼-inch disk drives.

KEY FEATURES — CONTROLLER
- Uses standard SCSI controller cabling.
- Supports SCSI Common Command Set (CCS-4B).
- Automatic ECC code generation that results in data integrity of 10^{-12}.
- Automatic retry on seek or read errors.
- Automatic defect mapping.
- Full disconnect/reconnect and arbitration capability.

- Average transfer data rate — 10 megabytes/sec.
- Supports 512 and 1024 byte sectors.

KEY FEATURES — MEDIA CARTRIDGE
- Removable, single-sided, 5¼-inch cartridge offering 1 gigabyte or 650 megabytes of formatted capacity.
- Data storage life in excess of 10 years.
- Protective hard-shell, plastic cartridge with sliding shutter for added media durability and protection.
- Inexpensive, removable, erasable disk media.
- Pre-formatted cartridges are ready to accept user data (pre-certified, media-user option).
- Write protect switch on cartridge provides for read-only operation.

SPECIFICATIONS

DRIVE AND CONTROLLER PERFORMANCE SPECIFICATIONS

Capacity, formatted (standard disk†) per side.
- (512 Byte sectors)   298 MB
- (1024 Byte sectors)   326 MB

Capacity, formatted (ZCAV disk, per side)
- (512 Byte sectors)   466 MB
- (1024 Byte sectors)   512 MB

SCSI bus transfer rate, maximum
- (megabytes/second)   4.0

Seek†† time, msec
- Average   30
- Track-to-track   1
- Maximum   60

Average latency (ms)
- Std. disk†   16.7
- ZCAV disk   13.6

FUNCTIONAL SPECIFICATIONS

Rotational speed (rpm)   1800/2200
Recording density (bpi)   25000
Track density (tpi) (ZCAV)   16933
Recording method used   (2,7) RLL
Guaranteed number of user-available sectors
per side (standard disk)
- (1024 Byte/sector)   316,500
- (512 Byte/sector)   576,400

per side (ZCAV)
- (1024 Byte/sector)   495,200
- (512 Byte/sector)   901,350

† Conforms to proposed ANSI standard.
†† Includes settling

SCSI COMMAND SET SUPPORTED

Erase	Request Sense
Format	Reserve Unit
Inquiry	Rezero Unit
Mode Select	Seek
Mode Sense	Seek (Extended)
Prevent/Allow	Send Diagnostic
Media Removal	Start/Stop Unit
Read (Gr 0, 5, 7)	Test Unit Ready
Read Capacity	Verify
Read Data Buffer	Write (Gr 0, 1, 5)
Read/Write Long	Write Data Buffer
Reassign Blocks	Write and Verify
Release Unit	

MEDIA CARTRIDGE SPECIFICATIONS

Disk Size	5.25 in. (130 mm)
Sensitive Layer Material	Rare earth, transition metal alloy
Substrate	Glass or plastic
Disk structure	Bonded sandwich
Archival life	>10 years
Write method	Magneto-Optics

OC-650MB		OC-1000MB	
Part #	Sector	Part #	Sector
*1015382	512B	*1015386	512B
*1015384	1024B	*1015388	1024B
**1015383	512B	**1015387	512B
**1015385	1024B	**1015389	1024B

substrate
* glass
** plastic

PHYSICAL SPECIFICATIONS

Environmental Limits (operating)
- Ambient temperature = 5° C to +45° C
- Relative Humidity (operating) = 8% to 80% with maximum gradient of 10% per hour, non-condensing

DC power requirements
- +12 VDC ±5%, 2A (maximum)
- +5 VDC ±5%, 2A (maximum)

Mechanical dimensions
- Height = 3.25 in. (82.5 mm)
- Width = 5.75 in. (146.0 mm)
- Depth = 8.2 in. (208.3 mm)
- Weight = 6 lbs. (2.7 Kg) (no media installed)

Heat dissipation = 35 watts (maximum)

RELIABILITY SPECIFICATIONS

MTBF: 30,000 POH, typical duty cycle
PM: not required
MTTR: 30 minutes
Component design life: over 5 years
Media archival life: over 10 years

Maxtor

Maxtor Corporation
211 River Oaks Parkway
San Jose, CA 95134
(408) 432-1700
TELEX 171074
FAX (408) 433-0457

™Tahiti 1 is a trademark of Maxtor Corporation

Specifications subject to change without notice.

Printed in U.S.A. 5/88

Copyright © 1988 Maxtor Corporation   20K   P/N1015349

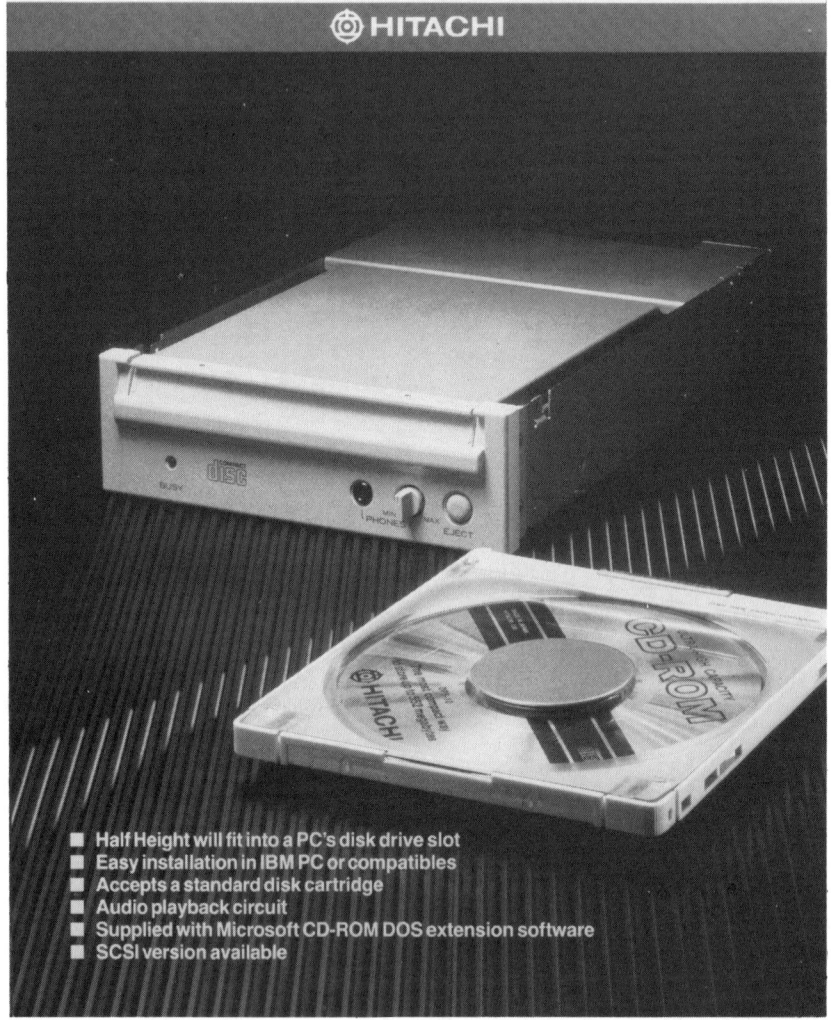

CDR3500

CDR3500 is a second generation half height CD-ROM player, which may be built into a personal computer.

CD-ROM is now established as a cost effective medium for the distribution of large quantities of machine readable data. Hitachi's CDR3500 allows access to 550 MBytes of information or up to 4 drives may be daisy chained to provide 2200 MBytes of on line memory. Miniaturised design and extensive use of LSI allow CDR3500 to be built into a computer's second floppy disk drive position.

- Uses a now accepted industry standard disk cartridge, which allows vertical or horizontal mounting and protects the disk from scratches or dirt.
- Audio output through a headphone jack at the front or an audio output terminal at the rear is provided to play back commentary recorded on CD-ROM as well as data for education, training or other interactive applications.
- Supply voltages are identical to those of conventional disk drives via a standard disk drive power plug, making installation simple.
- Hitachi CD-ROM drives are the fastest available on the market today and are stocked and supported by Hitachi New Media Products throughout Europe.

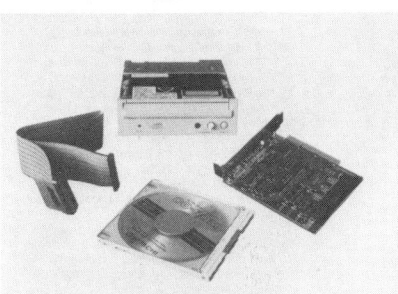

CDR3500 is supplied with interface cards and cables for connection to IBM PC or compatibles. All Hitachi's CD ROM products are supplied with Microsoft's MS-DOS extension software. The MS-DOS extensions allow your PC to access the CD-ROM in the same way as a magnetic disk drive when a standard CD-ROM disk is used.

SPECIFICATIONS

PERFORMANCE
Rotation speed:	200 – 535 rpm (CLV)
Recorded sides:	Single side
Transfer rate:	153 KBytes/sec
Seek time:	1 msec (track to track)
Access time:	0.8" sec (typical)
Average latency:	70msec (inner)
	150msec (outer)
Soft read errors (recoverable):	less than 10^{-9}
Hard read errors (non recoverable):	less than 10^{-12}
*Calculated from performing random access 200 times	

AUDIO SPECIFICATIONS
No of Channels:	2
Frequency response:	20 to 20,000 Hz ±3 dB
Distortion:	0.1% or less (at 1 kHz)
Output level:	
Headphones:	0.55 V rms typical (maximum volume level) (100 Ω load)
Line	0.8 V rms typical (47 kΩ load)
Output terminal:	
Headphones:	3.5 mm dia. minijack
Line	4-pin terminal (2.5 mm pitch)

DIMENSIONS
CDR-3500 (WxHxD):	146 × 41.3 × 205 mm (excluding the front panel)
Disc cartridge (WxHxT):	124.6 × 135 × 8 mm
Weight:	
CDR-3500	about 1.5 kg
Disc cartridge	about 75 g

POWER REQUIREMENTS
12 V DC power:	0.25 A (average), 1.3 A (maximum)
5 V DC power:	0.45 A (average), 0.7 A (maximum)

⊚ Hitachi
New Media Products

Hitachi Sales Scandinavia AB
Rissneleden 8, Box 7138 172 07
Sundbyberg, Sweden. Tel: 08 98 52 80

Hitachi Sales (UK) Ltd
Hitachi House, Station Road,
Hayes, Middx UB3 4DR, United Kingdom.
Tel: 01- 848 8787

Hitachi Sales Europa GmbH
Rungedamm 2, 2050 Hamburg 80,
West Germany. Tel: 040 734 110

Hitachi France SA
95-101 Rue Charles-Michels, 9320
Saint-Denis, France. Tel: 48 21 60 15

Hitachi Sales AG
Bahnhof Strasse 19, 5600 Lenzburg
Switzerland. Tel: 064 51 36 21

Hitachi Sales Italiana SPA
Via Christoforo Columbo 49
Trezzano Sul Naviglio, Milan, Italy.
Tel: 2 445 90 31

ODSR — OPTICAL DISK STORAGE & RETRIEVAL UNIT

Designed for Original Equipment Manufacturers (OEM)

The Optical Disk Storage and Retrieval Unit, ODSR, is commonly known in the industry as an optical "Jukebox". An ODSR incorporates up to two OSI LaserDrive 1200 JB Digital Optical Disk Drives, a 16 or 20 crypt tower for LaserDrive Media, and a microprocessor controlled electro-mechanical mechanism for selecting and transporting the cartridges. The ODSR can provide up to 32 GB (32,000 MB) or 40 GB (40,000 MB) of on-line storage with random access without human intervention.

The ODSR is designed for a standard office environment and requires a minimum amount of floor space. In addition, this device offers a very attractive low entry cost due to its simplicity of design and compact size. Up to 7 ODSR's can be modulary chained together to accommodate different storage applications and associated data throughput needs.

Applications

The ODSR offers a cost effective advantage over current methods of data storage. Key advantages are low cost, computer accessible, on-line random access, minimum human intervention and faster retrieval of information. Some application areas are Networked Centralized data bases, Image Processing, Transaction Processing, Document Filing/Storage, and the ever growing Archival Storage.

Interfaces/Systems Integration

Incorporated into the ODSR are several interfaces. The LaserDrive 1200JB optical drive inside the ODSR maintains either the Small Computer Systems Interface (SCSI) or the Intelligent Systems Interface (ISI). An RS232C interface is offered as the control interface to execute all motions commands for the ODSR. Separation of the RS232 control interface from the drive interface (SCSI or ISI) provides OEM's with flexibility in adapting to their unique systems integration requirements.

The separation also allows for the LD1200JB to perform data I/O functions on the drive interface while the RS232 control can transport other cartridges simultaneously to provide the user with a queued (overlapped) operation. These features provide easier systems integration, better systems throughput and in the event of an ODSR failure, the LD1200JB can still operate in a manual cartridge load mode.

Hardware Features

- Provide 16 (32 GB) or 20 (40 GB) cartridges of on-line storage
- Built-in micro processor controls for mechanism movement
- Built-in micro processor control for communications between LD1200JB drive(s) and ODSR mechanism
- Built-in power supply
- Dual-buffers for queued operation
- Fail-safe design to ensure safety during power failure
- 16 key operator key-pad and 16 character alphanumeric display
- I/O station makes it easy to load/unload cartridges externally

Software Features

- Simplified RS232C command protocol
- Self-diagnostic to isolate to Field Replaceable Units (FRU's)
- Self-calibrating capability
- Mechanism Error detection and correction with auto retries
- Reliability, Availability, Maintainability are built in
- Self-configuration during power-on

Copyright 1986, Optical Storage International

SPECIFICATIONS
Optical Disk Storage and Retrieval Unit (ODSR)

Functional
- Interface
  - Mechanism control: RS232C/RS485 (Optional)
  - Operator Interface: Key-pad (16-key board with Alphanumeric display).
  - I/O Station — dynamic mail station for place/retrieval a disk cartridge

Reliability
- Mean time between failure (MTBF): 10,000 hours; 12 month models
- Mean time between repair (MTTR): 1 hour
- Preventive Maintenance: Every 6 months

Physical Characteristics
- Height: 1371.6 mm (54 in)
- Width: 1524 mm (60 in)
- Depth: 711.2 mm (28 in)
- Weight: 250 kg (550 lb)

Regulatory and Safety Standards
- UL, CSA, IEC, VDE, FCC

Power Options
- AC:
  - 100V, 50/60 Hz
  - 110V, 60 Hz
  - 120V, 60 Hz
  - 200V, 50 Hz
  - 220V, 50/60 Hz
  - 240V, 50 Hz
- Power dissipation: Average 300 VA; Maximum 700 VA

Environmental
- Temperature
  - Operating: 10°C to 40°C (50°F to 104°F); 12°C/hr change
  - Storage: −10°C to 50°C (14°F to 122°F); 15°C/hr change
  - Shipping: −40°C to 60°C (−40°F to 140°F); 20°C/hr change
- Humidity
  - Operating: 20% to 80% RH
  - Storage: 10% to 90% RH
  - Shipping: 5% to 95% RH

Specifications subject to change without notice.

For more information, please call your Sales Representative at:
Optical Storage International
4425 Arrowswest Drive
Colorado Springs, CO 80907
303-593-7900

Index

Entries refer to the subject described by the words indexed, not necessarily to the exact words. Only significant entries are indexed; words which are very extensively used are indexed only at their most important entries. Principal entries are indicated by bold type.

access software for CD-ROM, **75**, 167, 193
access time, 45, 60, 77, 81
air incident, 27
angular velocity, **25**, 37, 60, 67
applications:
   archiving, 22, **52**, 99, 118, 120, 125
   back-up, 61, 120, 124
   data distribution, 84, 155, 162
   data interchange, 35, 52, 155; *see also* standards
   data storage, 113, 120, 122
   image storage, 52, 113–118, 123, 132, 186
   on-line storage, 61, 122
   program storage, 123
   publishing, 63, 84, 155, **157–162**, 179, 192
   transaction records, 52
applications of
   CD-ROM, 84, 155–180; *see also* applications — publishing
   jukebox, 96, 138
   optical card, 100, 163
   optical tape, 127
   rewritable disk, 61
   WORM disk, 52, 120–154
archiving, archival storage; *see* applications
audit trail, 22
automated disk library, **87–97**, 115, 116, 138
axial run-out, 37

beam splitter, 37
Bernouilli effect, 41
books, 192

caddy, 65, **79**, 81
capacity, 43, 68, 80, 93
card; *see* optical card
carriage, 39
cartridge, 30, 38
CAV (constant angular velocity), 25, 60
CD-I, **69**, 187, 189
CD-PROM, 36, **54**
CD-ROM, 19, **63–86**, 155–180, 189, 192, 193:
   in jukebox, 92, 95, 97
CD-ROM XA, **70**, 187, 189
character recognition, 114, 150
checking, 34
clamping, 37
CLV (constant linear velocity), **25–26**, 60, 67
command set, 104–105
Compact Audio, 63, 71, 77, 185
comparisons:
   CD-ROM with magnetic media, 160
   CD-ROM with microform, 159
   CD-ROM with on-line databases, 161
   CD-ROM with paper, 157
   WORM with magnetic disk and tape, 50, 121–127
compression, 114
conferences, 194
controller, 102, 106–108
copying, 32
current status:
   jukebox, 97
   read-only disk, 85
   rewritable disk, 62
   WORM disk, 53

DAT (digital audio tape), 124, 190
data coding, 33, 68
data lifetime, 32, 46, 100, 152
data rate, 45, 60, 80
data sheet, 43, 44, 80, 93, 201–213
defects, 32

delivery system, 72
detector, 37–41
device characteristics, 42–49, 60, 80–83, 92–95, 120, 155
Digital Paper, 29
directory, 44, 74
disk — spelling, 8
disk exchange time, 93
disk size, 15–17
disk structure, 29, 64
double-sided disk, 29, 89
DRAW (direct read after write), 34–35
DRDW (direct read during write), 35
DVI (digital video interactive), **70**, 189
dye-polymer; *see* recording technology

eccentricity, 37
ECMA; *see* standards organisations
ECMA-119, 72, **111**, 193
ECMA-130, 68
emulation of magnetic tape or disk, 117
entry slot or drawer, 88
environment, 47, 82, 94
erasable 19; *see also* rewritable
erase/rewrite cycle, 19, 58
error detection and correction; *see* error management
error management, 21, 32, **33–35**, 59, 70, 104, 115, 185, 193, 198
error rate, 32, 33–34, 46, 71, 81
exhibitions, 194

fatigue, 19, 58
file structure, 71–75
flexible media, 29, 41
focus, 39
focus spot, 22, 39
footprint, **17**, 47
format, 20, 24, 35, 59, 67, 70

gas laser, 37
Green Book, 69

header, 24
High Sierra, 72–74, 111
history, 181–186
holographic head, 76
holography, 182, 183, 190, **196–200**
hub, 36
hypertext, 76

IBM expansion card bus, 104; *see also* interface
information sources for CD-ROM, 164, 179
installations:
 Barclaycard, 128–132
 Bell and Howell, 172–177
 Bookland, 168–170, 172
 Britannia Building Society, 132–144
 Public Record Office, 144–148
 Shareware Marketing, 148–149
 Whitaker Bookbank, 166–172
interface, 48, 82, 94, **102–106**
ISO; *see* standards organisations
ISO-9660, 72, **111**, 193
ISO-10149, 68

journals, 194
jukebox (automated disk library), **87–97**, 115, 116, 138
jukebox for CD-ROM, 95, 97

label on CD-ROM disk, 64
land, 25
laser, 13, 37–38, 76, 189, 199
laser storage, 13
latency, 44, 45
library; *see* jukebox
lifetime, 31–32, 46, 100, 152
loading, 21, 78, 87–91

magneto-optic technology, 56
manufacture of CD-ROM disk, 65–67
manufacture of WORM disk, 29
mastering of CD-ROM disk, **65–67**, 170, 175
MCAV (modified constant angular velocity), 26
MCLV (modified constant linear velocity), 26
mechanism, 36–42, 59–60, 76–80, 87–91
media (*see also* recording technology):
 flexible, 29, 41
 photographic, 181
 read-only, 64
 rewritable, 58
 write-once, 26
media conversion, 118, 144
micrographics, 118, 159
mirror, 37, 39, 76
MS-DOS extensions, 105
MTBF; *see* reliability
multifunction, 18, 54, 55, 60, 80, 84

objective lens, 37, 42
optical card, 17, **100**, 106, 111, 163, 190
optical head, 37
optical storage — definition, 13
optical tape, 17, **98**, 111, 127, 190
OROM, 63

packaged systems, 113–119
packaging, 47, 81, 107
path, 67
performance, 45, 80, 93, 151

photodetector, 37–41
physical principles, 13, 192
picker, 88–90
polarisation, 14, 57
pre-groove, 25
preformatting, **24**, 28
price:
    CD-ROM, 82, 166
    jukebox, 94
    WORM, 48
publishing; *see* applications

radial run-out, 37
RAW (read after write), 34
read-only, 19, **63–86**, 155–180.
recording format; *see* format
recording method, 18; *see also* recording technology
recording technology:
    ablative, **233**, 183
    alloy, 24
    bubble, 24
    dye-polymer, **24**, 29, 56, 99, 189
    magneto-optic, 56
    moth-eye, 24, 29
    phase-change, **24**, 56, 189
    photochromic, 183
    read-only, 64
    thermoplastic, 24, 56
Red Book, **68**, 111
redundancy, 33–34, 115, 185
reliability, **46**, 81, 94, 96, 151
resolution, 150
rewritable, 19, 55–62, 187
ROM; *see* read-only and CD-ROM
ruggedised drives, 49
run-up, run-down, 45, 89, 93

SCSI 104; *see also* interface
sector, 19, 24, 68
seek time, 45

servo, 39, 76
smart card, 101
spindle run up/run down time, 45, 89, 93
standards, 35, 52, 59, 67, 68, 102, **109–112**, 186
standards organisations, 36, **109–110**
storage matrix, 87
strengths and weaknesses:
    jukebox, 95
    read-only disk, 83
    rewritable disk, 60
    WORM disk, 50
substrate, 17, 27, 64
substrate incident, 27
system area on CD-ROM, 75

tape; *see* optical tape
testing, 32, 67
track — special meaning in CD-ROM context, 67
track following, 39, 76

Uni-file, 72, 75
Unicon, 22, 183

videodisk, 19, 20, 63, 65, 71, 79, 83, 85, 163, 184, 187, 193
volume, 15
volume and file structure on CD-ROM, 71–75

wavelength; *see* laser
WORM; *see* write-once
write error recovery, 35, 45
write-once, 18, 22–54
write-protect, 31

Yellow Book, 68, 111